Paleolithic Zooarchaeology in Practice

Edited by

Jonathan A. Haws
Bryan S. Hockett
Jean-Philip Brugal

BAR International Series 1564
2006

Published in 2016 by
BAR Publishing, Oxford

BAR International Series 1564

Paleolithic Zooarchaeology in Practice

ISBN 978 1 84171 994 8

BAR Publishing is the trading name of British Archaeological Reports (Oxford) Ltd.
British Archaeological Reports was first incorporated in 1974 to publish the BAR
Series, International and British. In 1992 Hadrian Books Ltd became part of the BAR
group. This volume was originally published by Archaeopress in conjunction with
British Archaeological Reports (Oxford) Ltd / Hadrian Books Ltd, the Series principal
publisher, in 2006. This present volume is published by BAR Publishing, 2016.

Printed in England

BAR
PUBLISHING

BAR titles are available from:

BAR Publishing
122 Banbury Rd, Oxford, OX2 7BP, UK
EMAIL   info@barpublishing.com
PHONE   +44 (0)1865 310431
FAX   +44 (0)1865 316916
www.barpublishing.com

CONTENTS

INTRODUCTION: PALEOLITHIC ZOOARCHAEOLOGY

Jonathan A. Haws

Dept. of Anthropology, University of Louisville, Louisville, KY 40292

Understanding Paleolithic animal exploitation requires a multifaceted approach. Inferences may derive from research on paleoenvironments and taphonomy, the development of new methods for interpreting seasonality patterns, and ethnoarchaeological observations. A full understanding of Paleolithic economies also requires a multiregional perspective. This volume brings together a group of scholars with research interests from across the globe to understand the nature of animal exploitation practices through the lens of taphonomy. The chapters include case studies about the types of animals that Paleolithic peoples hunted and gathered through time and space and taphonomic analyses of non-human animal bone assemblages.

Jean-Philip Brugal and colleagues present their work on caves and other karstic cavities in southwestern Europe. They use taphonomic indicators to separate the occupation of Coudoulous, Unikoté and Atapuerca by hyenas and humans during the Middle and Late Pleistocene.

Roger Colten and Andrew Hill show the value of old museum collections. Despite the fact that excavation and curation methods may have been less rigorous than today, museum collections do contain useful materials to reconstruct prehistoric subsistence practices. They use the Middle Paleolithic faunal assemblage from La Quina housed in the Yale Peabody museum to illustrate the potential for using old museum collections.

James Enloe applies new methods for determining season of death using ungulate teeth. His analysis of Verberie uses a quadratic formula for measuring the eruption of permanent teeth and wear of deciduous ones. His methodological approach follows one developed by Pike-Tay *et al.* (2001) in order to avoid the problems associated with cementum annuli analyses.

Jonathan Haws and Maria João Valente apply a taphonomic study to the faunal assemblage from the Late Upper Paleolithic site of Lapa do Suão in Portugal. The site was excavated in the 1960s through the 1980s by Jean Roche who concluded the site was primarily a Magdalenian site. The faunal materials were never analyzed. For two decades, the species identified served as the sole evidence for Late Upper Paleolithic subsistence in Portugal. Recently, Zilhão reinterpreted the stratigraphy and lithic assemblage and claimed the main occupations were Solutrean. New radiocarbon dates and faunal analyses suggest Roche was correct.

Bryan Hockett presents the results of his study of the rabbit bone collection from beneath the Alvados roost in Portugal. This study is an important confirmation of his actualistic research in the Great Basin of the United States by an Old World case study. Understanding the formation processes of natural agents is critical to separating carnivore from human deposits of rabbit bones in caves and rockshelters.

Trent Holliday and Steven Churchill focus on the use of traps to capture animals and the archaeological signatures of trapping. They provide a rare study of the use of carnivores by Paleolithic humans. In this case, they focus of the processing of mustelids during the Upper Paleolithic in Central Europe.

Natalie Munro discusses the exploitation of gazelles during the Natufian period in the Levant. Her research is intended to shed light on the transition to agriculture by studying diachronic changes in faunal assemblages in the Natufian layers of Hayonim Cave, Israel.

Laura Niven evaluates the role of mammoth and wooly rhinoceros in the Middle Paleolithic and Aurgnacian of southern Germany. Using the faunal collections from Vogelherd she shows that mammoth and rhino bones exhibit minimal traces of human modification due to butchery despite the fact that they are more abundant than other taxa at Vogelherd. This suggests they were used as building materials or perhaps were introduced by natural agents.

Tim Prindiville and Nick Conard present the taphonomic analyses of the faunal assemblages collected from the Geelbok Dunes in South Africa. They discuss the likelihood that much of the faunal material derives from Upper Pleistocene human activity based on the skeletal element representation and occurrence of stone artifacts in several localities. The lack of obvious carnivore involvement does not preclude their role and the authors suggest the Geelbok Dunes have preserved a complex record of human/carnivore activity during the last glacial.

Each chapter is revised and expanded version of papers presented in a symposium titled, "Paleolithic Zooarchaeology: Paleoenvironments, Methods and Case Studies from Across the Globe," at the 66th annual meeting of the Society for American Archaeology in New Orleans, 2001.

KARSTIC CAVITIES, NATURAL BONE ACCUMULATIONS AND DISCRETE HUMAN ACTIVITIES IN THE EUROPEAN PALAEOLITHIC : SOME CASE STUDIES.

Jean-Philip Brugal*, Carlos Diez-Lomana**, Rosa Huguet Pàmies***, Patrick Michel[+] and Jordi Rosell Ardèvol[++]

*UMR6636 du CNRS, Maison Méditerranéenne des Sciences de l'Homme, BP647, F-13094 Aix-en-Provence cedex 02, brugal@mmsh.univ-aix.fr
**Area de Prehistoria, Dpt cc Historia, Fac. de Humanidades y Educacion C/ Villadiego s/n, E-09001 Burgos, clomana@ubu.es
***Becaria Fundación Atapuerca, Àrea de Prehistòria, Universitat Rovira i Virgili, Plaça Imperial Tarraco, 1, E-43005 Tarragona & Museo Nacional de Ciencias Naturales de Madrid, Jose Gutierrez Abascal, 2, E-28006 Madrid, rhuguet@mncn.csic.es
[+]UMR5808 du CNRS, Université de Bordeaux I, Bt. De Géologie, av. des facultés, F-33405 Talence cedex, p.michel@iquat.u-bordeaux.fr
[++]Àrea de Prehistòria, Universitat Rovira i Virgili, Plaça Imperial Tarraco, 1, E-43005 Tarragona, jrar@astor.urv.es

"…there is no advantage in killing preys if the animals could easily obtain good-quality meat by scavenging." (Houston, 1979 : p. 263).

INTRODUCTION

Archaeologists have long been concerned with the ecological interaction between human settlement systems and their environment, expressed in term of subsistence strategies. For the Palaeolithic, knowledge about hominid socio-economic adaptations depends mostly on the study of foraging strategies, raw material exploitation and technology systems analysed from the data collected in stratigraphic situations that are commonly called 'site' or 'deposit.'

The prehistoric sites found in two main topographic features: open-air sites often connected to humid deposits (fluvial, lacustrine, etc.) and karstic cavities, essentially found in limestone areas. These broad categories are quite generalized and linked particularly with site preservation in situ through time. So far, most of sites located in different geomorphologic or environmental contexts (such the shade of a tree in a plain or a plateau) would have less probability to survive until the present day. Exceptions are numerous, and the case of human occupations against cliffs with "éboulis" could be considered as a third category (rock-shelter s.l.) in the context of the European Palaeolithic.

Without going into detail about site classification, and considering the potential variety of places, past hunter-gatherer groups have accumulated various sets of lithic and organic remains in numerous contexts. These range from large and diversified accumulations of material to a few traces of human activities. It is the latter case we would like to focus attention: the existence of karstic sites generally rich in faunal material derived from non-anthropic origins and where few human activities are recorded. The karstic cavities of concern here are caves and pitfalls with deep subterranean network where Pleistocene bone accumulations occurred due to the action of biological or natural agents. They are generally considered as palaeontological sites. In some instances, the fossil deposits yield in association some evidence of human presence with a small series of stone artefacts and/or cut-marked bones implying a possible discrete occupation by prehistoric people. These examples have recently served to put the hypothesis that ancient European hominids may have used these peculiar, but regular, circumstances to exploit natural accumulated dead animals in order to obtain animal resources such as meat and/or marrow, possibly skin (?) (Brugal and Jaubert, 1991; Diez, 1993; Diez and Moreno, 1994 ; Diez and Rosell, 1998 ; Diez et al., 1999; Bermudez de Castro et al., 1995; Hughet 1998; Rosell et al., in prep.). This mode of resource acquisition would demonstrate an original foraging behaviour based on an active and controlled scavenging, directly related with some specific biologic and geologic environment (sensu territory).

Several issues can be raised about this problem: What is the density of potentially fossiliferous karstic sites in some area? How common is the frequency of natural bone assemblages in Pleistocene times? How to appreciate the site formation processes explaining the nature of lithic and bone associations? In which way or which part were human groups involved in such natural bone accumulations and modifications? Can we really demonstrate such minor human action and what kind of material and/or traces are evidenced? Is such behaviour equal among different hominid species or cultural groups? We cannot answer all the questions raised along these lines so we will confine our discussion to some relevant points exemplified by case studies from different periods of Palaeolithic.

KARSTIC ENVIRONMENTS (DENSITY AND FREQUENCY)

The term 'Karst' corresponds to a geographical notion (with reference to the landscape of the Trieste area in Slovenia: Kras or Carso) ascribed to a heterogeneous system (hydrological, chemical, geological, mechanical, etc.) mainly associated with carbonate geology with strong dissolution processes. So far, the processes involved are complex and combine aerial and subterranean components, mainly controlled by climatic features and also by local factors. The dynamic formation processes of sedimentary deposits in karstic environment are multiple, often considered as a sediment trap influenced by erosive and reworking forces. During the Quaternary, the morphologic and sedimentary evolution of karst was subjected to the climatic fluctuations according to the succession of glacial and interglacial phases (e.g., Nicod 1972; Renault 1976, 1987; Fabre, 1989; Campy, 1990, for more details).

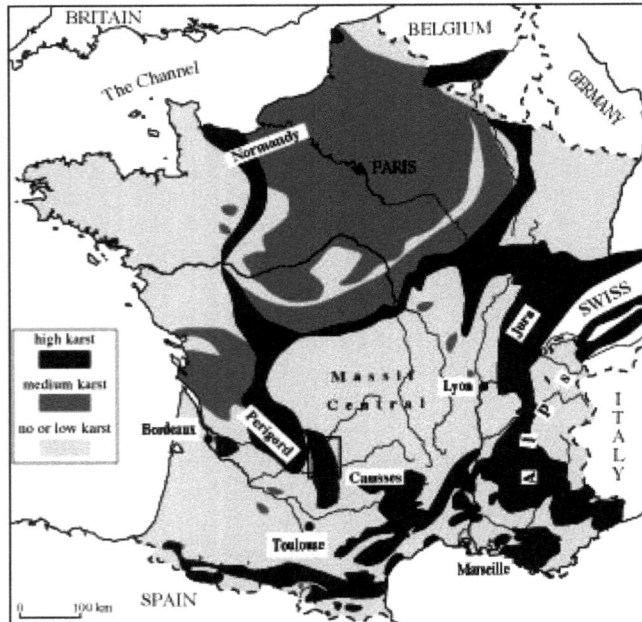

Figure 1. Karstic zones of France.

To simplify, we will consider aerial cavities (exokarst : entrance of the caves, deep rock-shelter, dolines or karstic circular depressions in a plateau) and subterranean cavities (endokarst : caves, sinkholes). In fact, it can be most relevant to distinguish these locations according to their horizontal (caves and their entrances) or vertical opening components (dolines, sinkholes or pitfalls). The overall geotopographic features, especially the orientation of the speleological network, involve the ease of access, which in turn have important issues in taphonomic processes and fossil accumulations (cf. infra). From a sedimentological point of view, it is noteworthy that cavities, especially sinkholes and dolines are filled with various sediments (detritic and chemical) and can be considered then as natural sediment traps.

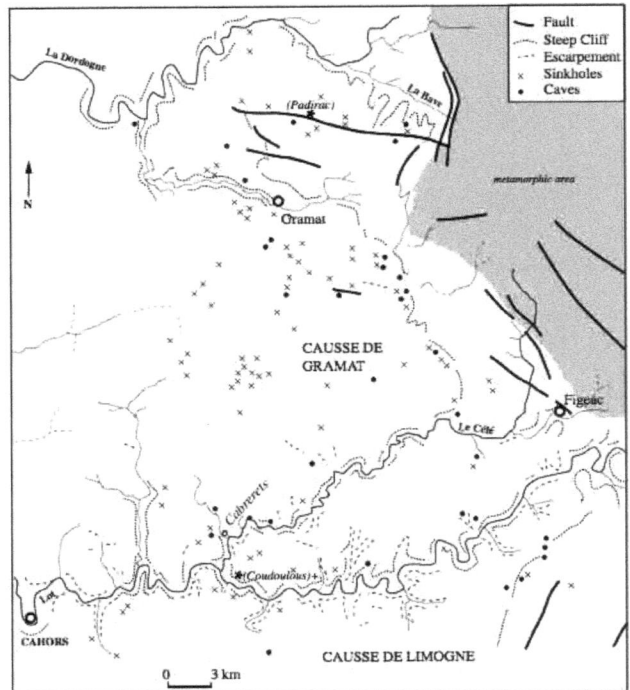

Figure 2. Geographic map of Coudoulous area and density of karstic cavities.

The carbonated (limestone, dolomite, chalk, etc.) regions are geologically dominant in Western Europe, and in some areas almost 25% of the surface is covered by limestone relief (ex. Mediterranean region) (Gilli 1995). Moreover, the karstification processes were especially important during the Plio-Pleistocene, having induced the formation of very numerous cavities. In France, it is possible to characterize three zones according to the frequency of cavities (fig.1): highly karstified, moderately karstified and few or no karstic cavities (Renault, 1976). As we can notice, almost half of the French country shows relatively abundant zones with cavities. It is then not a hazard if most of the prehistoric sites are located in the countries rich in karstic cavities (for ex. Perigord). Several specialized studies have been conducted in order to map all the hydro-karsto-speleological features for different regions (see studies and maps from Ambert, Delanoy, Maire, Nicod, etc.). In particular the region of the Causses, limestone plateaux situated from the south to southwestern border of Massif Central, yields numerous caves, dolines and sinkholes. Table 1 gives a general idea of their densities, from four main Causses (Larzac, Mejean, Noir, Sauveterre : e.750 to 900 m a.s.l.) covering an area of more than 2,000 square kilometres. Globally, the mean is respectively, one per two square kilometres for the sinkholes and one per one square kilometre for dolines (for a homogenous distribution). An enlargement of other portion of these Causses in Quercy (Gramat and Limogne), between the Dordogne and Lot rivers (fig.2), shows the density as well as the distribution of the cavities (only caves and sinkholes) in the landscape (Salomon et coll., 2000). We can again notice the importance of sinkholes relatively

CAUSSE*	Surf (Km2)	Number		Density	
		Sinkholes	Dolines	Sinkholes	Dolines
LARZAC	1,000	234	784	0.23	0.78
MEJEAN	330	273	647	0.82	1.96
NOIR	300	299	233	0.99	1.76
SAUVETERRE	550	357	889	0.64	1.61
Total	2,180	1163	2553	0.53	1.17

* limestone plateaux located in the south of the french Masif-Central

Table 1. Number and Density of karstic cavities (sinkhole and dolines) in Southwest France (surf.:surface).

well distributed as well as the relative partitioning of these plateaux due to cliffs near the main valleys, restricting the passage and movement of large mammals, such as ungulates. From these different examples, we can appreciate the high densities of karstic cavities, especially of sinkholes considered as natural pit falls. Moreover, in a very restricted zone of the Lot river where the site of Coudoulous is located (see fig.2), we have almost 30% of the sinkholes yielding Pleistocene fossil vertebrates, and among them we find a limited number which also contains few lithic materials shaped by humans.

These sinkholes frequently have small openings and deep collapse pits. It is not uncommon to find large amount of fossil material, especially bones of medium to large-sized ungulates, which have fallen into these natural traps. They can contain a limited number of individuals as well as yield large Pleistocene populations, in terms of ten or so individuals of horses, bison, occasionally cervids. Several examples are well known of this type of setting: in France, La Fage (e.g., Philippe, 1978), Vergranne (Campy, 1983), Les Rameaux (Rouzaud et al., 1990; Coumont, in prep.), Padirac (Philippe, 1994), La Berbie (Madelaine,...) Aven Bouet (Brugal, 1982), Privats (Bosch and Brugal, 1996), Jaurens and Siréjol (Philippe et al., 1980; Guérin et al., 1979), (see also Clot, 1989, Clot and Evin 1986 ; Philippe, 1986), etc.. Some of these sites have yielded few artefacts or even hominid remains themselves. The evidence of discrete use of cavities by prehistoric people is well known during Upper Pleistocene (Rouzaud, 1978, 1997). These sites span a wide time-range through the Pleistocene. It is important to note the regular and frequent process of trapping ungulates (individuals or partial populations), which correlate with the high densities of these cavities. Generally, bones are well-preserved and all parts of the skeleton are represented, without excluding strong post-depositional factors which can bias the skeletal representation (especially with reworking and erosive factors). Following the fatal fall and according to the temperature condition inside this deep underground cavity, acting as a refrigerator, carcass preservation, i.e. meaning the degree of tissue decomposition (decay), is much greater than in open-air settings.

FOSSIL RECORDS IN KARSTIC CAVITIES

The nature of what we will call by the generic term of cavities, have indeed several implications according to the origin of fossil materials s.l. (lithic artefacts, charcoal, bone of small to large vertebrates, etc.) and the behaviour of the occupants s.l. (as living places). Generally three cases, not exclusive, can be distinguished: caves and dolines used by humans (archaeological sites) and/or by carnivores (dens, lairs) seen as main agent accumulators, and sinkholes seen as natural traps (pitfalls) for small and large mammals (e.g., Morel, 1990, Brugal and Jaubert, 1991). In some degree, these three cases yield more or less dense bone and lithic assemblages.

Throughout all the Pleistocene sites interpreted either as carnivore dens in caves or natural accumulations in sinkholes are numerous. An initial survey of the literature allows us to identify nearly 20 dens and 18 pits from Western Europe containing a small number of lithic artefacts and/or human remains. These records are probably underestimated due to the low degree of research and observations conducted in such sites. Moreover, they are generally not considered as archaeological significant and usually remarks are limited if any. Most of these sites have not been subjected to taphonomic or complete palaeontological studies. The time-range is broad, extending from the lower, middle to early upper Pleistocene. In some instances, complex speleological networks are visible and often accessible from several places having one main pit (vertical) with secondary entrances (more or less horizontal). They probably would have functioned both as a den and as a sinkhole trap. It is often possible to discriminate these cases (e.g., Costamagno, 1999).

We would like to present three different case studies of multileveled sites still being excavated and under study: one instance of a cave hyena den (Unikoté) and two sinkholes (Coudoulous and Atapuerca). These examples give preliminary support to the hypothesis of scavenging opportunities for human groups to collect animal resources from karstic cavities. They have been chosen to illustrate the various potential combinations between topographic features, origins of bone accumulation and nature of human actions for different time periods. Moreover, multidisciplinary teams conduct the research on these sites and it is possible to envision an integrated approach of the different field studies.

1- Unikoté (Pyrénées Atlantiques, France)

Unikoté is a cave with three different loci chronologically attributed to the early last glacial (OIS 4-3). The oldest deposit (Unikoté I) is located inside the present cave and the two other loci (U II Base and U II top) are situated in a collapsed zone, in front of the cave (Michel, 1999, 2000; Fosse *et al.*, 1998). They are typical hyena dens, with a great number of *Crocuta* individuals and remains (e.31% of total NISP in levels 8-10 of U I to 13-9% in U II), a lot of coprolites, high percentage of gnawed bones and cylinders (fig.3a) from a diversified large ungulate faunas such as *Cervus*, *Rangifer*, *Equus*, *Bison*, etc. Some other carnivores are also present including *Canis*, *Vulpes*, *Meles*, *Ursus*, etc. All parts of the skeletons of herbivorous taxa are present with axial elements and long bones under-represented. The differences are mostly related to the degree of gnawing as well as age and size of the prey. The age mortality curves show a greater percentage of young and old animals for most of the ungulates (attritional profile), which are the favoured targets of hyenas.

Hominid bone remains and lithic artefacts verify the anthropic use of the cave. The former represents 15 bone remains from U I, and 40 from U II top. They show no evidence of carnivore marks on them (see *Tournepiche et al.*, 1996 for human remains with carnivore marks in hyena den). Stone tools and flakes, attributed to Middle Palaeolithic features (Dachary, 2000), are rare in U I and U II (respectively 19 and 13 artefacts) but they are more abundant in the upper levels of Unikote II. Generally, they are mostly from local raw material. There appears to be an inverse correlation (fig.3b) between the frequency of bones and artefacts through the sequence (although the level of U II base is weakly excavated), which suggest a lower occupation, probably more seasonal, by hyenas when hominids tend to stay longer. Moreover, U II top contains more evidence of knapping activities (with cores, Mousterian points and endscrapers, small debitage flakes) associated with evidence of the use of fire (burnt limestone, charcoals) in two different areas in close proximity to the actual entrance of the cave. Their concentrations suggest an absence of post-depositional reworking of the deposits.

The basal level of Unikote II is peculiar although little has been exposed (Michel, 2000: fig.5). The frequency of hyenids is still high and their action on bones is clearly visible. The level is interpreted as a *Crocuta* den. Only 13 flakes, rare fire traces and 5 cut-marked bone splinters in very close association with all the material allow us to establish a clear involvement of humans on the bone assemblage. One of the marked bones (large size

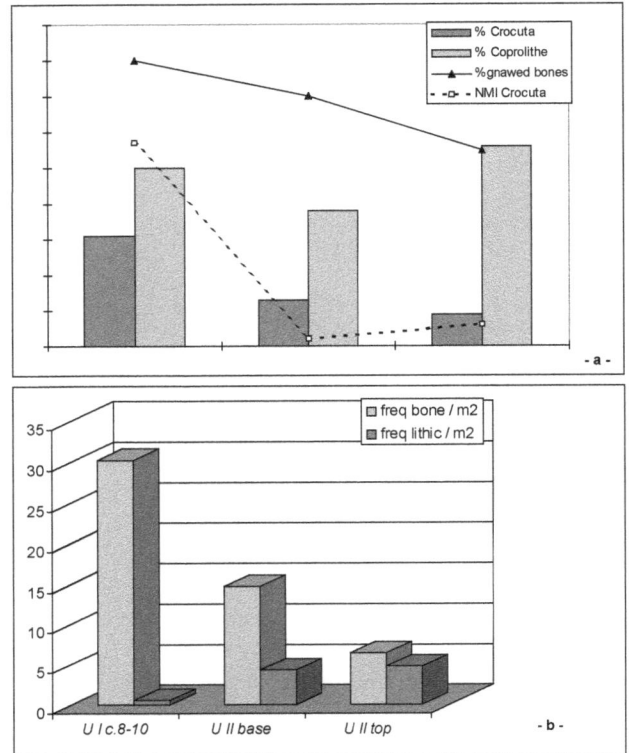

Figure 3a & b. Data supporting hyena denning activity and hominid occupation at Unikoté

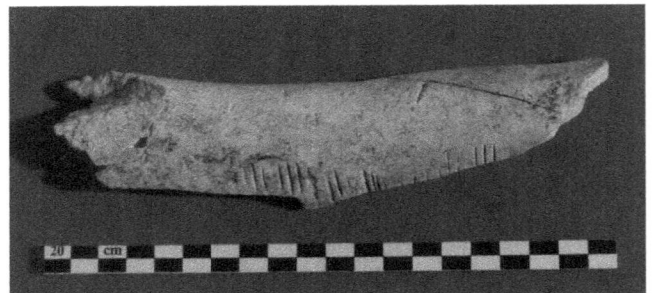

Figure 4a. Unikoté II: Long bone splinter of large size ungulates with incisions (detail)

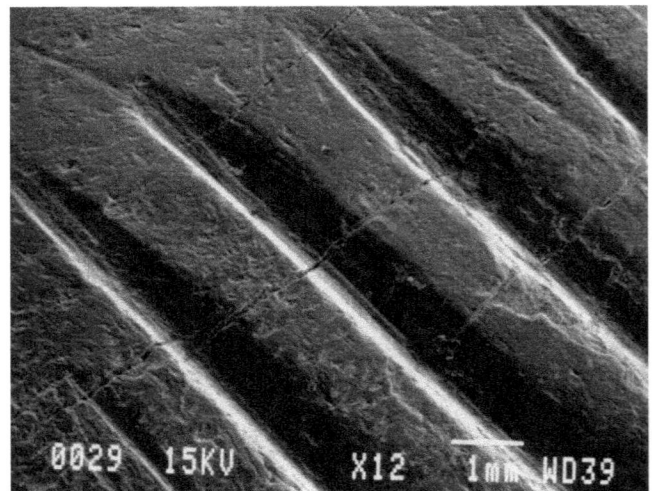

Figure 4b

4

		Level 5	Level 6	Level 7
	% NISP	2.80%	1.70%	5.90%
	N Bones	3277	5786	12,316
Herbivores	Age	adults	fïtus+juvenil + adults	fïtus to old adults
Carnivores	Species	Canid	Canid	Canid+Ursid+Felid
	Gnawed bones	+	+	++
	Coprolithes	0	0	0 ?
Carn / Humans	Green fracture	-	+	++
Humans	Lithics	34	20	50
	Cut-marked bones	2	1	2
	burnt splinters	10	3	0
	flaked bones	-	-	+

Table 2. Coudoulous I: criterions (data until 2000) about herbivore assemblages, and carnivore and hominid evidences (NISP count on total bone assemblages), present (+) and absent (-).

ungulate) shows a sequence of 23 parallel incisions on the same side of the cortical surface (D'Errico in Michel, 1999) with carnivore marks superimposed (a direct date to this specimen gave a AMS date of 30 150+/- 700 uncal BP, P. Pettit, Oxford) (fig. 4a). It is not obvious to relate these marks as a procurement activity. However, other pieces show real butchering marks for meat acquisition and some are clearly overlying hyenid gnaw marks. They demonstrate a short and discrete stay of hominids in a cave occupied episodically by hyenids, which are the main agent of the bone accumulation.

2 – Coudoulous (Lot, France)

Coudoulous I is an important multicomponent site with a deep stratigraphic sequence dated between 250 and 130 Ky (OIS 8-6; Jaubert et al., 2001, 2005). It is located at the edge of a plateau (e. 250 m a.s.l.), which overlooks the Lot valley, and essentially functioned as a sinkhole for the upper part of the detritic deposits. Another filling is also present in a underground room, called Coudoulous II, with a stratigraphic sequence estimated to e.150 to 30 Ky (OIS 6-3), and most of the bone assemblage was naturally accumulated by trapping (Brugal et al., 1998, 2001; Costamagno 1999).

At Coudoulous I (levels 5-8), the post-depositional processes (compaction, freeze-thaw action and reworking) are extensive in these basal deposits (15 m2 excavated), which result in low percentages of identifiable specimens and very large quantities of small bone debris (<2 cm, with dry fine-mesh screening). However, if we excluded all the smallest debris, the percentage of anatomically identified remains are greater (e.40-50% NISP) than those found generally in archaeological levels (e.10-25%). The layers are

relatively thick (>50 cm) and can be subdivided according to minor sedimentary variations; they will be combined here. Several points of concern include a very high degree of breakage with rare complete elements and mainly isolated teeth, a large number of immature pieces (new-born, infants and juveniles) and relatively good representation of broken axial elements. These taphonomic factors limit the specific determination and most of the identifications are to a familial or size class (Equid, Cervid, etc.) or genus level (especially for carnivores). Analyses are still in progress but preliminary data are summarized in table 2.

Large ungulates are dominant with (by importance): large Bovid, Cervid, Caprid and Equid (e.20-25%), while among carnivores, Canids (*Canis, Vulpes, Cuon*) are the main species with Felids and rare Ursids (e.15-20%). So far, any Hyenid remains are present. The non-human predators are most abundant at the base of the sequence (levels 7+8) indicating a possible secondary entrance. The filling-in of the cavity through time probably closed this opening. The bone assemblages are essentially natural, with very young, young and old individuals for the herbivores (attritional profiles). The existences of very young individuals suggest a seasonal process in animal trapping, with a probable suite of death events over a large time period. No juveniles and no coprolites are evidenced for carnivores, with some exceptions for levels 7 and 8. This suggests an easier access to the cavity and argues for natural deaths for carnivores related to reproduction and hibernation (Felid and Ursid). Moreover, the actions of carnivores on bones (gnawing and punctures marks) are present in all levels, induced by canid-size predators, which could indicate not only access into the cavity but also some degree of inter- and intra-specific competition.

The human activities are relatively restricted but demonstrate discrete activities on the bone assemblages. The deposits yielded a small number of lithic artefacts (34, 20 and 50 respectively in levels 5 to 7). These lithic materials exhibit a strictly local origin with quartz and basalt derived from the terrace, 100 meters down the valley. They are all heavy-duty tools produced on cobbles, attributed to Acheulean. Some very small, burnt splinters document a limited use of fire (levels 5 and 6). Cut-marked bones on bone shafts are rare; one instance seen on a femoral condyle of a caprid (cf. *Hemitragus*) indicates a

clear dismembering action (fig.5). This kind of evidence, replaced in the context of the butchery reduction sequence, show first an early access to carrion followed secondly by more intense removal of meat and marrow. Indeed, green fractures on large ungulates shafts and few typical flaked bones can be connected to these butchering activities, without totally excluding non-hominid actions for the fractures. We would remind that mostly medium-size carnivores, *Canis* or *Cuon* , are the modification agents, and they do not have the ability (contrary to Hyenids) to break thick and large long bones.

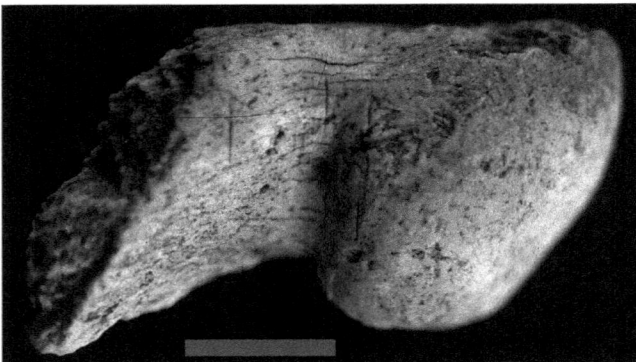

Figure 5: Cut-marked caprid femoral condyle

We can briefly mention the case of Coudoulous II, which yielded a small set of lithic products in level 7 of the

sequence (OIS 5): 23 artefacts, with few cores, modified pebbles and flakes, mostly in quartz. They are associated with natural Cervid populations (*Cervus* and *Dama*) composed of a lot of juveniles) with very few carnivores (*Vulpes, Lynx*). The Cervid elements show seven cut-

marked bones (ribs and vertebras), impacted long bones and bone flakes; three very small bone pieces are probably burnt (charcoal is also present). This level shows obvious evidence of discrete human activities on different part of carcasses, contrary to the upper levels where very few lithic artefacts were present but without any clear traces on bones (Brugal et al., 2000, 2001; Costamagno, 1999). In this later level, site formation processes acted to mix unrelated bones and lithics, as noted for other den sites (ex. Bois Roche, Villa and Soressi, 2000).

3- Atapuerca complex (Burgos, Spain)

The Sierra of Atapuerca has become famous due to the richness and complexity of the sites (almost 37 different cavities are recorded), because of the age of their sequences (beginning around 1 My) and the numerous human remains found. It is a complex of multileveled sites with different pits and fissures filled up with fine or coarse grained interbedded sediments. The karst is located on a limestone plateau or Sierra (e.1,000 m a.s.l.), not far from the Douro basin rich in terraces and raw material. The discussion here concerns two different sinkholes: Galeria with the level GII, dated around 350-300 ky (OIS 10-8) and Gran Dolina with the base level of TDW4, dated around 800-900 ky (OIS 26-25). The dates are determined by ESR, U/Th, paleomagnetic and biostratigrahic analyses: ex. Mimomys extinction occurs in TD6 and Bruhnes-Matuyama boundary is situated at the top of TD7 (see Made, 1998 ; Parès and Pérez Gonzalez, 1995, 1999 ; and others in Carbonell, Rosas and Diez, 1999; Carbonell and Rodriguez Alvarez, 1994). The main characteristics of the fossil assemblages from these levels are given in Table 3.

The extent of excavation surfaces varies from 7 square meters in TDW4b, 25 m2 for TDW4 and 64 m2 for unit GII. This last unit is thick (nearly 2 m) and contains 6 different levels, with the main assemblages coming from levels 10 and 11. Bone preservation is excellent, without weathering and preliminary studies (Huguet, 1998; Rosell Ardévol, 1998) have demonstrated the primary context of the deposits. There is no evidence for displacement of materials by rolling, which is also confirmed by the existence of connected anatomical units of ungulate limbs (fig.6a).

The number of identifiable remains is high (e.20-35% NISP) as well the number of individuals (ex. 167 for Galeria: Cervid, Equid and Bovid, which is a maximum here). Among herbivores, we found all size classes, from Rhinocerotid, Equid, large Bovids and several species of Cervids. The ungulate accumulations have a natural origin in all these levels, partly explained by the vertical nature of the karst systems and the skeletal and age patterns. All skeletal parts are present with the frequent existence of articulated complete bones (especially in Gran Dolina). Moreover, the mortality profiles tend to be more catastrophic than attritional with the systematic presence of adults and a predominance of juveniles.

The carnivores are relatively diversified but not so frequent (ex. only 2% of remains at Galeria). They are essentially a Canid, a wolf-like form, in Galeria and Ursid *(Ursus dolinensis nov.* sp. : Garcia and Arsuaga, 2001)) in Gran Dolina. So far, no hyenid remains have been recorded, as at Coudoulous. The absence of coprolites and young Canids argues against the use of Galeria as a den. On the other hand, the presence of juvenile and old bear at Grand Dolina indicates the use of the cavity by this hibernating species. The Atapuerca

		TDW 4	TDW 4b	G II (6 sublevels)
	% NISP	20.1%	24.5%	31.0%
	N Bones	1115	278	3207
Herbivores	Age	juvenil + adult + old adult	juvenil + adult	juvenil + adult + old adult
Carnivores	Species	Ursid	Ursid	Canid
	Gnawed bones	0.3%	1.7%	23.7%
	Coprolithes	0	0	0
Carn/humans	Green fracture	+	+	30%
Humans	Lithics	0	5	844
	Cut-marked bones	50	9	+
	Anthropic fractures	+	+(Herb.)	2.5%

Table 3. Atapuerca : Galeria (GII) and Gran Dolina (TDW4 and TDW4b) criterions (data until 2001) about herbivore assemblages and carnivore and hominid evidences (Huguet, 1998; Rosell Ardévol, 1998).

Figure 6a

Figure 6b. Atapuerca: Bone accumulations in TD4 and detail of bone splinters with puncture marks superimposed by cut-marks.

examples, as the case of the lower levels of Coudoulous, reveal a mixed case of accessibility into the cavity and to ungulate carcasses. However, the frequency of gnawed bones is low in Gran Dolina even though it is higher in Galeria. This suggests a possible entrance context for the latter and may also suggest rare carnivore trapping for the former.

The presence of a small quantity of stone tools, cut-marked bones and breakage patterns typical of human activities is good evidence of the intervention of hominids on the animal carcasses. The lithics exhibit no evidence of tumbling which serves to confirm the depositional integrity. Stone tools are made of quartzite, quartz and flint and all the raw materials occur within 2 km of the site. Most of them are finished tools. The TDW4b level yielded five quartzite artefacts attributed to a pre-Acheulean, which are the oldest evidence of hominid activity at Atapuerca. On the other hand, the GII level yields an abundant lithic assemblage with 844 pieces (but in fact only 6,6 pieces per m3), distributed in almost 2m thick deposits implying a succession of frequenting repetitive events. The lithics correspond to part of the reduction sequence with rare cores and more final products (cutting flakes). Unmodified pebbles are interpreted as heavy tools probably used as bone breakers or hammerstones.

According to the lithic quantities, cut-marked bones are more or less frequent, but their presence definitely indicates a relationship between humans and ungulate skeletal elements. In some cases, a sequence of puncture marks superimposed by cut-marks suggests an initial role of carnivores and subsequent scavenging by humans (Rosell *et al.*, 1998; Huguet *et al.*, 1999) (fig.6b). With respect to limb representation, and opposite to an in situ consumption by carnivores, hominids seems to spend a short time to recover parts of limbs in order to transport

7

them to an external place, out of the cavity (Rosell *et al.*, in prep.).

DISCUSSION

From these various features, it is important to emphasize three primary points: 1) the existence of large limestone area with high density of karstic cavities, especially sinkholes and dolines on plateaux; 2) relative common processes during the Pleistocene of natural ungulate deaths in these pitfalls (as for sediments too), as well as frequent use of caves by non-hominid predators which accumulated more or less dense bone assemblages, often on a seasonal basis; 3) the occurrence in some cases of small number of lithic artefacts in these sinkholes and cave dens, sometimes associated with evidence of cut-marked and impacted bones, more rarely fire traces.

At this point of the analysis, and without dismissing the possibility of fortuitous accumulation between lithics and bones, these several instances seem to demonstrate the repetitive and recurrent stay of human groups around these cavities. This can be explained by the natural transport processes of gravity and slope wash that combined the stone tools with natural bone accumulations (e.g., Villa and Soressi, 2000 for the hyena-den of Bois Roche, Costamagno, 1999 for upper levels of Coudoulous II). But, why would human groups be regularly present in such special locations, which do not represent a priori attractive resources (water, raw material, etc.)? Indeed, the causal association stone-tools/bones clearly indicates the frequenting of the inside cavity followed by minor exploitation of carcasses by hominids. The existence of carcasses from naturally dead animals represents the lone interest in this habitat. If we can question the relation for dens visited by scavenging humans "because there would not be much left to scavenge" (Villa and Soressi, 2000: 188), we can expect the opposite in sinkholes. However, animal exploitation can be diverse and hominids also have other resources to procure, such as animal skins (e.g., Diez *et al.*, 1998 for a leopard; Argant, in press. for bears) or durable raw materials (antler, bone, teeth, etc., as exemplified in the Upper Palaeolithic).

Different pictures emerge according to site specificity in terms of topographic features, presence of some predatory species and the intensity of hominid activities. But in all these cases, we notice the co-occurrence of small lithic series, technologically simple stone tools made on local materials, and food procurements characterized by cut-marks and breakage on ungulates long bones. They are found in clear association with natural bone accumulations in cavities, acting as a 'fridge' that benefits the body/nutrient conservation. The karstic trap and den occupations by humans were probably very short, even discrete. The evidence of anthropic action would be especially low and rather

'negative' related to the short duration of stay and the fast removal of edible pieces outside the cavity. We argue that these non-archaeological sites are relevant for assessing hominid food-management variability.

They can be integrated in a general adaptive framework of meat-eaters: predators and/or scavengers. The acquisition of animal food from large ungulates comes basically from three means (Houston, 1979: 265-266):
1 - by predation: to kill prey, which is often risky and requires time and energy;
2 - in scavenging from a predator kill or predator accumulations: food is generally poor and it can be risky as well to frequent dens;
3 - lastly, to locate and scavenge from animals that have died from some cause unconnected with predation: these means are, for instance, starvation, disease or accident...and this could introduce a seasonal factor to these kinds of mortality.
Indeed, mortality is not uniform through the year and increases during the dry season. In the East African plains, two third of ungulate deaths (often migratory species) fall into this category and it is the main food supply for non-human predators during some times of the year. This can be applied to karstic pits, which combined both high pit density and frequent animal trapping processes during Palaeolithic times. These sites are concentrated in restricted areas, easy to check and the risk of exposure to others predators is rather low. Though beyond the scope of this paper, we can briefly mention the open-air sites where large mammals can occurred due to natural trapping (marshland, peat bog, sludge, etc.). Instances of lower Pleistocene European sites with Proboscideans are well known in Spain and Italy (Villa, 1990; see papers in Cavarreta *et al.*, 2001 "The World of Elephants").

The main characteristics of the two forms of karst systems, caves and sinkholes, provide a contrasting picture, according to the origin of bone accumulations and human activities. The general features, as opposite extremes, are presented in Table 4. Geotopography is important when considering the location and accessibility of these features. This last point, accessibility, is especially relevant between quadruped and biped species. The mode and nature of bone accumulations are also variable, with complete carcasses and bones found in pits while more fragmented and dispersed materials are expected in the cave situation. Finally, the involvement of humans in terms of occupation and cultural debris again shows a different picture. The duration of human occupations in sinkholes would be short, just the necessary time for collecting the most recent and fresh dead animal. They would leave very few or no lithics artifacts. The examples given above support the evidence of discrete human involvement with some carcasses found in these natural accumulations (Brugal and Jaubert, 1991; Diez, 1993).

Characteristics	CAVES	SINKHOLES
Main Location	Valleys	Plateaux
Opening	Horizontal	Vertical
Acess	Easy	Difficult
Origin of Bone accumulations	Humans or Carnivores	Natural
Dominant species	Carnivores / Herbivores	Herbivores
Skeletal pattern 1	Cephalic + Limbs	Cephalic + Axial + Limbs
Skeletal pattern 2	Dispersed	Connection
Bone Completeness	Broken	Complete
Carcasse preserving	Short	Longer
Coprolithes	present	absent
Specific age Carnivores	new borns and old adults	youths and adults
Duration of human occupations	Short or Long	Short
Duration of opportunity	Variable	Short (Seasonal ?)
Human artefacts (lithic,cut-marks,..)	Abundant or Frequent	Rare or absent
Inter-specific competitions	High to Low	Low or Any

Table 4. General characteristics of cave *vs* sinkholes : topography, nature of bone assemblages and nature of human occupations.

Hominid food acquisitions using animals trapped in sinkholes could be considered as original subsistence behaviour, marked by the systematic inspection of restricted karstic territories on a regular and seasonal basis. From this hypothesis, related to the pit densities and frequent occurrence of trapping, we can also infer some degree of territoriality for these human groups as well as some degree of anticipatory behaviour. Indeed, the location and period of accident are relatively predictable in such karstic environment. Nevertheless, this tactical activity is mostly opportunistic although not marginal, but cannot constitute a reliable foraging strategy throughout the year for past human groups. They can however make up important food procurement for some stressful period such as wintertime in glaciated Europe. It is also a frequent season for naturally trapped animal accumulation processes. Moreover, this recurrent behaviour co-exists in many areas in Europe, and probably elsewhere (e.g., Asia, South Africa), and they occurred from the lower Pleistocene to more recent times. As pointed by P.Villa about the site (pitfall) of La Cotte St-Brelade (Jersey, see Callow and Cornford, 1986): "Occurrence of an organized approach to meat acquisition even in the scavenging context would seem to be appropriate precursor to the hunting behavior documented at that late Middle Pleistocene site." (Villa 1990: 304). In other words, hominids very likely made observations about ungulates felled down in natural pits. This probably gave them the basis to use this kind of location as a driving and communal hunt, such as the one precisely documented in level 4 of Coudoulous I (for *Bison priscus*: Brugal *et al.*, 1999)

This interpretation could represent a working hypothesis as a possible explanatory framework for some localities. However, this explanation relies on preliminary data and it is therefore necessary to refine and test it on others sites. For example, French sites such as Le Vallonet or l'Arago, Zhoukoudian in China or Swartkrans in South Africa, which are also characterized by collapsed pits and levels with few stone artefacts, could be evaluated utilizing this working hypothesis. Finally, we cannot avoid ignoring or minimizing the relative co-occurrence of a small number of lithic artefacts with natural bone accumulations. Hominids have highly adaptive subsistence strategies and since the earliest times have shown their cleverness and adventurous experiences. The prospecting and developed use of underground biotopes constitutes one example.

REFERENCES

BERMUDEZ DE CASTRO J.M., J.C. DIEZ FERNANDEZ-LOMANA, M. MOSQUERA MARTINEZ, M.E. NICOLAS CHECA, A. PEREZ-PEREZ, J. RODRIGUEZ MENDEZ, A. SANCHEZ MARCO. 1995. El nicho ecologico de los hominidos del Pleistoceno, medio de Atapuerca. *Complutum*, 6: 9-56.

BOSCH A.H., & J.-P. BRUGAL . 1996. Aveyron / Millau : Aven des Privats. Min. Cult. et Franc., Dir. Patrimoine, Serv. Rég. de l'Archéologie, Bilan Scientifique de la région Midi-Pyrénées 1995 pp. 51-52

BRUGAL J-P. 1982. Une faune du Tardiglaciaire dans l'Aven Bouet (Les Matelles,Hérault). *Et.Quatern.Languedoc.*, 2: 4-5.

BRUGAL J.P. 1999. Etude des populations de grands Bovidés européens : intérêt pour la connaissance des comportements humains au Paléolithique. In *Le Bison, gibier et moyen de subsistance des hommes du paléolithique aux paléoindiens des grandes plaines*, J.P.Brugal, F.David, J.Enloe, J.Jaubert (dir.), Antibes, ed. A.P.D.C.A: 7-10 (Actes du Colloque international, Toulouse, 6-10 juin 1995) pp. 85-103.

BRUGAL J.P. (ed.). 2000. *Rapport Trisannuel de Fouille Programmée : Bilan 1997-2000*, Pgm P1 Min. de la Culture, Service Régional de Midi-Pyrénées.

BRUGAL J-P., & J. JAUBERT. 1991. Les gisements paléontologiques pléistocènes à indices de fréquentation humaine : un nouveau type de comportement de prédation ? *Paléo,* 3: 15-41

BRUGAL J.P., S. COSTAMAGNO, J. JAUBERT, & V. MOURRE. 1998. Les gisements paléolithiques de Coudoulous (Tour-de-Faure, Lot, France). *Proceed. of the XIII Congress UISPP, Forli (Italia), 1996, Sect.5 'Paléolithique inférieur et moyen'*, éd. ABAZZI, vol. 2. pp. 141-145

BRUGAL J.P., D. COCHARD, B. ELLWOOD, M. GIRARD, J. JAUBERT, M. JEANNET, B. KERVAZO, A. LOUCHART, Y. QUINIF, & I. THERY-PARISOT. 2001. Tour de Faure : grotte de Coudoulous II (Lot). Min. Cult. et Franc., Dir. Patrimoine, Serv. Rég. de l'Archéologie, Bilan Scientifique de la région Midi-Pyrénées 2000. pp. 126-128

CALLOW P., & J.M. CORNFORD (eds.). 1987. *La Cotte de St.Brelade 1961-1979. Excavations by C.B.M.McBurney.* Norwich, Geo Books.

CARBONELL E., & X.P. RODRÍGUEZ ÁLVAREZ. 1994. Early Middle Pleistocene deposits and artifacts in the Gran Dolina site (TD4) of the 'Sierra de Atapuerca' (Burgos, Spain). *Journal of Human Evolution* 26: 291-311.

CARBONELL E., A. ROSAS, J.C. DÍEZ (eds.). 1999. *Atapuerca: Ocupaciones humanas y paleoecología del yacimiento de Galería.* Arqueología en Castilla y León. Zamora, Junta de Castilla y León.

CAMPY M. (ed.). 1983. L'aven de Vergranne (Doubs, France), Un site du Pléistocène moyen à hominidé. Extrait des Annales Scientifiques de l'Université de Besançon, Géologie, 4(5)

CAMPY M. 1990. L'enregistrement du temps et du climat dans les remplissages karstiques : l'apport de la sédimentologie. *Coll. Remplissages karstiques et Paléoclimats, Karstologia Mém.* n°2: 11-22

CLOT A. 1989. Les restes d'animaux piégés naturellement dans les cavités karstiques. in *Le Temps de la Préhistoire, S.P.F. Archeologia*, 1: 134-135

CLOT A., J. EVIN. 1986. Gisements naturels pléistocènes et holocènes des cavités des Pyrénées occidentales françaises : inventaire et datages 14C. *Munibe,* 38: 185-194

COSTAMAGNO S. 1999. Taphonomie d'un aven-piège : contribution des accumulations d'origine naturelle à l'interprétation des archéofaunes du Paléolithique moyen. *Anthropozoologica,* 29: 13-32

DACHARY M. 2000. Étude du matériel lithique recueilli à Unikoté (Iholdy, Pyrénées-Atlantiques) : campagnes 1995 à 1998. *Archéologie des pyrénées Occidentales et des Landes,* 19: 65-76.

DIEZ J.C. 1993. *Zooarqueología de Atapuerca (Burgos) e Implicaciones Paleoeconómicas del Estudio Tafonómico de Yacimientos del Pleistoceno Medio.* Departamento de Prehistoria y Etnología. Facultad de Geografía e Historia. Madrid, Universidad Complutense de Madrid.

DIEZ J.C., V. MORENO. 1994. El yacimiento Galeria (Atapuerca, Burgos): evolucion de un espacio en el Pleistoceno medio. Boletin del Seminario de Arte y Arqueologia, 60: 9-24.

DiEZ FERNANDEZ-LOMANA J.C., J.F. JORDA PARDO, A. ARRIBAS HERRERA. 1998. Torrejones (Tamajon, Guadalajara, Spain). A hyena den on human occupation. In *Economie Préhistorique : les comportements de subsistance au Paléolithique XVIIIe Rencontres Internationales d'Archéologie et d'Histoire d'Antibes, Sophia Antipolis.* éd. APDCA pp. 63-72.

DIEZ J.C., J. ROSELL ARDEVOL. 1998. Estrategia de subsistencia de los hominidos de la Sierra de Atapuerca. In *Atapuerca y la Evolucion Humana,* E.Aguirre (ed.), Madrid : Fundacion Ramon Areces, pp. 363-390.

DÍEZ J.C., V. MORENO, J. RODRÍGUEZ MÉNDEZ, J. ROSELL, I. CÁCERES, & R. HUGUET. 1999. Estudio arqueológico de los restos de macrovertebrados de la Unidad GIII de Galería (Sierra de Atapuerca)". E. Carbonell, A. Rosas and J.C. Díez (Eds.) *Atapuerca: Ocupaciones Humanas y Paleoecología del yacimiento de Galería.* Zamora, Arqueología en Castilla y León, 7: 265-281.

CAVARRETA G., P. GIOIA, M. MUSSI, M.R. PALOMBO. (eds.). 2001. *The World of Elephants. Proceed. 1st Internat.Congress,* Roma C.N.R.

FABRE G. 1989. Les karsts du Languedoc méditerranéen (S.E. de la France). *Z.Geomorph.N.F.,* suppl. 75: 49-81.

FOSSE Ph., J.-P. BRUGAL, J.L. GUADELLI, P. MICHEL, J.F. TOURNEPICHE. 1998. Les repaires d'Hyènes des cavernes en Europe occidentale: Présentation et comparaisons de quelques assemblages osseux. *Economie Préhistorique : les comportements de subsistance au Paléolithique.* J.P.Brugal, L.Meignen, M.Patou-Mathis (éds.), XVIIIème Rencontres Internationales d'Archéologie et d'Histoire d'Antibes, éd.APDCA: pp.43-61.

GARCIA N., & J.L. ARSUAGA. 2001. Ursus dolinensis : a new species of early pleistocene ursid from Trincehera Dolina, Atapuerca (Spain). *Compte Rendu de l'Académie des Sciences, Paris,* 332: 717-725.

GUERIN C., M. PHILIPPE, & R. VILAIN. 1979. Le gisement pléistocène supérieur de la grotte de Jaurens à Nespouls, Corrèze, France : historique et généralités. *Nouv.Arch.Mus.Hist.nat.Lyon,* 17: 11-16.

GILLI E. 1995. *La Spéléologie.* Paris, Presses Universitaires de France.

HOUSTON D.C. 1979. The adaptations of scavengers. In *Serengeti, Dynamics of an ecosystem,* A.R.E.Sinclair, M.Norton-Griffiths (eds.),Chicago and London: Univesrity of Chicago Press, pp. 263-286.

HUGUET R. 1998. Etude archéozoologique de l'unité GII du complexe de Galeria (Sierra de Atapuerca, Burgos, Espagne). In *Economie Préhistorique: les comportements de susbistance au Paléolithique,* J.P.Brugal, L.Meignen, M.Patou-Mathis (éds.), XVIIIème Rencontres Internationales d'Archéologie et d'Histoire d'Antibes, éd. APDCA, pp. 163-172.

HUGUET R., I. CACERES, J.C. DIEZ, J. ROSELL. 1999. Estudio tafonómico y zooarqueológico de los restos óseos de macromamíferos de la Unidad GII de Galería (Sierra de Atapuerca). E. Carbonell, A. Rosas, J. Díez: *Atapuerca: Ocupaciones Humanas y Paleoecología del yacimiento de Galería.* Zamora, Arqueología en Castilla y León, 7: 245-264.

JAUBERT, J., J.P. BRUGAL, M. JEANNET, B. KERVAZO, V. MOURRE. 2001. Tour de Faure : grotte de Coudoulous I (Lot). Min. Cult. et Franc., Dir. Patrimoine, Serv. Rég. de l'Archéologie, *Bilan Scientifique de la région Midi-Pyrénées 2000* pp. 123-126.

J.JAUBERT, B. KERVAZO, J.-P. BRUGAL, C. FALGUERES, M. JEANNET, A. LOUCHARD, H. MARTIN, F. MAKSUD, V.MOURRE, Y.QUINIF 2005. La séquence Pléistocène moyen de Coudoulous I (Lot). Bilan pluridisciplinaire. In *Les premiers peuplements en Europe: Données récentes sur les modalités de peuplement et sur le cadre chronostratigraphique, géologique et paléogéographique des industries du Paléolithique ancien et moyen en Europe,* N.Molines, M.H.Moncel, J.L.Monnier (éds), (Actes du Coll.intern.Rennes, 22-25 septembre 2003), Oxford. BAR, International Series 1364: 237-251.

MADE J. van der, 1998. Ungulates from Gran Dolina (Atapuerca, Burgos, Spain). *Quaternaire,* 9(4): 267-281.

MADE, J. van der. 1999. Ungulates from Atapuerca TD6. *Journal of Human Evolution,* 37 (3/4): 389-413.

MICHEL, P. 1999. La grotte d'Unikoté (Commune d'Iholdy, Pyrénées-Atlantiques): un repaire d'Hyènes avec des restes humains dans des niveaux würmiens. Rapport de fouille programmée. Direction régionales des Affaires Culturelles, Aquitaine, Service Régional de l'Archéologie.

MICHEL, P. 2000. Une grotte repaire d'hyènes des cavernes avec des indices de présence humaine dans des niveaux würmiens: la grotte d'Unikoté à Iholdy (Pyrénées-Atlantiques). *Archéologie des Pyrénées Occidentales et des Landes,* 19: 39-64.

MOREL, P. 1990. Aspects zoologiques et paléontologiques: possibilités et limites d'une interprétation paléoclimatologique. *Coll. Remplissages karstiques et Paléoclimats, Karstologia Mém.* n°2: 33-35

NICOD, J. 1972. *Pays et paysages calcaires.* Paris, Presses Universitaires de France, 244 p.

PARÉS, J. M., A. PÉREZ GONZÁLEZ. 1995. Paleomagnetic age for hominid fossils at Atapuerca archaeological site, Spain. *Science,* 269: 830-832.

PARÉS, J. M., A. PÉREZ GONZÁLEZ. 1999. Magnetochronology and stratigraphy at Gran Dolina section, Atapuerca (Burgos, Spain). *Journal of Human Evolution* 37 (3/4): 325-342.

PHILIPPE, M. 1978. Présentation du gisement pléistocène moyen de l'aven II des abîmes de La

Fage, à Noailles, (Corrèze), *Nouvelles Archives du Museum d'Histoire Naturelle de Lyon*, pp. 3-8

PHILIPPE, M. 1986. Les cavités du Lot et la Paléontologie du Quaternaire. In *Recherches sur les karsts du Quercy et du Sud-Ouest de la France*, Commission scientifique de Midi-Pyrénées du Comité de Spéléologie Régional, pp. 61-68.

PHILIPPE, M. 1994. *L'autre Padirac. Spéléologie, karstologie, paléontologie et préhistoire dans l'affluent du Joly.*, Fédération Française de Spéléologie et Muséum de Lyon.

PHILIPPE, M., C. MOURER-CHAUVIRE, & J. EVIN. 1980. Les gisements paléontologiques quaternaires des Causses de Martel et de Gramat (Corrèze et Lot) : faunes et chronologie *Nouv.Arch.Mus.Hist.nat.Lyon*, suppl. 18: 57-67.

RENAULT, P. 1976. Les karstifications pendant le quaternaire. In *La Préhistoire Française*, Lumley H.d. (ed.), Paris, vol.1, pp. 192-200.

RENAULT, P. 1987. Phénomènes karstiques. In *Géologie de la Préhistoire: Méthodes, techniques, applications*, J.C.Miskovsky (ed.), Paris: ed. GEOPRE . 169-196.

ROSELL ARDEVOL, J. 1998. Les premières occupations humaines à la Sierra de Atapuerca (Burgos, Espagne) : les niveaux TDW4 et TDW4B. In *Economie Préhistorique: les comportements de susbistance au Paléolithique*, J.P.Brugal, L.Meignen, M.Patou-Mathis (éds.), XVIIIème Rencontres Internationales d'Archéologie et d'Histoire d'Antibes, éd. APDCA : pp.153-162.

ROSELL J., I. CACERES, R. HUGUET. 1998. Systèmes d'occupation anthropique pendant le Pléistocène Inférieur et Moyen à la Sierra de Atapuerca (Burgos, Espagne). *Quaternaire*, 9 (4): 355-360.

ROSELL J., R. HUGUET, J.C. DIEZ, J.P. BRUGAL. in prep. – Human scavenging at the archaeological site of Atapuerca (Burgos, Spain).

ROUZAUD F., 1978. *La Paléospéléologie. L'homme et le milieu souterrain pyrénéen au Paléolithique supérieur*, Toulouse, Ecole des Hautes Etudes en Sciences Sociales. (Archives d'Ecologie Préhistorique)

ROUZAUD F., 1997. La paléospéléologie, in *Proceedings of the 12th International Congress of Speleology*, P.Y.Jeannin (ed.), La Chaux-de-Fonds, pp. 49-50

ROUZAUD F., M. SOULIER, J.-P. BRUGAL, & J. JAUBERT. 1990. L'Igue des Rameaux (Saint-Antonin-Noble-Val, Tarn-et-Garonne): un nouveau gisement du Pléistocène moyen. Premiers résultats. *Paleo* , 2 : 87-104.

SALOMON J.N., (with C.Messud & A.Tarisse), 2000. Le Causse de Gramat et ses alentours: les atouts du paysage karstique. *Karstologia*, 35.

TOURNEPICHE F., C. COUTURE, J.L. GUADELLI, P. MICHEL. 1996. Les restes néandertaliens du repaire d'hyènes de la grotte de Rochelot (Saint-Amant-de-Bonnieure, Charente, France). *Compte Rendu de l'Académie des Sciences, Paris,* 322: 429-435.

VILLA P., 1990. Torralba and Aridos: Elephant exploitation in Middle Pleistocene Spain. *Journal of Human Evolution,* 19: 229-309

VILLA P., M. SORESSI. 2000. Stone tools in carnivore sites: the case of Bois Roche. *Journal of Anthropological Research,* 56: 187-215.

NEW DATA FROM MUSEUM COLLECTIONS: MOUSTERIAN MAMMALS FROM LA QUINA IN THE PEABODY MUSEUM OF NATURAL HISTORY

Roger H. Colten* and Andrew Hill**

*Peabody Museum of Natural History, Yale University
**Department of Anthropology and Peabody Museum, Yale University

INTRODUCTION

Museum collections contain a great wealth of information that is often underutilized. Despite the widespread bias towards new excavations, analysis of existing collections can provide significant information at modest expense, and these collections are of increasing importance for several reasons. First, as our understanding of taphonomy, preservation, and recovery biases increase, we can better evaluate factors that may influence the analysis of museum collections and make more informed use of them. Second, as more archaeological sites (and paleontological and other types of sites) are lost through erosion, development, and excavation, the portion of the archaeological record that is housed in museums grows proportionally, and in its scientific importance. Third, as new scientific techniques are developed, it is possible to gather greater amounts of information from museum collections, some of great antiquity and possibly more suited to such analyses than modern collections. In this paper we review some issues related to the analysis of museum collections, and provide an example of a faunal analysis of Pleistocene fauna from the Mousterian site of La Quina, in France.

A wide variety of new methods, many not discovered when objects were acquired, are now available for studying museum collections and providing new information. For example, the application of modern genetic analysis to museum specimens is one of the most exciting uses of museum collections that has been applied to a variety of taxa and diverse research questions. Numerous scholars have extracted DNA to study the relationship between older historic and modern populations, and to study "genetic bottlenecks" among taxa that were nearly extinct but have recovered. Some of the most well-known of these studies involved Whooping Crane (Glenn, et al. 1999), Right Whale (Rosenbaum, et al. 2000), wombat, dog and wolf (Roy, et al. 1994) and kangaroo rat (Thomas, et al. 1990).

More traditional anthropological studies of museum collections can also yield useful information, occasionally altering the results of earlier generations of researchers. Museum collections may have been curated without analysis, or simply cataloged with simple generic descriptions, such as "stone tools," "bones," or "shells." More precise identification and summarizing of catalog data can provide otherwise unavailable data. Re-analysis of human skeletal remains, producing new results, is one of the strongest arguments for retention of human skeletal collections (Buikstra and Gordon 1981).

Before the discovery of radiocarbon dating, absolute dates for sites, artifact types, and entire prehistoric cultures were based on relative dating methods, such as seriation. Carbon 14 dating of museum collections, as well as newly recovered material, can provide more rigorous chronological control allowing more refined anthropological problem oriented research. This avenue of inquiry is particularly important for collections from destroyed or otherwise inaccessible sites. Advances in radiocarbon data allow the direct dating of individual artifacts or small samples of organic material recovered from the surfaces of artifacts. For example, radiocarbon dating of food residues from the surface of ceramics allowed Lovis (1990a, 1990b) to re-evaluate the ceramic sequence for the Saginaw River valley in lower Michigan. Another interesting application of radiocarbon dating focused on shells from museum collections derived from archaeological sites in southern California. More precise chronological control for these sites has added significantly to our understanding of culture history and cultural ecology in that region (Erlandson 1991; Erlandson et al. 1988; Rick et al 2000). Many of these sites were identified before radiocarbon dating, and some lack diagnostic artifacts or stratification that would allow relative dating.

Quantitative analysis of numerous small collections from existing museum collections can provide information on regional patterns of ecological adaptations, culture history, and biogeography (Colten 1989, 2002).

THE SITE OF LA QUINA

La Quina, in Charente, France was first identified by Gustave Chauvet in 1872 and excavated over many years by three teams. The first excavation was directed by Dr. Henri-Martin, the second phase by his daughter Germaine Henri-Martin, and more recently by Arthur Jelinek and André Debénath (Bierwirth 1996). Former Peabody Museum curator George Grant MacCurdy was one of the founders of the American School for Prehistoric Research in France, and during the first two seasons of this training and research program (1921 and 1922), students excavated at La Quina (MacCurdy 1922b; Peabody 1923) while Dr. Henri-Martin was supervising excavation of the site.

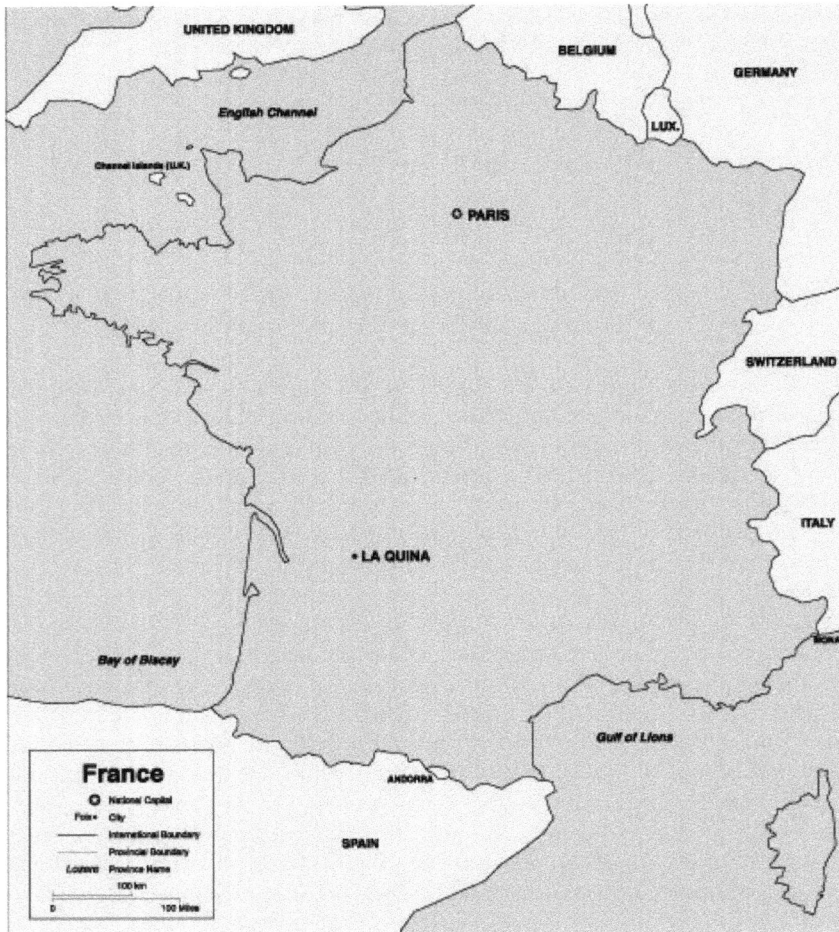

Figure 1: Map of France with location of La Quina

La Quina is located in southwestern France in the Charente region (Figure 1). The site is essentially a collapsed rock shelter adjacent to the Voultron River, a distant tributary to the Dordogne River in the Périgord region. This site can be dated by a variety of methods, including the stone tool typology, the presence of extinct fauna (including Neanderthal remains) and radiocarbon dates. The flaked stone industry has been described in great detail by Bierwirth (1996) and can be characterized as Mousterian with abundant points, scrapers, and evidence of the Levallois technique. The site has yielded the remains of at least 21 Neanderthal (Homo neanderthalensis) individuals, including a nearly complete adult skeleton and one child (Oakley, et al. 1971). In this part of Europe, Neanderthal remains have been dated from roughly 110,000 to 35,000 years before present. La Quina has also been the source of several radiocarbon dates which range from 34,130 +/- 700 BP to 35,250 +/- 530 BP (Bierwirth 1996:21; Henri-Martin 1964). This places the site towards the end of the age range for Neanderthal remains in Europe.

THE YALE PEABODY MUSEUM LA QUINA COLLECTION

The YPM collections include faunal remains and stone tools. There are 34 catalog entries representing 287 stone tools primarily described as scrapers, points, or cores. The portion of the collection described in this paper consists of 520 bones of large mammals originally listed under 116 catalog entries. While there are a very few bones of small mammals, and possibly birds, fish and amphibians in small numbers, they are not discussed in this paper. Our complete catalog of the macro-mammals will be published elsewhere (Colten and Hill, n.d.).

While some of the faunal material was identified to element and correct taxonomic categories, most of the large mammal bones were initially cataloged as "bones of large game animals." Many of these catalog entries included numerous limb fragments that we believed could be more precisely identified, and some of the identified bones appeared to be incorrectly categorized. All of the bones were labeled with catalog numbers, and they were initially sorted by skeletal element and size. Few Pleistocene mammals of European origin are present in the museum's collections, and we therefore relied on the Peabody Museum vertebrate zoology division's modern osteology collection for comparative material. The only significant problems encountered with this approach were differentiating Bos and Bison, and identification of the species of equids present in the collection. Given the well-known difficulty of differentiating between European Bos and Bison from teeth and fragmentary remains, we elected to combine these taxa under the designation Bos/Bison. For similar reasons, we categorized all equid remains only to genus, as Equus. However, it is likely that all the equid remains are E. caballus.

Taxonomically, the collection is formed primarily of bovids, equids and cervids, with a few carnivores (Tables 1 and 2). There are at least three cervids, most likely reindeer (Rangifer tarandus), red deer (Cervus elaphus), and one smaller cervid. The carnivores include Hyena (Crocuta), canids, possibly wolf (Canis), fox (Vulpes), and cave bear (Ursus spaeleus). Some of the hyena remains had previously been described as lion, and a bear tooth had been mis-identified as pig.

The skeletal elements are primarily teeth and other cranial elements. Lower limb bones are the next most abundant category of element, other portions of the skeleton being present in small numbers (Table 3). Most of the skeletal elements classified as "miscellaneous" are fragmentary limb bones that were not identified more precisely.

Taxon	%NISP
Bos/Bison	43%
Unassigned	29%
Equus	14%
Rangifer	12%
Crocuta	1%
Vulpes	1%
Ursus	<1%
Canis	<1%

Table 1: Large mammal taxa from La Quina

Taxon	%NISP
Bos/Bison	60%
Equus	20%
Rangifer	17%
Crocuta	1%
Vulpes	1%
Ursus	1%
Canis	1%

Table 2: Large mammal genera from La Quina (excluding unassigned bones)

Skeletal element	%NISP
Cranial	51%
Distal limb	21%
Miscellaneous	14%
Proximal limb	9%
Axial	5%

Table 3: Large mammal skeletal elements from La Quina

The collection methods are unknown, so it is not possible to determine if the body part distribution is due to taphonomic factors, such as density mediated attrition or collecting bias, or due to cultural factors, such as site function or butchery practices. The Yale Peabody Museum (YPM) material from trench M differs from a more recently collected faunal sample in which cranial elements were under-represented (Chase *et al.* 1994), which could indicate different collecting methods or some intra-site variability in cultural or taphonomic factors. The YPM collection also differs from previously reported samples in lacking burning or surface encrustations. It is highly likely that field collection methods influenced the pattern of skeletal elements in this collection, and MacCurdy may have specifically collected objects that he felt were appropriate for the Peabody Museum collections.

Because most of the Peabody collections was derived from Trench M, it is possible to consider change through the stratigraphic sequence in the taxonomy and skeletal elements in the faunal sample. While there is some variation through the three levels in Trench M, the

general patterns of taxonomic abundance and body part distribution are the same as in the collection as a whole. Bos/Bison is most abundant taxon in all three levels, although this category is relatively less abundant in the uppermost level, M1. M1 also contains the highest percentage of Rangifer bones, which could indicate a change in hunting strategy or climate. Cranial elements are the most abundant type of bones in all three levels of Trench M, although they are noticeably more prominent in M3, the deepest level in the trench. While these patterns may be intriguing, it is important to keep in mind the small sample size of the collection as a whole, and the variation in sample size between the levels. M2 in particular has very few bones, compared to the other two levels.

	Bos/Bison	*Equus*	*Rangifer*	other
M1	51.39%	20.83%	23.61%	4.17%
M2	75.00%	0.00%	12.50%	12.50%
M3	76.47%	18.72%	1.07%	3.74%

Table 4: Mammal taxa in different levels of trench M, La Quina

	Cranial	Distal limb	Misc.	Axial	Proximal limb
M1	41.46%	20.33%	20.33%	8.13%	9.76%
M2	42.86%	7.14%	28.57%	0.00%	21.43%
M3	66.80%	13.04%	9.49%	2.37%	8.30%

Table 5: Mammal skeletal elements in different levels of Trench M, La Quina

A fair number of bones have cut marks, suggesting either intensive butchering, selection by the excavators for butchered bones, or a combination of factors. Some of the cut marks and bone modification, such as the cut antlers, probably indicate tool manufacture and not processing for food consumption (David Reese, pers. comm. 2001). Previous studies suggest that the bones may have been used as tools themselves, perhaps in lithic artifact production or re-sharpening, which might account for some of the modification to the bones. While Charles Peabody (1914) suggests that 26 percent of the faunal material from La Quina shows evidence of cut marks, the current sample appears to have a much higher incidence of such modifications. Virtually all of the YPM collection is fragmented, with no complete long bones present. The only complete elements are teeth and foot bones.

This study demonstrates that older museum collections have potential to provide new information concerning anthropological research problems. Once collections of the type described here are cataloged and published, application of modern technical studies can be used to yield additional information. For example, radiocarbon dating, trace element analysis and other methods may produce information about chronology and paleoenvironments at the time of site occupation. One particularly interesting possibility is the recovery of plant remains from the surface of teeth in the La Quina collection. Many of the bovid teeth have thick layers of calculus (tartar) that has been shown to contain phytoliths (J. MacCormack, pers. comm. 2001). With a systematic effort to sample and study these remains, we may be able to provide detailed information about the environment in the region around La Quina during the later Pleistocene.

SUMMARY

In summary, the Peabody Museum holds numerous small collections of Paleolithic material, including a collection of about 800 objects from the Mousterian site of La Quina. Analysis of the faunal material demonstrates some similarity, and some differences, from more recent collections from that site. Taxonomically, the collection is similar to recently acquired material, being dominated by bovids, equids, and cervids. In terms of body part representation, cranial bones are the most abundant skeletal elements. The prevalence of these skeletal portions in most likely a result of collector preference, although our analysis has not formally evaluated whether or not taphonomic factors or prehistoric behavior could have produced this pattern. We hope this study will inspire other researchers to look at museum collections with an eye towards productive analysis and application of modern methods to older collections.

ACKNOWLEDGMENTS

We thank the following individuals for their assistance and contributions to this study: Richard Burger, Chris Chandler, Larry Gall, Diane Gifford-Gonzalez, Frank Hole, Daria Lucas, Barbara Narendra, Sally Pallato, Rick Potts, David Reese, James Rossie, Bill Sacco, Max Shpak, and Paul Whitehead.

REFERENCES

BIERWIRTH, S. L. 1996. *Lithic Analysis in Southwestern France. Middle Paleolithic Assemblages from the site of La Quina.* BAR International Series 633.

BUIKSTRA, J. E., AND C. C. GORDON. 1981. The study and restudy of human skeletal series: The importance of long-term curation. *Annals of the New York Academy of Sciences* 376:449-465.

CHASE, P.G., D. ARMAND, A. DEBÉNATH, H. DIBBLE, AND A.J. JELINEK. 1994. Taphonomy and zooarchaeology of a Mousterian faunal assemblage from La Quina, Charente, France. *Journal of Field Archaeology* 21:289-305.

COLTEN, R.H. 1989. Prehistoric shellfish exploitation around the Goleta Lagoon. *Journal of California and Great Basin Anthropology* 11:203-214.

COLTEN, R. H. 2002. Prehistoric marine mammal hunting in context: Two Western North American examples. *International Journal of Osteoarchaeology* 12:12-22.

COLTEN, R.H., AND A. HILL. n.d. Mousterian Mammals from La Quina in the Yale Peabody Museum Collections. Ms. In preparation for Postilla.

ERLANDSON, J. 1991. A radiocarbon series for CA-SBA-1 (Rincon Point), Santa Barbara County, California. *Journal of California and Great Basin Anthropology* 13(1):110-117.

ERLANDSON, J., R. COLTEN, AND M. GLASSOW. 1988. Reassessing the chronology of the Glen Annie Canyon Site (CA-SBA-142). *Journal of California and Great Basin Anthropology* 10(2):237-245.

GLENN, T. C., W. STEPHAN, AND M. J BRAUN. 1999. Effects of a population bottleneck on whooping crane mitochondrial DNA variation. *Conservation Biology* 13(5):1097-1107.

HENRI-MARTIN, G. 1964. La dernière occupation moustérienne de La Quina (Charente). Datation par le radio-carbone. *Comptes Rendus De L'Academie Des Sciences De Paris. Série D.* 258:3533-3535.

LOVIS, W. 1990a. Curatorial considerations for systematic research collections: AMS dating a curated ceramic assemblage. *American Antiquity* 55(2):382-387.

LOVIS, W. 1990b. Accelerator dating the ceramic assemblage from the Fletcher Site: Implications of a pilot study for interpretation of the Wayne Period. *Midcontinental Journal of Archaeology* 15(1):37-50.

MACCURDY, G.G. 1922a. New discoveries of Neanderthal Man at La Quina and La Ferrassie. *American Journal of Physical Anthropology* 5(1):1-3.

MACCURDY, G. G. 1922b The first season's work of the American School in France for Prehistoric Studies. *American Anthropologist* 24:61-71.

MILLER, E.H. (ed.) 1985. *Museum Collections: Their Roles and Future in Biological Research.* Occasional Papers of the British Columbia Provincial Museum No. 25.

OAKLEY, K.P., B.G. CAMPBELL, T.I. MOLLESON. 1971. Catalogue of Fossil Hominids. Part II: Europe. London: Trustees of the British Museum (Natural History).

PEABODY, C. 1914. Ten days with Dr. Henri Martin at La Quina. *American Anthropologist* 16:257-268.

PEABODY, C. 1923. Annual Report of the American School in France of Prehistoric Studies, 1922-23. *Bulletin of the Archaeological Institute of America* 14:115-118.

RICK, T., ERLANDSON, J., AND R. VELLANOWETH. 2000. A radiocarbon chronology for the Arozena site (CA-SBA-141), Eastern Santa Barbara County, California. *Journal of California and Great Basin Anthropology* 22(2):353-360.

ROSENBAUM, H. C., M. G. EGAN, P. J. CLAPHAM, R. L BROWNELL, JR., S. MALIK, M. W. BROWN, B. N. WHITE, P. WALSH, AND R. DESALLE. 2000. Utility of North Atlantic right whale museum specimens for assessing changes in genetic diversity. *Conservation Biology* 14(6):1837-1842.

ROY, M. S., D. J. GIRMAN, A. C. TAYLOR, AND R. K. WAYNE. 1994. The use of museum specimens to reconstruct the genetic variability and relationships of extinct populations. *Experientia* 50:551-557.

THOMAS, W.K., S. PÄÄBO, F. X. VILLABLANCA, AND A. C. WILSON. 1990. Spatial and temporal continuity of kangaroo rat populations shown by sequencing mitochondrial DNA from museum specimens. *Journal of Molecular Evolution* 31:101-112.

REEVALUATIONS OF REINDEER KILL SEASONALITY AND IMPLICATIONS FOR SITE FUNCTION AT VERBERIE

James G. Enloe

Department of Anthropology, University of Iowa, Iowa City, IA 52242, james-enloe@uiowa.edu

INTRODUCTION

Rangifer tarandus has been argued (Mellars 1989) to be the basis of specialized hunting strategies throughout the Upper Paleolithic. It has been demonstrated (Enloe 1993) that this species was also taken as territorial game as a function of availability during severe climatic regimes during the early Upper Paleolithic. Nonetheless, the occupation of the Paris Basin at the end of the Pleistocene was a pioneering settlement into formerly unoccupied territory. Mellars (1994:76) has argued that an adaptive response to rapidly changing environmental conditions at the end of the Pleistocene was to retreat northward from the classic Paleolithic regions such as the Périgord, to colonize newly emerging environments in northern Europe, such as the Paris Basin, in order to maintain a grip on open environments and to continue to exploit the same animal species.

The mere presence or even predominance of Rangifer in the assemblage is insufficient to characterize the exploitative aspects of human subsistence patterns. We must ask more specific questions. What problems in adaptation were being solved by this expansion of territory? How were these animal species being exploited? Rangifer can be exploited in a variety of ways, not just as variation in hunting tactics, such as stalking, ambush, drives, etc., but also as fundamental variation in hunting strategies. The difference between tactics and strategies lies in understanding what fundamental subsistence need the resource fulfills in the environmental context. Are single or small numbers of prey being taken for immediate consumption, regardless of the species? Or, are certain species being targeted because they can help solve a problem posed by the environment? Because of its seasonally migratory behavior, Rangifer tarandus can provide a predictable large quantity of food, for which sufficient labor forces for hunting and processing can be organized at a predictable location and time. In short, food can be stored for the winter. Rangifer can also be hunted as any other species available at hand, with no overall strategic consideration, as was probably the case at the Abri Pataud (Spiess 1979) or le Flageolet (Enloe 1993).

In order to assess the strategic considerations of Rangifer exploitation patterns, it is necessary to examine closely population parameters of the target species. In particular, the seasonality of hunts and the mortality profile of the targeted prey can give important information for understanding the overall strategy of Magdalenian hunters in northern Europe. The late Magdalenian site of Verberie can give us some insight into this problem.

VERBERIE

Verberie (Audouze et al. 1981; Audouze 1987; Audouze and Enloe 1997) is located approximately 60 km north of Paris, on the low first terrace of the left bank of the Oise, a tributary of the Seine. Radiocarbon dates range from 12,900 + 180 to 12,450 + 850 BP (Audouze 1987:185). Verberie is characterized by several hearths with dense associated artifactual and faunal debris. The well-preserved fauna at Verberie is dominated by reindeer (Rangifer tarandus), comprising over 98% of the assemblage (David 1994; David and Enloe 1992; Enloe 1994).

Level	Elevation	Artifacts	Individuals
II-1	-1.212	4047	29
II-2	-1.272	6995	30
II-21	-1.292	10744	28
II-22	-1.340	2680	9
II-3	-1.373	9445	24
II-4	-1.413	3390	8
II-5	-1.440	440	?
II-6	-1.460	200	?

Table 1: Occupation levels at Verberie with counts of reindeer individuals

Although Verberie has been excavated since 1976, during the last dozen years that we have discovered than in certain areas of the site remains from multiple levels of occupation have been preserved under the original occupation described by Audouze et al. (1971). Since preliminary analyses were completed in 1994 (Enloe 1997), four occupation levels and 31 new individuals have been added to our sample. This warrants this current analytical presentation. Level designations have been reassigned for previously excavated material. The levels in the Pleistocene stratum II are designated by historical accident as II1, II2, II21, II22, II3, II4, II5, and II6 (table 1). Obviously, more surface area has been excavated for the upper occupation surfaces ca. 220 m_ for II1 and ca. 120 m_ for II2, and correspondingly less for the lower ones, ca. 80 m_ for II21, ca. 80 m_ for II22, ca. 35 m_ for II3 and less than 10 m_ II4, II5 and II6. The structure and content of the deeper, earlier occupations appear to be somewhat different, raising questions about potential differences in site role in annual economic rounds, most particularly for its role as a fall migration interception hunting camp. The differences may be due to sampling bias attributable to the smaller excavation area.

These different occupation surfaces offer the opportunity to examine details of the hunting strategies of the Magdalenian occupants of the site. Multiple occupations allow us to examine repeated episodes of hunting, from which we may be able to discern possible strategies. Single incidents may be distorted, masked by periodic anomalies in prey herd structure, such as missing cohorts of young animals, due to late spring storm kill off of new calves. Was there a consistent demographic target in the reindeer prey? Could information on the prey population shed light on specific tactics of the hunt at Verberie and on general strategy of Magdalenian hunting in the Paris Basin?

All elements of the skeleton are present at Verberie, but there appears to be differential representation of skeletal elements, particularly when compared with Pincevent, the only other Magdalenian site in the region with well-preserved reindeer remains. Of particular interest are the numerous articulated segments of vertebral columns. Ethnoarchaeological evidence suggests that these elements are frequently abandoned at close proximity to the kill site, where initial butchering for transport might take place. Such elements are absent at Pincevent, suggesting that it was more a consumption location than one of primary acquisition. In contrast, Verberie appears to be a hunting campsite, more closely concerned with direct acquisition and initial processing of carcasses. As such, it may yield information about hunting strategies more directly, without having passed through the filter of transported assemblages.

This analysis is focused on the mandibular dental remains of the reindeer. Dental remains are the best preserved and best represented skeletal element present. It is also the most useful for determining age and seasonality, which are critical factors in understanding the exploitation of a highly seasonal food resource like reindeer.

MINIMUM NUMBER OF INDIVIDUALS

The Minimum Number of Individuals is derived from the frequency of right P3's from adults and D3's from immature individuals. This minimal frequency MNI totals 70. This figure can be refined by several procedures. First, deciduous dental series were separated from fully permanent series. This yielded 53 right permanent M2's and 32 right deciduous D4's, increasing the total to 85. Second, the first year individuals were separated from the second year individuals in the deciduous dentition, based on wear on the deciduous teeth and eruption of the permanent molars. This yielded 8 left D3's in the first year and 26 right D4's in the second year, increasing the total MNI to 89.

One goal of this investigation is the elucidation of actual number of individuals killed and processed at the site. Therefore Poplin's comparison method of calculating the minimum number of individuals was employed. The hemi-mandibles, dental series and individual teeth were examined for side and tooth identification. Teeth were placed into dental series when specimen fragments had matching breaks. Left and right mandible halves and teeth were matched according to size and similarity of cusp and wear patterns. These proved to be sufficiently individualized to determine that a given isolated tooth could not be derived from a particular individual, so that another individual could be recognized. This procedure was employed in the first year calves, the second year sub-adults and the adults with fully permanent dentition. Partial overlaps of teeth in dental series within each broad age class were used further to identify additional individuals. A total of 128 individuals, represented by from one to twelve teeth each, was achieved. This population was the basis for the study of age parameters. This includes 29 individuals for level II1, 30 individuals for level II2, 28 individuals for level II21, 9 individuals for level II22, 24 individuals for level II3, and 8 individuals for level II4. No significant dental remains have been discovered in the limited excavation area of levels II5 and II6.

SEASONALITY

Seasonality is a crucial variable in the exploitation of Rangifer. Hunting during the winter or summer cannot yield the same predictable massive food resource for the strategic goal of potential winter storage as can hunting during the fall migration. Hunting during the spring migration yields prey in a depleted nutritional state, and is thus both qualitatively and quantitatively inappropriate for long term strategic goals. Hunting throughout the year may be responsive to different short or long term goals. Therefore, determination of seasonality is a crucial prerequisite for examining hunting strategy.

Seasonality can be determined by a number of indicators. One of these deals with antlers. Rangifer is the only cervid characterized by antlers on adults of both sexes, but there are different schedules for the growth and shedding of antlers for each sex. Bulls carry antlers from late March or April until the end of the rut in late October. Nonpregnant cows and young males carry their antlers from May until the following may. Pregnant cows carry their antlers until parturition in early June, and begin regrowth soon thereafter (Skoog 1968, Spiess 1979). The antlers from Verberie are bois de massacre, indicating kills between June and late October. The technological utility of bull antler, however, necessitates our considering the possibility that those antlers could have been transported to the site from other locations occupied at other times of the year.

Bryan Gordon's (1988:86) analysis of cementum annuli of teeth from Verberie yielded equal increments from summer, fall and late winter. This type of analysis has been criticized due to loss of the outermost annuli during specimen preparation. Spiess (1979:69) reported that only 10 of 171 specimens from Abri Pataud were successfully sectioned and readable. Contradictions between annuli counts and other age determinations at Pincevent suggest (Enloe 1991:134-135) that problems exist also for reading of the final annulus to determine seasonality. My analyses indicate different results from Gordon's findings at Verberie.

The best indicators of seasonality can be found in the eruption of permanent teeth and wear of the deciduous dentition. Since Rangifer exhibits highly synchronized births, tooth eruption age determinations can yield fairly precise determinations of age at death. Miller (1974) observed the timing of permanent dentition eruption in several herds in North America and Asia. The first permanent molar erupts between 3 and 5 months, while the deciduous teeth have high, sharp cusps. The second permanent molar erupts between 10 and 15 months, while the cusps of the deciduous teeth have become worn and flattened. The majority of second molars are in occlusion by 13 months and all are in occlusion after 15 months. The third permanent molar can erupt between 15 and 29 months, and is not useful for seasonality determinations.

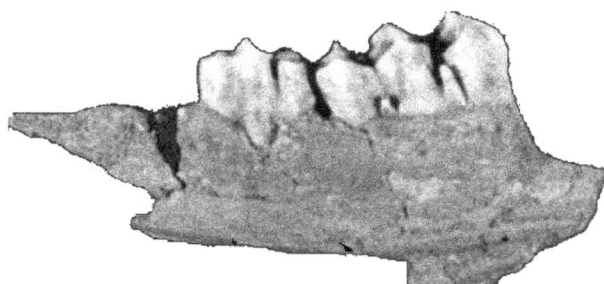

Figure 1

In the Verberie fauna, there are 11 individuals that exhibit very lightly worn deciduous teeth and erupting first molars (e.g. Figure 1), corresponding to calves of their first year. There is another group of 33 individuals with well worn deciduous teeth, slightly worn first permanent molars, second molars just coming into occlusion, and occasional buds or erupting third molars (e.g. Figure 2); these correspond to yearlings, individuals in the second year. The similarity in eruption and wear within each of these groups suggests limited seasonality. Spiess (1979:78) noted that "Deciduous molar wear patterns will only appear discrete in sites of limited season hunting." This is clearly the pattern that can be seen for the first and second year cohorts. It becomes a little blurred into the third year, when wear rates on deciduous teeth slow down and very worn deciduous teeth may be maintained while second permanent molars are in full occlusion and wear and even third molars and some premolars may be coming into wear.

We can go to measurement of the wear of the deciduous teeth for a more precise determination of seasonality.

Crown heights were measured for D4, the most frequently occurring tooth in juvenile remains. The frequency distribution of these measurements is plotted in Figure 3. It can be seen that there are two very strong peaks in the

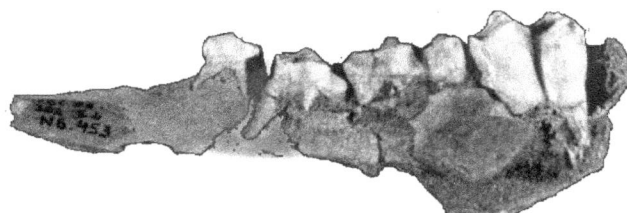

Figure 2

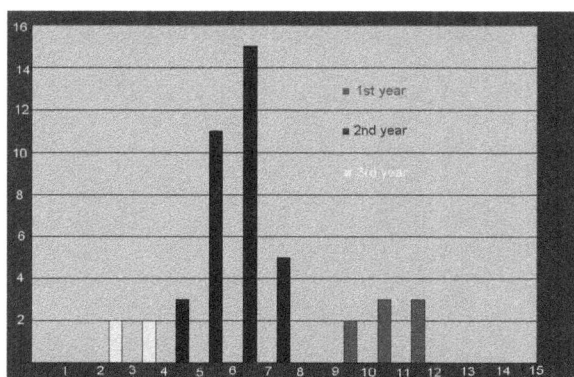

Figure 3

frequency of wear, at 11-12 mm and at 6-7 mm. These peaks correspond to the first and second year cohorts and indicate that each cohort was killed during a very restricted time period. In conjunction with the eruption of the first and second permanent molars, these data indicate synchronized mortality at 3 to 5 months and at 15 to 17 months for the second year, death between mid-August and mid-October, corresponding to the fall migration. The third group of crown heights falls below 4mm. These probably indicated late retention of deciduous teeth into the third year by some members of the third year cohort.

Do the data from the different levels indicate consistent seasonality for each occupation? Each level includes from 3 to 9 individuals from first and second year cohorts, which gives sufficient information to confirm a consistent seasonal pattern for each occupation. This begins to suggest a strategic goal for Rangifer hunting at Verberie.

AGE STRUCTURE

Age structure or mortality profiles have been frequently used to interpret hunting patterns of early humans and other carnivores (Kurtén 1953; Voorhies 1969; Klein 1982, Stiner 1990). While epiphyseal fusion can provide some clues to age, it is again the dentition that has the most complete and most reliable information.

Table 2: Revised formulas for the Verberie crown heigh calculations for tooth age.

For P3:
$$Age=200-(2(200-24)(CH/19.49))+((200-24)(CH1.5)/(19.491.5))+(((19.49-CH)2)/1.25$$

For P4:
$$Age=200-(2(200-24)(CH/20.67))+((200-24)(CH1.5)/(20.671.5))+(((20.67-CH)2)/1.25)$$

For M1:
$$Age=200-(2(200-5)(CH/19.83))+((200-5)(CH1.6)/(19.831.6))+(((19.83-CH1)2)2/3)$$

M2 :
$$Age=200-(2(200-12.5)(CH/19.87))+((200-12.5)(CH1.6)/(19.871.6))+(((13.87-CH)2)2/3)$$

For M3 :
$$Age=200-(2(200-24)(CH/18.11))+((200-24)(CH1.6)/(18.111.6))+(((18.11-CH)2)2/3)$$

Bouchud's (1966) wear stages have been shown to be inadequate for determining the ages of individual mandibles (Spiess 1979:70-75). Modern biological studies (Miller 1974; Skoog 1968) indicate too much variation in the eruption schedule of permanent molars and premolars and significant differences in rates of wear over the lifespans of different individuals. The mandibular material from Verberie demonstrates the inapplicability of such simplistic wear stages. There are great differences among individuals in the motor habits of chewing that have resulted in greatly different patterns of wear on mandibular teeth. On some individuals (Figure 4 top), once all of the permanent teeth have erupted and come into occlusion, the tooth row appears to wear fairly evenly. On others (Figure 4 bottom), however, the back teeth wear faster than the front teeth and wear out while the premolars are relatively unworn. On still other individuals, the premolars appear to wear faster than the molars.

Because tooth wear is not linear, occurring faster on the smaller surface area of high crowns than on the increased surface area of worn teeth, Klein et al. (1983) proposed the application of a quadratic equation to crown height measurements of Cervus elaphus to determine age and mortality profiles for prey populations. Pike Tay *et al.* (2001) tested the quadratic regressions of age on a large, known age sample of Rangifer, and then modified them to achieve a better fit to the curve of the known age population. Their equations for third and fourth premolars and for first, second and third molars were used as a basis

for age calculations. Due to differences in original crown heights between their control sample and our archaeological sample, the equations were adjusted to account for the empirically determined originally higher crowns at Verberie. The revised formulas for the Verberie material are presented in Table 2.

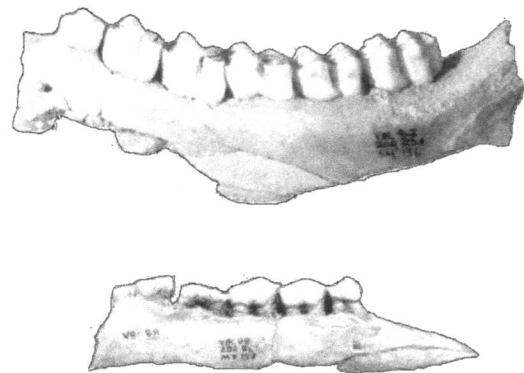

Figure 4

The modified equations were used to calculate age for each tooth specimen for which a measurement of crown height was possible in the Verberie dental material. Due to variations in wear on the teeth in a single mandible, all of the individual tooth calculations were averaged for each individual animal.

Pike-Tay et al. (2001) suggest that problems in extreme height variability in youngest age classes necessitate calculation of their age by other means, so deciduous wear and permanent eruption stages were used to place individuals in the first three age classes. There were 11 first year individuals and 36 second year individuals. Similarly, the very oldest age class calculations were based on such small samples that precise determination of months of age by their equation could not be considered highly reliable. For the Verberie's oldest mandibles, maximum age calculations indicated up to 199, 237, and even 279 months. Averaged ages were calculated for 90 adults (Table 3).

Table 3: Age classes of Rangifer tarandus by occupation level at Verberie.

	0-1	1-2	2-3	3-4	4-5	5-6	6-7	7-8	8-9	9-10	10+	Total
II-1	1	11	4	4	2	0	1	3	0	1	2	29
II-2	0	9	8	3	3	0	1	2	2	2	0	30
II-21	3	4	4	5	2	2	0	2	3	2	1	28
II-22	2	2	1	2	2	0	0	0	0	0	0	9
II-3	4	6	5	3	1	0	1	0	2	1	1	24
II-4	1	1	2	2	1	0	0	1	0	0	0	8
Total	11	33	24	19	11	2	3	8	7	6	4	128
%	8.59	25.78	18.75	14.84	8.59	1.56	2.34	6.25	5.47	4.69	3.13	100

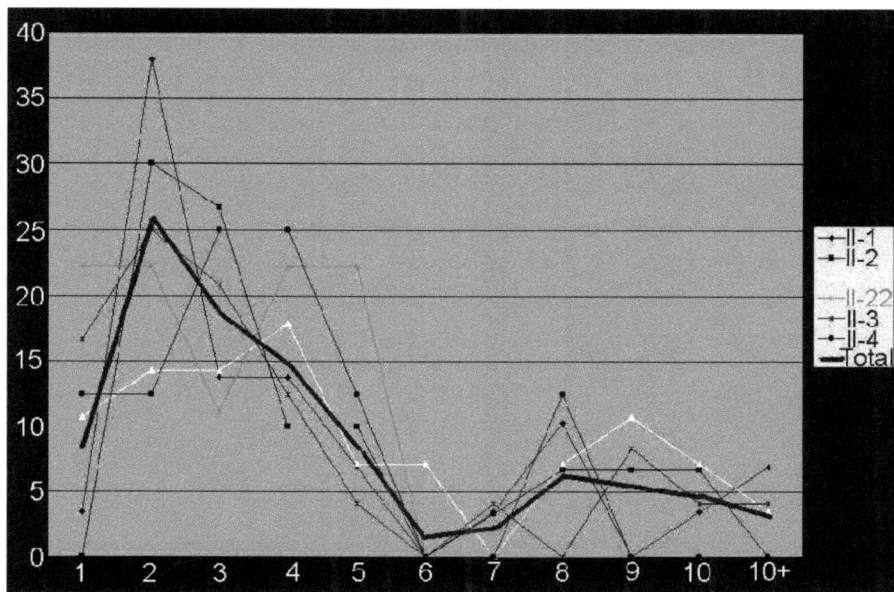

Figure 5

Figure 5 shows the frequency of individuals assigned to age classes of one-year intervals, for the total assemblage, and also for each occupation level. The highest bars for each age class represent the total assemblage. A trimodal distribution can be seen, with the largest frequencies for the second, sixth and oldest age classes.

Because of the different numbers of individuals represented in each level, these frequencies were normalized to percentages in each age class (table 4, figure 6. With the exception of II3, which had the smallest excavation surface and lowest number of individuals and, thus, the greatest problem of sampling bias, all of the levels exhibit the same pattern, already noted for the total assemblage. Individuals of the second and third year cohort are very strongly represented, while older adult cohorts comprise much smaller proportions within each level. Does this constitute a specialized selection?

The age distribution can be compared to the proportions of age classes reported by Skoog (1968:515) for the Nelchina herd during the fall migration (Table 5 and Figure 7). The differences in proportions of age groups are highly significant, with a Chi-square value of 29.0212** for five degrees of freedom. Comparisons between the occupation levels contain too many zero cells to have statistical significance. The differences in the total population are most marked in the over-representation of the second and third year cohorts and the 6-10 year age individuals, and the under-representation of the first and 3-6 year age classes.

If we do not consider the first age class, the cohort under one year of age which is most susceptible to taphonomic subtraction from an archaeological assemblage, and recalculate the chi-square for the distribution among the age classes, we still get a smaller, but still significant difference from the living population age distribution (table 6). The most significant deviations are the over-representations of the yearlings and older adults, and the under-representations of the prime age adults.

Table 4: Proportions of age classes of Rangifer tarandus by occupation level at Verberie.

%	0-1	1-2	2-3	3-4	4-5	5-6	6-7	7-8	8-9	9-10	10+
II-1	3.45	37.93	13.79	13.79	6.90	0	3.45	10.34	0	3.45	6.90
II-2	0	30.00	26.67	10.00	10.00	0	3.33	6.67	6.67	6.67	0
II-21	10.71	14.29	14.29	17.86	7.14	7.14	0	7.14	10.71	7.14	3.57
II-22	22.22	22.22	11.11	22.22	22.22	0	0	0	0	0	0
II-3	16.67	25.00	20.83	12.50	4.17	0	4.17	0	8.33	4.17	4.17
II-4	12.50	12.50	25.00	25.00	12.50	0	0	12.50	0	0	0
Total	8.59	25.78	18.75	14.84	8.59	1.56	2.34	6.25	5.47	4.69	3.13

Table 5: Comparison of age groups between Nelchina herd and Verberie assemblage.

Age	Nelchina			Verberie			
Class	%	O	E	%	O	E	Total
0-1	21	210	195.92	8.59	11	25.08	221
1-2	17	170	179.96	25.78	33	23.04	203
2-3	15	150	132.98	18.75	24	19.74	174
3-6	35	350	338.65	25.00	32	43.35	382
6-10	10	100	109.93	18.75	24	14.07	124
10+	2	20	17.73	3.13	4	2.72	24
Totals		1000			128		1128

$X_= 29.0212**$ at $p<0.001$ for df=5

Table 6: Comparison of age groups (excluding first year cohort) between Nelchina herd and Verberie assemblage.

Age	Nelchina			Verberie			
Class	%	O	E	%	O	E	Total
1-2	17	170	176.81	25	33	26.19	203
2-3	15	150	151.55	18	24	22.45	174
3-6	35	350	332.72	24	32	49.28	382
6-10	10	100	108.00	14	24	16.00	124
10+	2	20	20.90	3	4	3.10	24
Totals		790			117		907

$X2=14.0052$ at $p<0.010$ for df=4

24

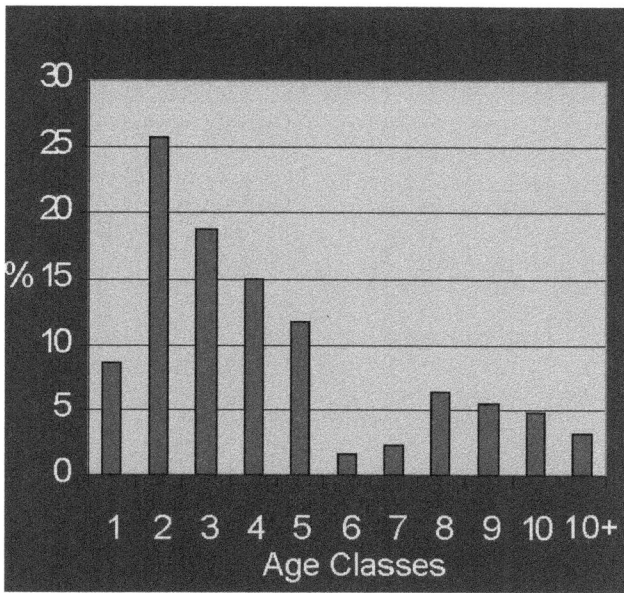

Figure 6

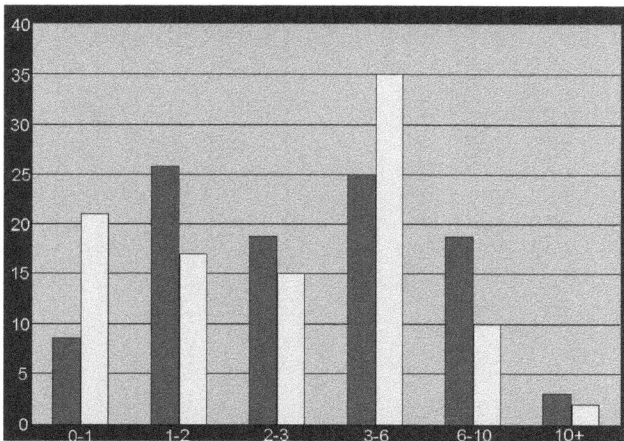

Figure 7

While this does not correspond to Stiner's (1990:309) prime-dominated mortality pattern, it nonetheless suggests a certain selectivity by hunters. While Stiner argues that the prime-dominated procurement focuses on the age group with the highest reproductive potential, the case at Verberie seems to differ from that pattern. This may not be the only desirable demographic target among the prey. This targeting may be toward pre- and post-reproductive herd members. The highest representation of second and third year animals may not be those with the highest reproductive potential. McEwan (1963) reported that reproductive success in females increases after the third year, and does not decrease even with extreme age. Males may form harems with 3 to 15 females associated with a dominant male, effectively excluding many of the subdominant males from reproductive participation. Reproductive behavior is not consistent with nutritional criteria for prey choice. Males participating in the rut lose most of the summer's accumulation of fat and up to 20% of their body weight.

Younger females are less likely to produce offspring. Thus, selection of the younger adults and larger subadults may not result in decreases in reproductive success of the prey population.

Stiner (1990:317) noted that prime-dominated harvesting probably involves considerable selection by sex as well as by age, requiring a large measure of selective control. Since dental measurements of Rangifer are not reflective of sexual dimorphism, other data must be sought to address this point. Postcranial measurements from this assemblage indicate that ca. 60% of the population is composed of males. Summarizing biological reports, Kelsall (1968:154) concludes that adult male to female ratios in breeding populations average 27 to 100. This suggests very heavy selection from within the potential prey population. This selectivity for young, non-reproducing males would be consistent with conscious conservation of a key resource, and it would also yield the highest quality meat, from which fat reserves would not be depleted.

CONCLUSION

These data, when taken together, suggest a very specific tactics to acquire substantial quantities of meat. Exploitation of Rangifer at this site occurred consistently during the fall migration. There is no discernible variation in the season of hunt among the six occupation levels, although small sample size from the lower levels may distort their patterns. Hunters obviously anticipated coming to a specific location at a specific time of the year in order to harvest a predictable resource. This amounts to a planned strategy, rather than a haphazard encounter.

A specific portion of the population was targeted to maximize both the quantity and quality of the food resource. Other species were being exploited by the Magdalenians of the Paris Basin. At Verberie, there is also evidence of horse and ground squirrel. While the latter was undoubtedly killed on the spot, the horse remains are so sparse and fragmentary that they probably represent food that was brought into the site before the hunt for the reindeer. While analyses of the rest of the faunal assemblage are continuing, the differential representation of skeletal elements seems to indicate that the proceeds of the hunt were taken elsewhere, quite possibly for storage and consumption through the winter. As such, this does constitute evidence of a strategy of planned hunts for storage, rather than random events of encounter hunting and immediate consumption. This suggests that Magdalenians may have been exploiting reindeer in a slightly different way than can be seen in the Périgord, supplying fewer people for longer periods of time. This may be seen as a means of adapting to a more northern and potentially harsher open environment during the rapidly changing environment at the close of the Pleistocene.

ACKNOWLEDGEMENTS

This research was made possible through the support of an Arts and Humanities Initiative Grant from the Office of the Vice President for Research, University of Iowa. Substantial work on the measurement (and remeasurement) of the teeth could not have been accomplished without the assistance of Vincent Warner, Michele Schoenfeld and Kent Brockman. The errors in procedures and interpretation belong solely to the author.

REFERENCES

AUDOUZE, F. 1987 The Paris Basin in Magdalenian Times. *The Pleistocene Old World: Regional Perspectives* (O. Soffer, ed.). Plenum Press, New York and London. pp. 183-200.

AUDOUZE, F., D. CAHEN, L.H. KEELEY, AND B. SCHMIDER. 1981. Le site magdalénien du Buisson Campin à Verberie (Oise). *Gallia Préhistoire* 24:99-143.

AUDOUZE, F., AND J.G. ENLOE. 1991. Subsistence strategies and economy in the Magdalenian of the Paris Basin. *The Late Glacial of Northwest Europe: Human Adaptation and Environmental Change at the End of the Ice Age.* (R.N.E. Barton, A.J. Roberts, and D.A. Roe, eds.) Council for British Archaeology Report 77:63-71.

AUDOUZE, F., AND J.G. ENLOE. 1997. High resolution archaeology at Verberie: Limits and interpretations. *World Archaeology* 29 (2):195-207.

BOUCHUD, J. 1966. *Essai sur le Renne et la Climatologie du Paléolithique Moyen et Supérieur.* Imprimerie Magne, Périgeux.

DAVID, F. 1994. Les faunes de Verberie et Pincevent. In: *Environnements et habitats magdaléniens dans le centre du Bassin Parisien* (Y. Taborin, ed.) Documents d'Archéologie Française, N° 43, Paris.

DAVID, F., AND J.G. ENLOE. 1992. Chasse saisonnière des Magdaléniens du Bassin parisien. *Bulletin et Mémoire de la Société d'Anthropologie de Paris* 4:167-174.

ENLOE, J.G. 1991. Subsistence organization in the Upper Paleolithic: Carcass refitting and food sharing at Pincevent. Doctoral dissertation, University of New Mexico. University Microfilms, Ann Arbor.

ENLOE, J.G. 1993. Subsistence organization in the Early Upper Paleolithic: Reindeer hunters of the Abri du Flageolet, couche V. *Before Lascaux: The Complex Record of the Early Upper Paleolithic,* (H. Knecht, A. Pike-Tay and R. White, eds.) CRC Press, Boca Raton. pp. 101-115.

ENLOE, J.G. 1994. Comparaison entre les troupeaux de rennes de Pincevent et de Verberie. *Environnements et Habitats Magdaléniens dans le centre du Bassin Parisien* (Y. Taborin, ed.), Documents d'Archéologie Française, N° 43, Paris. pp. 115-117.

ENLOE, J.G. 1997. Seasonality and age structure in remains of Rangifer tarandus: Magdalenian hunting strategy at Verberie. *Anthropozoologica* 25-26:95-102.

ENLOE, J.G., AND F. DAVID. 1997. Rangifer herd behavior: seasonality of hunting in the Magdalenian of the Paris Basin. *Caribou and Reindeer Hunters of the Northern Hemisphere* (Jackson, L.J. and Thacker, P., eds.) Avebury Press, Aldershot. pp. 47-63.

GORDON, B. C. 1988. *Of Men and Reindeer Herds in French Magdalenian Prehistory.* British Archaeological Reports International Series 390.

KELSALL, J.P. 1968. *The Migratory Barren-Ground Caribou of Canada.* Canadian Wildlife Service Monograph **3**.

KLEIN, R. G. 1982. Age (mortality) profiles as a means of distinguishing hunted species from scavenged ones in Stone Age archaeological sites. *Paleobiology* 8(2):151-158.

KLEIN, R. G., ALLWARDEN, K. AND WOLF, C. 1983. The calculation and interpretation of ungulate age profiles from dental crown heights. *Hunter-gatherer Economy in Prehistory: A European Perspective,* (Ed. Bailey, G.N.) Cambridge Univ. Press, Cambridge. pp. 47-58.

KURTÉN, B. 1953. On the variation and population dynamics of fossil and recent mammals. *Acta Zoologica Fennica* 76. Helsinki.

MCEWAN, E.H. 1963. Seasonal annuli in the cementum of the teeth of the Barren Ground caribou.Canadian Journal of Zoology 41(1).

MELLARS, P.A. 1989. Major issues in the emergence of modern humans. *Current Anthropology* 30(3):349-385.

MELLARS, P. 1994. The Upper Paleolithic Revolution. In: B. Cunliffe, ed., *The Oxford Illustrated Prehistory of Europe,* pp. 42-78. Oxford University Press, Oxford.

MILLER, F.L. 1974. *Biology of the Kaminuriak population of barren-ground caribou*, Part 2. Canadian Wildlife Service Report Series 31.

PIKE-TAY, A., C. A. MORCOMB & M. O'FARRELL. 2001. Reconsidering the Quadratic Crown Height Method of Age Estimation for Rangifer from Archaeological Sites. In: A. Pike-Tay, editor, *Assessing Season of Capture, Age and Sex of Archaeofaunas*. ArchaeoZoologia monograph series,vol. no. XI, La Pensée Sauvage, Paris

SKOOG, R. O. 1968. *Ecology of the caribou in Alaska*. Doctoral dissertation, University of California.

SPIESS, A. E. 1979. *Reindeer and Caribou Hunters: An Archaeological Study*. Academic Press, New York.

STINER, M.C. 1990. The use of mortality patterns in archaeological studies of hominid predatory adaptations. *Journal of Anthropological Archaeology* 9:305-351.

VOORHIES, M. R. 1969. *Taphonomy and population dynamics of an early Pliocene vertebrate fauna, Knox County, Nebraska*. Contributions to Geology, Special Paper No. 1. University of Wyoming, Laramie.

ANIMAL CARCASS UTILIZATION DURING THE LATE UPPER PALEOLITHIC OCCUPATION OF LAPA DO SUÃO (PORTUGAL)

Jonathan A. Haws* and Maria João Valente**

*Department of Anthropology, University of Louisville, Louisville, KY 40292
**Faculdade de Ciências Humanas e Sociais, Universidade do Algarve, Campus de Gambelas, 8000 Faro, PORTUGAL

Until recently, much of what was known about Upper Paleolithic subsistence derived from the excavations at Lapa do Suão in central Portugal. When Jean Roche published his brief description of the site in 1982, Suão became the definitive record of Magdalenian subsistence. Yet despite its significance the faunal assemblage was never systematically studied and reported. Roche (1979, 1982) only reported the identified taxa. No quantitative information was ever published. In addition, Roche never obtained radiocarbon dates for the site despite the recovery of bone and charcoal. In this paper, we present the first behavioral analysis of the faunal assemblage and radiocarbon dates. Using these data, we place Lapa do Suão in its archaeological context for the first time.

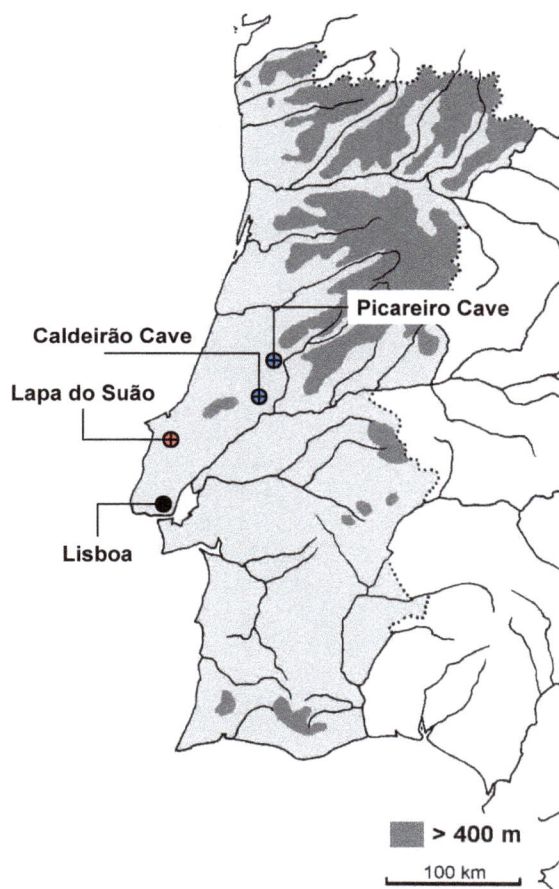

Figure 1. Map of key sites mentioned in the text.

Lapa do Suão is located in a narrow limestone valley about 40 km north of Lisbon and approximately 15 km from the Atlantic Ocean (Figure 1). The cave lies about 50 m above the Roto valley floor and its opening faces NE (Zilhão 1997). The cavity has a long passage with a SW inclination (Figure 2). There is a $25m^2$ room at the end.

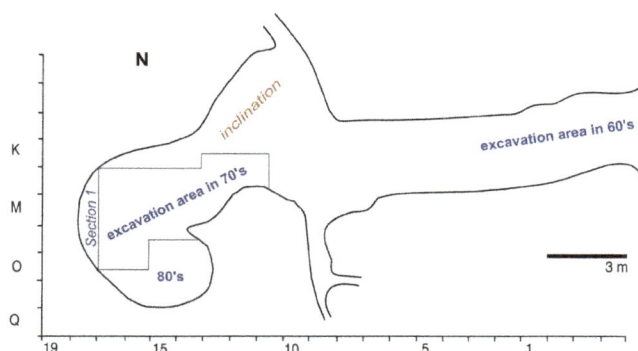

Figure 2. Lapa do Suão excavation plan

The geologist Carlos Ribeiro first investigated the cave in the late 19th century (Rocha 1907). Several years later Santos Rocha viewed the materials from the cave entrance and concluded that they were from the Iron Age (Rocha 1907). In the 1960s, Furtado et al. (1969) excavated Neolithic and Calcolithic deposits in the entrance and passage. They reported finding numerous microliths, possibly Mesolithic, and a *pointe à cran* or shouldered point typically Upper Solutrean in Iberia (Cortes et al. 1977). Subsequently, Abbé Jean Roche excavated the Upper Paleolithic deposits at the end of the passage and room 1974 to 1987.

Roche's excavations revealed 12 stratigraphic levels (Figure 3) that he interpreted in preliminary reports (Roche 1979, 1982). His archaeological interpretation was based only on the typological and technological analysis of lithic material since no radiocarbon dates were obtained. Nevertheless, Level 3 was considered Epipaleolithic and Levels 4-9, Upper Paleolithic. Levels 8 and 9 were classified as Magdalenian based on the presence of sagaies.

Roche (1982) interpreted the association of two human teeth with a cache of pierced marine shells, lynx canines, red ochre and charcoal as an intentional human burial. He then interpreted Level 9 as a prepared Magdalenian "floor." Faunal remains from the Upper Paleolithic levels included red deer, ibex, horse, wild boar, lynx, small rodents, small carnivores, birds, and fish. Despite years of excavation and deep soundings, Roche never reported finding evidence of a Solutrean occupation as suggested by the earlier excavators.

Zilhão (1997) re-analyzed the lithic assemblages and concluded that Levels 8 and 9 were Solutrean based on the presence of a few bifacial trimming flakes in the collections from the 1960s. This was supported by a reinterpretation of the stratigraphy and consideration of the *pointe à cran*. Zilhão further argued that the Solutrean occupation was located mainly near the cave entrance since the *pointe à cran* was found there. He concluded that the Solutrean materials in the back of the cave must have been redeposited since the lower deposits are marked by a dip. These deposits filled the SW corner of the cave, leveling the area in which the subsequent Magdalenian occupations took place.

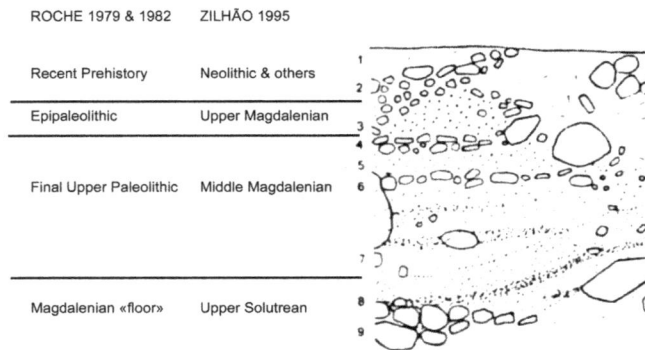

Figure 3. Stratigraphic interpretation.

In 2000 and 2001 we undertook the study of the Upper Paleolithic faunal assemblages. The materials were kept for several years at the Universidade de Porto where Roche worked. In the late 1980s, the collections were moved to a small regional museum in Bombarral, a municipality located near the cave. These materials are on loan to the National Museum of Archaeology in Lisbon where the analysis took place. Unfortunately, no fauna or charcoal was marked Level 3, the lone Epipaleolithic occupation. Also, many bags from upper levels lacked source tags, forcing us to leave several aside. As a consequence, the majority of the material came from Levels 7, 8 & 9.

Charcoal samples were sent to Geochron Laboratories for conventional radiocarbon dating. Although the dates are not in sequence all are Pleistocene and fall within the Portuguese Magdalenian between 16,000 and 10,000 years bp (Table 1). Prior to dating, the charcoal samples were identified by Marjeta Jeraj and one of us (Haws) at the University of Wisconsin-Madison. The work is still in progress, however the bottom two levels are complete. Levels 8 and 9 both contain wood charcoal from species comprising a mixed Atlantic and Mediterranean

vegetation cover. These include deciduous oak, pine, juniper, Rosaceae (wild fruit trees), olive, and other Mediterranean varieties. The Suão charcoal is similar in composition to the Magdalenian assemblage identified by Figueiral at Cabeço de Porto Marinho, with the exception of evergreen oak and wild strawberry. The microfauna from all levels are a typical Mediterranean suite including *Microtus lusitanicus*, *Arvicola terrestris* and *Eliomys quercinus*. If one accepts the Level 8 date of c. 15,000 bp, then the charcoal and microfaunal data fit the notion that the post-LGM warming trend was well underway in Portugal prior to the Dryas I.

Level	Years bp	Lab number
5	12,950 ± 100	GX-27591
6	14,380 ± 90	GX-27589
7	10,900 ± 70 12,410 ± 80	GX-27590 GX-275-92
8	15,110 ± 90	GX-27593
9	12,590 ± 80	GX-27594

Table 1. Radiocarbon dates for Lapa do Suão.

LAPA DO SUÃO FAUNAL REMAINS

The large mammal remains total 339 specimens of which 83 were identified to species or genera (Table 2). The majority of these are red deer, followed by Iberian lynx (*Lynx pardina*) and wild boar. Additional species include fox, wolf and unidentified mustelid (cf. *Meles meles*), equid and caprid. As Table 2 shows, Levels 4, 5 and 6 contained few specimens. In contrast, Levels 7, 8 and 9 were much richer in the number and variety of species.

Little can be said of the upper levels due to the scarcity of faunal remains. A burned and cut-marked Iberian lynx ulna was recovered in Level 6. This might be interpreted as evidence for the use of lynx for pelts or teeth but it could have been for food. Though lynx are rare in Portugal today, they were hunted and eaten by rural people until the 1940s.

The Level 7 herbivores include both adult and juvenile red deer and wild boar. Only one burned portion was recovered and four fragments had cut marks, three of them limb shafts. Carnivores are represented by lynx, wolf, fox and a mustelid. No cut marks were found on the lynx.

Levels 8 and 9 contained two adults and one juvenile red deer, a single wild boar, horse and ibex. As in the previous layer, burned bone is rare. Cut marks were observed on red deer and wild boar bones, plus a few indeterminate specimens. Most of these are shallow, oriented diagonal or perpendicular to the longitudinal axis of the bone and likely from defleshing the carcass of the animal.

	Level 4	Level 5	Level 6	Level 7	Level 8+9
Red Deer	1	0	4	13	17
Wild Boar	0	0	2	8	3
Caprinae	0	0	1	0	1
Auroch	0	0	0	1	0
Horse	0	0	0	0	1
indet.	5	3	12	100	166
Wolf	0	1	0	2	1
Fox	0	0	0	3	3
Lynx	0	0	1	5	3
Mustelid	0	0	0	1	0

Table 2. NISP for Lapa do Suão.

Some of the wild boar, fox and indeterminate specimens exhibit tooth marks consistent with carnivore gnawing. In all three levels, some limb shafts show impact fractures and other breakage indicative of marrow extraction. One red deer phalanx was split longitudinally as at Picareiro. While carnivore activity may have impacted the assemblage, density-mediated attrition is unlikely given the near-complete absence of ungulate teeth. These observations suggest that humans deposited the majority of large herbivore remains, possibly even the lynx.

The low NISP for the macrofauna makes comparisons with other contemporary sites difficult. If Magdalenian hunters were bringing significant numbers of red deer and wild boar into the cave, they only minimally processed them and transported entire carcasses away. Because Suão is located in a narrow valley that opens onto a broad coastal plain, residential base camps may have been located close enough to obviate the need for extended occupations in the cave. This may explain why so few large animal remains were recovered. On the other hand, the large mammal bones may have been discarded outside the cave and destroyed by post-depositional processes.

RABBITS

As with Picareiro, rabbit remains numerically dominate the Suão assemblage. Over 5,000 rabbit bones were recovered from Lapa do Suão, representing at least 234 individuals (Table 3). Five hare bones were also identified.

Hockett (1991, 1994, 1995, 1996, 1999) has observed bone damage and skeletal element patterns typical of raptors, carnivores and humans. A general discussion can be found in Hockett and Haws (2002). His actualistic studies of raptor nests show distinct, regular

types of damage to rabbit bones by owls and eagles. The eagle owl (*Bubo bubo*) commonly nests at the entrances of caves and above rockshelters in Iberia. Hockett (1995) found a predominance of hindlimbs over forelimbs in owl assemblages. Eagle owl assemblages in Spain display considerable variability (Sanchis Serra 2000). Some lack forelimbs others contain more forelimbs than hindlimbs. Cranial elements are more common in some than others. Lumbar vertebrae and sacra often greatly outnumber cervical and thoracic vertebrae. The assemblages studied by Sanchis Serra lack abundant foot elements but that may be due to collector bias. High degrees of breakage are typical of owl assemblages. Damage typically occurs on the limb epiphyses (especially the greater trochanter of the femur), vertebrae and innominates (primarily near the acetabulum) (Hockett 1991, 1994, 1995; Sanchis Serra 2000). Spiral fractures are common but bone cylinders are rare. Broken limbs are generally characterized by epiphyses with attached shaft portions. Beak and talon punctures occur on 2-3% of bones, usually on one side (Hockett 1991, 1995).

	4	5	6	7	8+9	Total
Mand	5	13	32	118	317	546
Max	2	1	15	57	155	259
Innom	4	2	18	96	227	384
Pat	0	0	0	0	0	0
Fem	4	10	21	97	236	421
Tib	4	4	31	139	323	565
Calc	0	1	10	24	67	111
Astr	0	0	1	5	4	10
Scap	1	2	13	53	116	200
Hum	4	7	15	48	87	184
Rad	1	4	11	45	130	216
Ulna	0	3	10	54	109	198
Car/Tar	0	0	0	0	1	1
Mtp	2	13	46	99	412	637
Phal	5	7	5	45	61	132
Rib	0	3	9	24	15	57
Vert	3	7	25	67	177	314
Sac	0	1	2	3	7	16
Total	35	78	264	974	2444	3795

Table 3. Rabbit MNE at Lapa do Suão.

Rabbit bones from carnivore dens and scats typically show signs of etching and polishing. Large carnivores such as wolves and coyotes completely destroy rabbit bones during consumption (Schmitt and Juell 1994). Small carnivores often leave bones intact but with characteristic damage such as tooth punctures on both sides limb bones (Hockett 1989, 1995; Pérez Ripoll 1993; Valente 2000). In Iberia the two main predators of rabbits are the Iberian lynx and fox. No actualistic studies of rabbit consumption patterns by Iberian lynx have been undertaken. Sanchis Serra (2000) conducted a study of rabbit bones from three zones within a single fox den. Hockett (1999) analyzed the bone assemblage from a carnivore den at the entrance to Picareiro. Punctures occurred on less than 1% of the total assemblage. These were located on both sides of limb epiphyses and the innominate. Valente (2000) studied the faunal remains including rabbit from the Early Upper Paleolithic site, Pego do Diabo. This site contained a carnivore-accumulated assemblage that was thought originally to have been associated with lithic artifacts (Zilhão 1995).

Human-created rabbit bone assemblages are known from definite cultural contexts within archaeological sites in the Great Basin of the United States, the Spanish Mediterranean Region and now Portugal (Vila *et al*. 1985; Drews and Schmitt 1986; Hockett 1989, 1991, 1992, 1995; Schmitt 1990; Rowley-Conwy 1992; Pérez Ripoll 1992, 1993; Hockett and Bicho 2000; Hockett and Haws 2002). Studies of these sites reveal a great deal of similarity in skeletal element patterns when humans process and consume rabbit carcasses. Three sites in the Great Basin all had high representation of mandibles, tibiae, scapulae, skulls and ribs (Hockett 1994, 1995). Vertebrae and sacra were present in very low frequencies. The long bones, mainly tibiae, were processed for marrow extraction by breaking or biting off the epiphyses creating cylinders through which marrow could be pushed through or sucked out (Figure 4). The tibia in the rabbit is the largest limb bone and thus contains the most marrow. This explains why tibia cylinders occur in greater frequencies in archaeological sites than other limb bones. Ethnographic observations of Great Basin Shoshone groups by Steward led Hockett (1995) to conclude that the paucity of vertebrae and sacra at archaeological sites was due to bone meal processing. The Shoshone regularly pounded and ground axial elements and soft greasy epiphyses on milling stones.
Tibiae cylinders have also been recovered in large numbers from Upper Paleolithic sites in Iberia (Vila *et al*. 1985; Pérez Ripoll 1993; Hockett and Bicho 2000; Hockett and Haws 2002). At Cingle Vermell in Catalunya, Faro noted an overwhelming majority of rabbit tibiae were fractured near both epiphyses (Vila *et al*. 1985). Though Faro does not suggest marrow removal, the pattern implies the creation of tibia cylinders. Fractures at the distal ends of the radius, ulna and tibia were interpreted as evidence for the removal of the feet. Pérez Ripoll (1992, 1993), working independently (and seemingly unaware of Hockett's work) came to very similar conclusions as Hockett concerning rabbit butchery patterns. At the Magdalenian sites, Santa Maira, Tossal de la Roca and Cueva de Nerja, he attributed the distinct pattern of rabbit long bone cylinders to marrow removal. Magdalenian and Epipaleolithic hunters created numerous shaft cylinders on the tibia, femur and much less frequent ones on the humerus (Pérez Ripoll 1993).

Additional taphonomic traces of human agency in rabbit bone assemblages are the presence of cutmarks and burning. In his analysis of the bones from Santa Maira, a

Late Upper Paleolithic site in southeast Spain, Pérez Ripoll (1993) found up to 60% of the bones had identifiable cutmarks. There is, however, considerable variability in cutmark frequencies (Hockett and Haws 2002). Evidence of burning on the feet and distal ends of lower limbs is also common in archaeological rabbit bone assemblages (Hockett 1991; Pérez Ripoll 1993). Only 3-6.5% of the rabbit bones from Cingle Vermell were burned. Though distributed evenly across skeletal parts, many distal tibiae and radii had been burned. Conversely, at Picareiro, phalanges, metapodials, calcanei and astragali were the most common element burned indicating whole carcasses were probably roasted with the feet still attached (Hockett and Bicho 2000).

Figure 4. Rabbit tibia cylinders.

The majority of rabbit specimens from Lapa do Suão are mandibles, limb bones, in particular tibiae and femora, and innominates. The abundance of these elements is not due to differential transport or raptors, which often deposit greater numbers of hind limbs than fore limbs as shown above. Most of the radii and ulnae are broken in half and distal humeri, so common in Picareiro, are infrequent. The absence of small elements is probably due to the use of a wide mesh screen during the excavation as well as curation bias. In Table 3, it is clear that there is a strong bias against small skeletal elements at Suão. This is almost certainly due to the excavation and screen methods used at each site. At Picareiro, elements as small as phalanges were piece-plotted. All other small elements were collected in the fine-mesh screen. Figure 5 compares rabbit %MAU in Suão with Picareiro. There are important differences between the two sites. At Suão, both Level 7 and 8+9 have remarkably similar body part profiles. The small foot bones aside, Picareiro has better forelimb representation. Both sites lack axial elements except the pelvis. Hockett and Haws (2002) compared vertebra representation between accumulators. Human-created assemblages typically lack vertebrae compared to raptors and carnivores. It would appear that prehistoric people at both sites ground the vertebrae, sacra and ribs into bone meal as Hockett (1994, 1995) has noted in the Great Basin and at Picareiro (Hockett and Bicho 2000).

	Up.	Low.	E	F	G/I	J	Total
Mand	5	10	143	62	2	225	
Max	0	1	111	37	8	157	
Innom	9	9	201	83	8	313	
Pat	4	16	49	5	5	79	
Fem	9	10	86	65	7	179	
Tib	13	10	98	53	8	188	
Calc	33	28	146	89	5	308	
Ast	29	20	109	44	13	216	
Scap	2	5	156	60	4	227	
Hum	11	9	105	45	7	178	
Rad	16	10	152	72	2	254	
Ulna	9	12	172	67	2	263	
Car/Tar	12	16	109	29	3	169	
Mtp	37	64	610	148	20	883	
Phal	110	169	1012	287	25	1607	
Rib	6	9	145	42	7	210	
Vert	4	8	141	27	4	187	
Sac	0	0	6	0	0	6	
Total	309	406	3551	1215	130	5612	

Table 4. Rabbit MNE from Lapa do Suão.

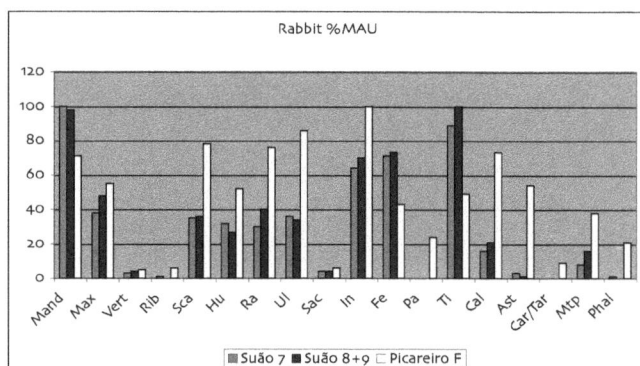

Figure 5. Rabbit skeletal element representation at Lapa do Suão and Lapa do Picareiro.

Alternatively, density-mediated attrition due to chemical weathering or carnivores may have played a role in the Suão assemblage formation. Pavao and Stahl (1999) used a photon absortiometer to measure bone density in several species of leporids. They made two calculations: one based on Lyman et al.'s (1992) methodology for marmots which normed volume density using squares or rectangles, and their method of shape-adjusting using circles, triangles, etc. to reduce air space in the estimation of volume density (Pavao and Stahl 1999). Though positive, significant correlations were found between their shape-adjusted VD (VD$_{SA}$), the scan site density rank shows some striking differences between the two methods. The results using the Lyman et al. (1992) method match those expected from other taxa. That is to say, limb epiphyses are generally the weakest structurally and limb shafts are strongest (Table 4 and 5). Counterintuitively, however, the VD$_{SA}$ results show that

some of the weakest portions in the traditional method are strongest. For example, the proximal humerus epiphysis ranks as one of the densest scan sites, higher than the distal epiphysis which is often one of the strongest limb epiphyses. Both methods show the proximal tibia is denser than the distal end. The densest portion using the traditional method is the femoral midshaft, whereas it ranks 10th in the VD$_{SA}$ method. Figure 6 shows there is no clear pattern between VD$_{SA}$ and limb portion representation. Figure 7 shows rabbit limb MNE for Suão Level 7. It is clear that the rabbit limb portions most under-represented are those traditionally thought of as the weakest structurally. Therefore, it would appear that something in the shape-adjusted method is badly skewing the results (Hockett pers. com.). Given the absence of small, usually dense foot bones due to screen size, full comparisons between skeletal element representation and bone density using either method cannot be made.

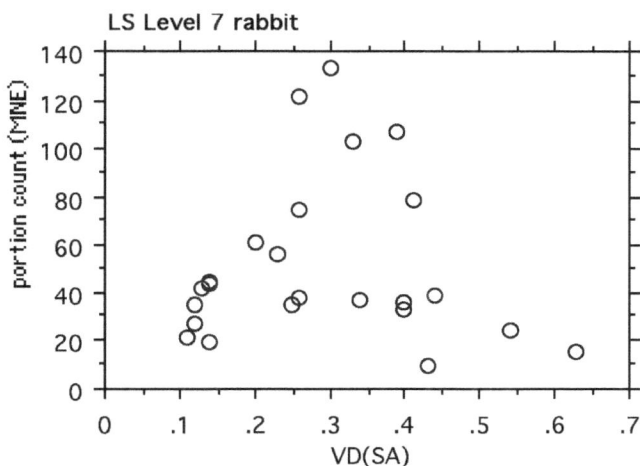

Figure 6. Rabbit bone density vs. MNE.

With regard to carnivores, Walter (1984) documented the tremendous destructive action by dogs of small game bones
in hunter-gatherer sites in Australia. However, the sheer numbers of bones left suggests medium/large carnivores did not impact the rabbit assemblage. The lack of physical traces such as thinning and polishing, and element survivorship effectively eliminates carnivores as agents of post-depositional destruction (Payne and Munson 1984; Schmitt and Juell 1994).

Additional evidence of human consumption is the high degree of fragmentation of the appendicular rabbit bones. In contrast to raptors and humans, carnivores often deposit a high number of complete or near complete appendicular elements. At Suão only about 1% of the humeri, femora and tibiae are complete. We observed a number of proximal and distal long bone fragments but shaft cylinders and fragments (about 60%) were more common. These data support idea that the majority of breakage occurs on the meat-bearing extremities to facilitate the removal of the marrow as observed by Hockett at Picareiro (Hockett and Bicho 2000) and Pérez Ripoll (1992, 1993) in the Spanish Mediterranean Region.

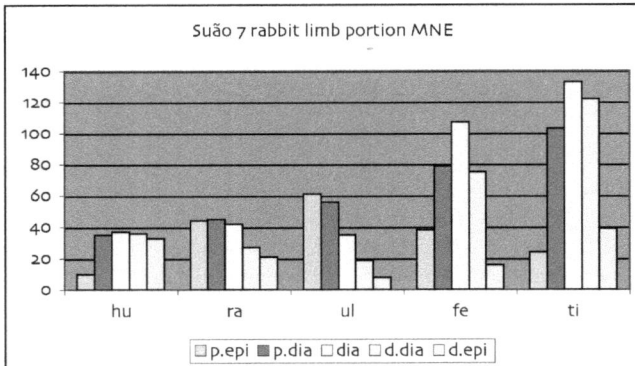

Figure 7. Rabbit limb portion MNE.

Valente (n.d.) also studied the bones for cutmarks in order to confirm human agency. She concluded that about 10% of long bones had cut marks in Levels 7 and 8+9. Most of these were tibiae, normally on the ventral side of the proximal diaphysis. On these and other long bones, the marks are normally diagonal to the longitudinal axis, with some deeper perpendicular marks. Cutmarks on the mandible are diagonal to the anterior/posterior axis. She interpreted these data as evidence for skin removal rather than disarticulation or fracturation, which may have produced deeper marks.

Based on work by Hockett (1991, 1994, 1995, 1996, 1999), humans likely deposited most of the rabbits. Only a few modifications by raptors and small carnivores were observed. These include a few bones with multiple and single punctures. How were rabbits procured? There is no evidence for nets or cordage from any Upper Paleolithic site in Portugal. However, this technology is known archaeologically from at least the Gravettian in central Europe if not much earlier in other parts of the Old World (Adovasio et al. 1996). There is little doubt that all Upper Paleolithic peoples utilized fibrous material to makes nets and cordage useful in traps and snares. Rabbit drives are known ethnographically from the Southwest and Great Basin of the United States (Shaffer and Gardner 1995). Schmidt (1999) used element representation in rabbit assemblages from Arizona to determine whether or not drives were used prehistorically. One site, the Five Feature site, contained high NISP and overall percentage of rabbit bones in the faunal assemblage. Interestingly, the elements represented are distal tibiae, calcanei, astragali, tarsals, metapodials and phalanges. Only two bones out of 802 came from another skeletal element. This patterning led Schmidt (1999) to conclude that the Five Feature site was the processing location for rabbits collected in a prehistoric communal drive. If this element representation pattern can be seen as diagnostic, then neither Picareiro nor Suão would fit into this category.

Further evidence suggestive of rabbit drives in prehistory is provided by Hudson (1994). At one site in California (KER-526) she noted that cranial elements far outnumbered limbs and other parts. Hudson (1994) concluded that large numbers rabbits had been taken through drives with the heads subsequently removed prior to transport. A few were probably consumed onsite accounting ·for the additional elements. This pattern, if considered diagnostic, is also not apparent at Picareiro or Suão.

Considering rabbit ecology, there are behavioral differences between the European rabbit and hares that probably make drives unlikely for the former and more likely for the latter (Hockett 1992; Hockett and Haws 2002). The European rabbit is a territorial animal that forms harems and lives in burrows (Garson 1981; Soriguer and Rogers 1981). They are best hunted by stalking individuals, trapping and snaring, or digging them out of their holes. Because rabbit warrens are easily recognizable to the trained eye, prehistoric hunters would have known their locations and regularly exploited them. Hares, on the other hand, are solitary and live in nests on the ground surface. Hare hunting would probably have been less profitable than rabbit because they would be too infrequent to hunt individually. They do, however, congregate and migrate in large numbers during stressful times (Angerman 1981). Hunters could much more easily drive large numbers of hares into nets at various times of the year (Hockett and Haws 2002).

Rabbits at Picareiro and Suão were more than likely taken by traps, snares and possibly with bow and arrow (Hockett and Bicho 2000). Net hunting was unlikely due rabbit behavior (Lupo and Schmitt 2002). In all likelihood, rabbits were hunted by individuals or small groups who set out traps or snares while engaged in other activities. As with Picareiro, numerous rabbits were stripped of meat and probably consumed onsite. The fact that marrow was removed from the humeri, femora and tibiae provides further evidence of immediate consumption. It is very likely that additional carcasses, possibly smoked rabbit meat and axial parts of the skeleton were transported to other locations nearby.

AVIFAUNA

Several species of birds were present in the Upper Paleolithic levels. A total of 118 bones were recovered in Level 7 (Table 5). The most representative species are *Anas platyrynchos* (mallard) and *Alectoris rufa* (red-legged partridge). No remains of raptors were found. Some of the duck bones have cut-marks, mostly on the humerus, coracoid and ulna (Figure 8 cutmark). According to Bochenski et al. (1999) golden eagles and other raptors that prey on other birds, leave higher percentages of sterna, coracoids, scapulae and humeri in the unswallowed portion than other elements. Owls typically leave higher proportions of wing elements. At Suão, the most frequent bird bones are humeri, radii, coracoids, carpo-metacarpi and ulnae. The latter are usually missing both epiphyses forming bone cylinders though not for the same reason as those from rabbits. Bird bones do not contain marrow. Instead they are hollow to aid in lift and flight. In this case, the missing epiphyses are probably due to eating habits whereby the soft epiphyses are chewed off (cf. Steadman *et al.* 2002). Still, the possibility for bird bone stock is open for suggestion. Garcia Petit (1995) has argued for such a practice during the Magdalenian at Bora Gran in Catalunya. Several limb elements from geese and bustard were recovered as bone cylinders. A similar pattern is documented at the Magdalenian site Grotte de les Églises in southern France (Laroulandie 1998). Lefèvre (1992) observed this phenomenon in prehistoric and historic sites in Patagonia. She attributed the lack of epiphyses to human chewing behavior eased by incomplete fusion. Raptors or carnivores cannot be ruled out as agents in the deposition of bird bones at Suão but the element representation, presence of cutmarks and breakage patterns strongly suggests predominately human agency.

	6	7	8+9
Alectoris rufa		+	+
Anas platyrhynchos	+	+	+
Corvidae	+	+	+
Corvus monedula		+	+
Garrulus glandarius			+
Pyrrhocorax pyrrhocorax			+
Tordus sp.			+

+= present

Table 5. Bird species from Lapa do Suão.

AQUATIC FAUNA

As for the marine fauna, Roche (1982) reported a variety of molluscan species, clams, mussels, limpets and gastropods and a single fish, gilthead (Table 6). The marine shells were almost certainly all ornamental as there was no shellmidden reported and the number of shells is low. Many are perforated, especially the *Littorina* and *Nassarius*. Nevertheless, the collection of these species, mostly from littoral environments, suggests a fairly large exploitation territory for Suão. Given the screen size used, the fish remains may be greatly under-represented.

To summarize, the Suão fauna is numerically dominated by rabbit. Red deer, wild boar, equids, caprids and carnivores are also present. Additional small animals include birds, molluscs, fish, reptiles, bats, voles and dormice. Given that most of the cave sediments were excavated it is likely that the existing sample of Magdalenian artifacts and food refuse represents the nature of site function. However, the possibility that many of the animal bones were discarded outside the entrance of the cave could mean that the sample from the interior is strongly biased in favor of smaller, more fragmented remains.

	6	7	8+9
Cerastoderma edule	+	+	+
Mytilus edulis	+	+	+
Scrobicularia plana		+	
Solen marginatus		+	+
Tapes decussata	+	+	+
Patella sp.			
Cerithium vugatum			+
Littorina obtusata			+
Nassarius reticulata			+
Trivia monacha			+
Turritela sp.			+
Semicassis undulata	+		+
Theodoxus fluviatilis			+

Table 6. Shellfish species from Lapa do Suão.

DISCUSSION

The preponderance of rabbit fits the general pattern in Upper Paleolithic caves and rockshelters. For ungulates, red deer is most abundant, as it is in the Magdalenian levels at Caldeirão and Picareiro. The absence of auroch is perhaps strange since Suão is located much closer to prime auroch habitat than Picareiro. The fauna, wood charcoal and radiocarbon dates conform to Roche's conclusion that the site is Magdalenian and the Solutrean artifacts derive from an occupation that eroded away. That Roche ignored the numerous rabbit bones in his publication may be due more to the fact that most of these were found in later, unpublished excavations than a dismissal that humans hunted rabbits.

Birds are relatively rare in Magdalenian sites in central Portugal. Suão and Caldeirão are the only sites where waterfowl and partridges, common prey types in Spanish Magdalenian sites, have been found. Picareiro has a few bird bones but these are of songbird size (Bicho *et al.* 2000). Suão is located upslope from a small stream winding through a narrow valley. Within a kilometer or two, this valley opens to a low coastal plain. This is a fairly unique location for a fauna-bearing Late Upper Paleolithic site in Portugal and perhaps explains the presence of several avian prey types. However, it may also relate to differences in the season of occupation of Suão compared to other sites further inland.

Determining seasonality at Suão is made difficult due to the absence of teeth for sectioning or crown height measurements. The primary evidence lies in the rabbit mortality profile. The rabbit assemblage is dominated by adults but does contain a few juveniles, unlike Picareiro which is almost entirely comprised of adults. Of a total of 2,444 rabbit elements in Suão Level 8+9, Valente (n.d.) identified 94 juvenile rabbit elements from approximately 13 individuals, about 9% of the total

MAU. At Picareiro, Hockett has reported that 99.4% of the rabbit limb epiphyses were fused (Hockett and Bicho 2000). Rabbit seasonality at Picareiro was determined by comparison of the mortality pattern and modern rabbit ecology. Rabbits in Spain and Portugal have two birthing peaks coinciding with fall and spring rainfall (Soriguer and Rogers 1981). There is a high mortality rate for juvenile rabbits so that within a few months the juveniles have either matured or been killed by predators. Therefore, archaeological assemblages dominated by adult rabbits may have been formed during winter and/or summer unless, of course, hunters were selectively targeting adults (Hockett and Bicho 2002). Lupo and Schmitt (2002) have argued that traps and snares tend to catch adults more often than not because juveniles either do not follow adults into traps or are too small to trip snares. If however, one accepts the use of mortality patterns to determine season of capture, then Suão may have been occupied slightly earlier or later during the year than Picareiro when subadult rabbits were still present, perhaps the early Fall or late Spring.

REFERENCES

ANGERMAN, R. 1972. Hare, rabbits and pikas. *Grzimek's Animal Life Encyclopedia* 12:419-462.

BICHO, N. F., B. HOCKETT, J. HAWS, AND W. BELCHER. 2000. Hunter-gatherer subsistence at the end of the Pleistocene: preliminary results from Picareiro Cave, Central Portugal. *Antiquity* 74:500-506.

BOCHENSKI, Z. M., K. HUHTALA, S. SULKAVA, AND R. TORNBERG. 1999. Fragmentation and preservation of bird bones in food remains of the Golden Eagle *Aquila chrysaetos*. *Archaeofauna* 8:31-39.

CORTES, V., O. D. V. FERREIRA, A. FURTADO, A. S. MAURICIO, AND J. A. MONTEIRO. 1977. A Lapa do Suão (Bombarral): relatório da campanha de escavações de 1970. *Boletim Cultural* 83:219-237.

FRANÇA, J. C., J. ROCHE, AND O. D. V. FERREIRA. 1961. Sur l'existence probable d'un niveau solutréen dans les couches de la grotte de Casa da Moura (Cesareda). *Comunicações Serviços Geológicos de Portugal* 45:365-370.

FURTADO, A., A. S. MAURÍCIO, V. CÔRTES, AND J. A. MONTEIRO. 1969. Lapa do Suão (Bombarral). *O Arqueólogo Português* III:63-69.

GARCIA I PETIT, L. 1995. Preliminary study of Upper Pleistocene bird bone remains from L'Arbreda Cave (Catalonia). *Courier Forschungsinstitut Senckenberg* 181:215-227.

GARCIA PETIT, L. 1997. Les restes d'oiseaux des sites de Serinyà (Pays Catalans). in *El Món Mediterrani després del Pleniglacial (18,000-12,000 BP)*. J. M. Fullola and N. Soler,Eds. Girona: Sèrie Monogràfica, 17, Museu d'Arqueologia de Catalunya-Girona. pp. 329-344.

GARSON, P. 1979. Social organization and reproduction in the rabbit: a review. in *Proceedings of the World Lagomorph Conference*. K. Myers and C. D. MacInnes,Eds. Guelph: University of Guelph. pp. 256-270.

HOCKETT, B. S. 1989. Archaeological significance of rabbit-raptor interactions in southern California. *North American Archaeologist* 10:123-139.

HOCKETT, B.S. 1991. Toward distinguishing human and raptor patterning on leporid bones. *American Antiquity* 56:667-679.

HOCKETT, B.S. 1994. A descriptive analysis of the leporid bones from Hogup Cave, Utah. *Journal of California and Great Basin Anthropology* 16:106-117.

HOCKETT, B.S. 1995. Comparison of leporid bones in raptor pellets, raptor nests and archaeological sites in the Great Basin. *North American Archaeologist* 16:223-238.

HOCKETT, B.S. 1996. Corroded, thinned and polished bones created by golden eagles (*Aquila chrysaetos*): taphonomic implications for archaeological interpretations. *Journal of Archaeological Science* 23:587-591.

HOCKETT, B.S. 1999. Taphonomy of a carnivore-accumulated rabbit bone assemblage from Picareiro Cave, Portugal. *Journal of Iberian Archaeology* 1:225-230.

HOCKETT, B. S., AND N. F. BICHO. 2000. The rabbits of Picareiro Cave: small mammal hunting during the Late Upper Paleolithic in the Portuguese Estremadura. *Journal of Archaeological Science* 27.

HOCKETT, B. S., AND J. A. HAWS. 2002. Taphonomic and methodological perspectives of leporid hunting during the Upper Paleolithic of the western Mediterranean Basin. *Journal of Archaeological Method and Theory* 9:269-302.

HUDSON, J. 1993. The impacts of domestic dogs on bone in forager camps; or, the dog-gone bones. in *From Bones to Behavior: Ethnoarchaeological and Experimental*

Contributions to the Interpretation of Faunal Remains. J. Hudson,Eds. Carbondale: Center for Archaeological Investigations, Occasional Paper No. 21. pp. 301-323.

LAROULANDIE, V. 1998. Études archéozoologique et taphonomique des lagopèdes des saules de la grotte magdalénienne des Égilses (Ariège). *Anthropozoologica* 28:45-54.

LEFÈVRE, C. 1992. Punta Maria 2: los restos de aves. *Palimpsesto. Revista de Arqueologia* 2:71-98.

LEFÈVRE, C. 1997. Sea bird fowling in southern Patagonia: a contribution to understanding the nomadic round of the Canoeros Indians. *International Journal of Osteoarchaeology* 7:260-270.

PAYNE, S., AND P. J. MUNSON. 1982. Ruby and how many squirrels? The destruction of bones by dogs. in *Palaeobiological Investigations: Research Design, Methods and Data Analysis.* N. R. J. Fieller, D. D. Gilbertson, and N. G. A. Ralph,Eds. Oxford: BAR International Series 266. pp. 31-39.

PÉREZ RIPOLL, M. 1992. *Marcas de Carnicería, Fracturas Intencionadas y Mordeduras de Carnivoros en Huesos Prehistóricos del Mediterráneo Español.* Alicante: Instituto de Cultura Juan Gil-Albert.

PÉREZ RIPOLL, M. 1993. Las marcas tafonómicas en huesos de lagoformos. in *Estudios sobre Cuaternario.* M. P. Fumanal and J. Bernabeu,Eds. Valencia: Asociación Española para el Estudio del Cuaternario. pp. 227-231.

PÉREZ RIPOLL, M., AND R. M. VALLE. 2001. La caza, el aprovechamiento de las presas y el comporttanmiento de las comunidades cazadores prehistóricas. in *De Neandertales a Cromañones: El Inicio del Poblamiento Humano en las Tierras Valencianas.* V. Villaverde,Eds. València: Universitat de València. pp. 73-98.

ROCHA, S. 1907. Novas explorações na gruta da Lapa do Suão. *Boletim da Sociedade Archeologica Santos Rocha* 1:150-153.

ROCHE, J. 1979. Le Magdalenien portugais. in *La Fin des Temps Glaciaires en Europe.* D. D. Sonneville-Bordes,Ed. Paris: CNRS. pp. 753-58.

ROCHE, J. 1982. A gruta chamada Lapa do Suão (Bombarral). *Arqueologia* 5:5-18.

ROWLEY-CONWY, P. 1992. The early Neolithic animal bones from Gruta do Caldeirão. in *Gruta do Caldeirão. O Neolítico Antigo,* vol. 6. J. Zilhão,Ed. Lisboa: IPPAR, Trabalhos de Arqueologia, 6. pp. 231-257.

SANCHIS SERRA, A. 2000. Los restos de *Oryctolagus cuniculus* en las tafocenosis de *Bubo bubo* y *Vulpes vulpes* y su aplicacíon a la caracterizacíon del registro faunístico arqueológico. *Saguntum-PLAV* 32:31-49.

SCHMIDT, K. M. 1999. The Five Feature site (AZ CC:7:55 [ASM]): evidence for a prehistoric rabbit drive in southeastern Arizona. *The Kiva* 65:103-124.

SCHMITT, D. N., AND K. E. JUELL. 1994. Toward the identification of coyote scatological faunal accumulations in archaeological contexts. *Journal of Archaeological Science* 21:249-262.

SORIGUER, R. C., AND P. ROGERS. 1979. The European wild rabbit in Mediterranean Spain. in *Proceedings of the World Lagomorph Conference.* K. Myers and C. D. MacInnes,Eds. Guelph: University of Guelph. pp. 600-613.

VILA, A., R. YLL, J. ESTÉVEZ, G. ALCALDE, A. FARO, J. OLLER, AND P. VILETTE. 1985. *El "Cingle Vermell": Assentament de Caçadors-recollectors del Xé. Milleni B.P. Excavacion Arqueològiques a Catalunya 5.* Barcelona: Generalitat de Catalunya.

WALTERS, I. 1984. Gone to the dogs: a study of bone attrition at a central Australian campsite. *Mankind* 14:389-400.

ZILHÃO, J. 1995. O Paleolitico Superior da Estremadura Portuguesa. Doctoral dissertation, Universidade de Lisboa.

PALEOLITHIC SUBSISTENCE AND THE TAPHONOMY OF SMALL MAMMAL ACCUMULATIONS IN THE IBERIAN PENINSULA

Bryan Hockett

Bureau of Land Management, 3900 East Idaho St., Elko, NV 89801, USA

INTRODUCTION

Small mammal bones, and in particular those of the European rabbit (*Oryctolagus cuniculus*), are ubiquitous components of Paleolithic faunal assemblages recovered from caves and rockshelters throughout the Iberian Peninsula (Aura *et al.* 2002; Hockett and Haws 2002). Leporids (rabbits and hares [*Lepus* spp.]) were occasionally hunted by European Neanderthals (Aura et al. 2002; Blasco 1997), but it is not until the Upper Paleolithic in central and southern Europe, after ca. 30,000 BP, that these animals became mainstays of the diet (Aura et al. 2002; Hockett and Haws 2002; Musil 1994). Leporids were actively hunted in the early Upper Paleolithic throughout Iberia and central Europe, but in the eastern Mediterranean hares were taken in greater frequency much later, nearer to the Pleistocene-Holocene transition (Stiner and Munro 2002).

It has long been recognized by archaeologists that leporids are also the favorite prey of a variety of avian and mammalian predators in Iberia and elsewhere (Hockett 1989, 1991, 1999; Hockett and Haws 2002; Serra 2000; Perez-Ripoll 1993; Schmitt and Juell 1995; Schmitt 1995). In Iberia, over 30 mammalian and avian predators are known to hunt rabbits (e.g., Jaksic and Soriguer 1981; Mathias et al. 1998; Revilla and Palomares 2002). These predators include the eagle owl (*Bubo bubo*), lynx *(Lynx pardina)*, wild cat (*Felis silvestris*), polecat or wild ferret (*Mustela putorius*), genet (*Genetta genetta*), red fox (*Vulpes vulpes*) and the badger (*Meles meles*).

Previous research suggests that eagle and owl pellets contain greater relative frequencies of forelimb bones (scapula, humerus, radius, ulna) compared to hindlimb bones (innominate, femur, tibia) (Hockett 1991, 1995; Hockett and Haws 2002; Serra 2000). Rabbit bones accumulated under the nesting or roosting sites of golden eagles (*Aquila chrysaetos*) and martial eagles *(Polemaetus bellicosus)* in North America and southern Africa, respectively, display the opposite pattern: hindlimb bones outnumber forelimb bones (Hockett 1995; Schmitt 1995; Cruz-Uribe and Klein 1998). Non-scatological rabbit bone assemblages accumulated by small carnivores in Iberia also tend to contain larger frequencies of hindlimb bones (Hockett 1999; Hockett and Haws 2002).

Raptors sometimes puncture rabbit bones during the kill or during feeding with their beaks and talons; small carnivores also puncture bones during feeding. Raptors, however, generally leave a single puncture mark, and they tend to puncture the innominate and sacrum more frequently than other bones. Small carnivores, in contrast, often create multiple puncture marks primarily on limb bones and innominates. As many as 10-12 individual puncture marks may be present on the ends of rabbit limb bones damaged by small carnivores (Hockett 1999). Additionally, raptors generally puncture only about 2-3% of the rabbit bones left behind at a nesting or roosting site; small carnivores puncture up to 25% of the non-scatological rabbit bones they may deposit in a cave or rockshelter (Hockett 1999; Hockett and Haws 2002).

These taphonomic patterns are in contrast to those created by Upper Paleolithic foragers in Iberia. In the Upper Paleolithic of Iberia, humans often butchered, consumed, and discarded complete or near-complete carcasses in caves and rockshelters, although foot elements are sometimes rare. Therefore, forelimb bones, hindlimb bones, and head parts such as mandibles all tend to be recovered in relatively large numbers. These patterns are displayed in Tables 1 and 2.

In addition, beginning in the early Upper Paleolithic human foragers in Iberia systematically extracted marrow from the tibia, femur, and humerus of rabbit carcasses (Pérez Ripoll 1993, 2001; Hockett and Bicho 2000; Hockett and Haws 2002). The marrow was extracted by snapping or biting the ends off these bones, creating diaphysis cylinders that sometimes number in the hundreds in Iberian Upper Paleolithic caves. Raptors and carnivores sometimes inadvertently create leporid diaphysis cylinders as well during feeding (Hockett 1991), but they are infrequent compared to the number of rabbit long bones with attached epiphyses (Hockett and Haws 2002). In these latter accumulations, as mentioned above, they will be accompanied by bones displaying puncture marks, particularly the innominate, sacrum and the ends of long bones.

Table 1. Relative frequencies of rabbit head, hindlimb, and forelimb bones from five
nonhuman predator assemblages (data summarized in Hockett and Haws 2002).

	Eagle Nests	Eagle Pellets	Owl Small Carnivore – Picareiro Cave	Small Carnivore – Buraca Glorioso	Alvados Raptor Nest
Head:					
mandible	.23	.54	.48	.39	.21
Hindlimb:					
innominate	.60	.41	.73	1.0	1.0
femur	.51	.58	.67	.67	.89
tibia	1.0	.57	1.0	.89	.70
Forelimb:					
scapula	.06	.59	.19	.11	.08
humerus	.18	1.0	.33	.28	.16
radius	.22	.77	.25	.00	.16
ulna	.19	.91	.31	.17	.08

Table 2. Rabbit bones accumulated by a variety of nonhuman and human predators
grouped into three blocks by relative frequencies.

Relative Frequency	Small Carnivore Not Swallowed	Small Carnivore Scats	Raptor Pellets	Raptor Nests	Picareiro Cave Upper Paleolithic
1.0					
	innominate	mandible	humerus	innominate	mandible
	femur	femur	radius	femur	tibia
	tibia		ulna	tibia	scapula
					humerus
					radius
					ulna
.60					
	mandible	innominate	mandible	mandible	femur
	humerus	tibia	innominate		
	ulna	scapula	femur		
		humerus	tibia		
		radius	scapula		
		ulna			
.20					
	scapula				
	radius				
0.0					

This short note reports on the analysis of rabbit bones collected under a degraded raptor nest in the Estremadura region of central Portugal. Although the taphonomic patterning of leporid bones accumulated under raptor nests have been reported from the Great Basin of North America (Hockett 1995; Schmitt 1995; Hockett and Haws 2002) and from Africa (Cruz-Uribe and Klein 1998), I sought a similar assemblage of bones from central Portugal for comparative purposes. Serra (2000) has reported on rabbit bones extracted from eagle owl pellets in Spain, but this study did not include an assemblage of unswallowed bones typically left behind at eagle owl nesting sites. The bones described below

Table 3. Rabbit bones of the axial skeleton and limbs from the Alvados Roost, central Portugal

Element	Complete	Proximal	Distal	Midshaft	Totals (NISP)	Totals (MNE)
mandible		8		1	9	8
maxilla	12				12	12
sacrum	9				9	9
innominate	38				38	38
femur	12	21	11	4	48	33
tibia	2	16	24	6	48	26
scapula		3			3	3
humerus	7	3	2		12	10
radius	4	2	2		8	6
ulna	1	2			3	3
vertebra	54				54	54
Totals	139	55	39	11	244	202

demonstrate continuity in taphonomic patterning of rabbit bones accumulated by raptors under nesting or roosting sites on three continents, building on the earlier research of Hockett (1989, 1991, 1995, 1996), Schmitt (1995), Cruz-Uribe and Klein (1998), and Hockett and Haws (2002).

ALVADOS ROOST

During the summer of 2001, approximately 250 rabbit bones were found lying alongside a steep cliff face near Buraca Glorioso, a collapsed 'rockshelter' in central Portugal that also serves as the opening to a large cave system (Table 3). The surface of Buraca Glorioso contained a number of rabbit bones accumulated by small carnivores (Hockett and Haws 2002). The rabbit bones reported on here were located along a narrow ledge and side slope below a nearly vertical cliff face. Although no active raptor roost was present, the rabbit bones most probably derived from a collapsed roost as the cliff face would have provided ideal ledges for the construction of an owl or eagle nest, but it afforded no room or protection for carnivores to den and accumulate bones. All bones from the surface were collected, and the top 2-3cm of sediment was scraped in order to collect bones that had been covered by recent vegetation. All bones were tightly clustered within an area measuring only 1-2m in diameter, again suggesting that they had fallen from a raptor nest built above the slope. Further, none of the bones exhibit the taphonomic traces of polishing, thinning, and corrosion characteristic of bones deposited in raptor pellets or carnivore scats. These bones allow for comparison to leporid bones recovered from eagle roosts in North America (Hockett 1995; Schmitt 1995; Hockett and Haws 2002) and southern Africa (Cruz-Uribe and Klein 1998).

Table 3 shows that hindlimb bones greatly outnumber forelimb bones, and head parts are relatively rare at Alvados Roost. The greater relative frequencies of hindlimb bones compared to forelimb bones matches that of other reported raptor nest and non-scatological small carnivore assemblages; the relative scarcity of head parts (mandible, maxilla) matches the patterning of raptor nest

assemblages from North America and Africa. I have previously noted that golden eagles in North America often decapitate and 'skin' hare carcasses before feeding them to their young (Hockett 1995), which would account for the scarcity of head parts being accumulated under these nests. This behavior may have been repeated by the raptor that nested within Alvados Roost. Additionally, eagles often 'houseclean' their nests of rotting carcass parts not consumed by chicks in order to prevent potentially dangerous insects from invading roosts. This behavior tends to remove the upper body segment of leporid carcasses from nesting sites, while the lower limb segment from the tibia downward tends to remain at the nest and become incorporated into the nest as building material along with sticks, twigs, and the like. This would account for the consistently high relative frequencies of rabbit hindlimb bones under raptor nesting sites.

Similar to raptor-accumulated rabbit bone assemblages, only 3% of the bones from Alvados Roost display puncture marks, and all of these bones exhibit a single puncture. This is consistent with bones that have been punctured by raptor beaks and talons either during the kill or during feeding, in contrast to the multiple puncture marks caused by small carnivore teeth during feeding. Overall, then, these data suggest that leporid bone assemblages accumulated under raptor nests exhibit consistent taphonomic patterning across three continents: North America, Africa, and Europe. This patterning consists of 1) higher relative frequencies of hindlimb bones compared to forelimb bones; 2) relatively low frequencies of head parts; 3) 2-3% of bones exhibiting puncture marks; and 4) bones displaying single puncture marks; bones with multiple puncture marks will be relatively rare.

SIGNIFICANCE AND RELATION TO PALEOLITHIC SUBSISTENCE

These data are important because small carnivores and raptors probably both accumulated large numbers of rabbit bones in some archaeological sites in the Iberian Peninsula, particularly before ca. 30,000 BP. In fact, in some cases it conceptually may be better to state that Neanderthals deposited some artifacts in carnivore dens and under raptor nests rather than to state that nonhuman predators accumulated bones in archaeological sites inhabited by Neanderthals. For examples, previous studies in central Portugal near Alvados Roost suggest that some pre-30,000 BP faunal assemblages were accumulated primarily by small carnivores, such as at Pego do Diabo Cave (Valente 2000). Preliminary results of the analysis of more than 10,000 rabbit bones from the early Middle Paleolithic site Galeria Pesada in central Portugal (Hockett 2001) suggests that the majority of these bones may have accumulated under a raptor nest, despite the fact that large mammal bones cut by stone tools and hundreds of lithic artifacts were found amongst the rabbit bones (Marks et al. 2002).

In contrast, rabbit bone assemblages dating to the Upper Paleolithic in Portugal consistently display patterns suggesting that all or nearly all of these bones were deposited by humans rather than by nonhuman predators. Upper Paleolithic sites such as Picareiro Cave, Anecrial, and Lapa dos Coelhos (Hockett and Bicho 2000; Hockett and Haws 2002) contain thousands of rabbit bones accumulated by humans. There is scant evidence that nonhuman predators occupied these caves and deposited rabbit bones within them when they were unoccupied by Upper Paleolithic foragers. Central Portuguese caves that contain both Middle Paleolithic and Upper Paleolithic deposits such as Caldeirão Cave tell the same tale: during the Middle Paleolithic fewer rabbit bones were deposited into the cave, and those that are present exhibit good evidence that the majority of them were accumulated by nonhuman predators. In contrast, the Upper Paleolithic deposits of Caldeirão contain many more rabbit bones, the majority of which exhibit no evidence of nonhuman predator modification such as puncture marks (e.g., Davis 2002). This general pattern is repeated in caves throughout much of Spain, such as the central, eastern, and southern regions (Pérez Ripoll 2001; Aura et al. 2002).

These data in turn suggest that Upper Paleolithic foragers in Iberia may have occupied caves and rockshelters for longer periods of time than did the Neanderthals. The Iberian Neanderthals had more competition for food from a wider variety of principally large mammalian carnivores than did Upper Paleolithic foragers (Valente 2000). These combined data may support earlier interpretations that Iberian Neanderthals were more mobile than many populations of Upper Paleolithic foragers (e.g., Villaverde et al. 1996). While reductions in mobility may have been a contributing factor to the increase in rabbit hunting during the Upper Paleolithic of Iberia, this explanation seems inadequate to entirely explain the virtual absence of rabbit hunting at cave sites inhabited by H. heidelbergensis or Neanderthals such as Galeria Pesada. In the latter case, these early humans occupied the cave during a time in which rabbits were clearly abundant near the cave, just as they were during Upper Paleolithic times. Yet the early human occupants focused on large mammalian herbivores, ignoring a wide variety of small animals such as rabbits and birds (Marks et al. 2002) that probably could have been taken while the cave was occupied. Because there is no evidence for a decrease in the abundance of large herbivores in the region during the Upper Paleolithic, it seems that the virtual absence of rabbit hunting in central Portugal before the Upper Paleolithic may be due to a combination of mobility patterns and differences in cognitive choice between early and later humans about which animals to pursue and eat. I reject the notion that large-scale rabbit hunting required specialized technology such as nets or snares, although these tools certainly would have made their capture more efficient than digging rabbits out of their burrows or ambushing the animals along their easily defined trails (e.g., Hockett and Haws 2002).

CONCLUSION

The brief discussion presented above regarding differences in subsistence and mobility patterns between the Middle and Upper Paleolithic occupation of Iberia based on small game hunting would have no substance without the taphonomic details necessary to adequately distinguish between rabbit bone assemblages deposited by nonhuman predators from those accumulated by humans. Taphonomic analysis of rabbit bones, including patterns of element frequencies and puncture marks, must occur before interpretations are offered about the hunting of small fauna during the Paleolithic of Iberia and elsewhere. Taphonomic data from 'naturally' accumulated sites such as Alvados Roost assist in formulating these interpretations.

Yet additional work is needed. Controlled experiments in which rabbit carcasses are fed to small carnivores such as lynx and wild cat would be a valuable addition to the 'naturally' accumulated assemblages that I have reported on from the Great Basin in North America and from Portugal (Two Ledges Chamber, Matrac Roost, Waterfall Roost, Dondero Cave, Mineral Hill Cave, Picareiro Cave, Buraca Glorioso, Alvados Roost). In each case, these actualistic assemblages represent bones accumulated in cave and rockshelter settings, although I have witnessed the accumulation of thousands of leporid bones in open-air contexts as well, particularly in sand dunes in Nevada and Oregon and near coastal settings in California (e.g., Hockett 1989). While the precise species of predator was not always known to me, I purposively chose this class of actualistic data in order to most closely approximate the end result of rabbit bone accumulations on the landscape. These complex biotic and abiotic interactions cannot be duplicated by feeding carcasses to caged raptors or mammalian carnivores; but I recognize that this latter class of actualistic data has offered key insights into the taphonomic patterning of predator damage to large mammal bones. While this latter experimental research has been conducted on a variety of large carnivores, such studies are relatively rare on predator-prey relationships involving smaller carnivores and rabbits. These data, as well as those from sites such as Alvados Roost, will continue to be critical to the development of models that account for differences in the subsistence patterns of the early and later Paleolithic foragers of the Iberian Peninsula.

REFERENCES

AURA TORTOSA, J. E., BONILLA, B., RIPOLL, M., MARTINEZ VALLE, M., AND CALATAYUD, P. (2002). Big game and small prey: Paleolithic and Epipaleolithic economy from Valencia (Spain). Journal of Archaeological Method and Theory 9:215-268.

BLASCO, M. F. (1997). In the pursuit of game: The Mousterian cave site of Gabasa I in the Spanish Pyrenees. Journal of Anthropological Research 53:177-217.

CRUZ-URIBE, K., AND KLEIN, R. G. (1998). Hyrax and hare bones from modern South African eagle roosts and the detection of eagle involvement in fossil bone assemblages. Journal of Archaeological Science 25:135-147.

DAVIS, S. (2002). The mammals and birds from the Gruta do Caldeirão, Portugal. Revista Portuguesa de Arqueologia 5:29-98.

HOCKETT, B. (1989). Archaeological significance of rabbit-raptor interactions in southern California. North American Archaeologist 10:123-139.

HOCKETT, B. (1991). Toward distinguishing human and raptor patterning on leporid bones. American Antiquity 56:667-679.

HOCKETT, B. (1995). Comparison of leporid bones in raptor pellets, raptor nests, and archaeological sites in the Great Basin. North American Archaeologist 16:223-238.

HOCKETT, B. (1996). Corroded, thinned, and polished bones created by golden eagles (Aquila chrysaetos): Taphonomic implications for archaeological interpretations. Journal of Archaeological Science 23:587-591.

HOCKETT, B. (1999). Taphonomy of a carnivore-accumulated rabbit bone assemblage from Picareiro Cave, central Portugal. Journal of Iberian Archaeology 1:225-230.

HOCKETT, B. (2001). The rabbits of Galeria Pesada: Small mammal hunting during the Middle Paleolithic of Central Portugal? Paper presented at the XIV Congress of the International Union of Prehistoric and Protohistoric Sciences, Liège, Belgium.

HOCKETT, B., AND BICHO, N. (2000). The rabbits of Picareiro Cave: Small mammal hunting during the late Upper Paleolithic in the Portuguese Estremadura. Journal of Archaeological Science 27:715-723.

HOCKETT, B., AND HAWS, J. (2002). Taphonomic and methodological perspectives of leporid hunting during the Upper Paleolithic of the western Mediterranean basin. Journal of Archaeological Method and Theory 9:269-302.

JAKSIC, F., AND SORIGUER, R. (1981). Predation upon the European rabbit (Oryctolagus cuniculus) in Mediterranean habitats of Chile and Spain: A comparative analysis. Journal of Animal Ecology 50:269-281.

MATHIAS, M., SANTOS-REIS, M., PALMEIRIM, J., AND GRACA RAMALHINHO, M. (1998). Mamíferos de Portugal. Edições Inapa: Lisboa.

MARKS, A. E., MONIGAL, K., CHABAI, V., BRUGAL, J-P., GOLDBERG, P., HOCKETT, B., PEMÁN, E., ELORZA, M., AND MALLOL, C. (2002). Excavations at the Middle Pleistocene cave site of Galeria Pesada (Estremadura, Portugal): first results. Paleo 14:77-99.

MUSIL, R. (1994). The fauna. In Svoboda, J. (ed.), Pavlov I, Excavations 1952-1953, ERAUL 66, Université de Liège, Liège, pp. 181-209.

PÉREZ RIPOLL, M. (1993). Las marcas tafonomicas en huesos de lagoformos. Estudios sobre Cuaternario 1993:227-231.

PÉREZ RIPOLL, M. (2001). Marcas antrópicas en los huesos de conejo. In: V. Villaverde (Ed.), de Neandertales a Cromañones: El Inicio del Poblamiento Humano en las Tierras Valencianas, pp. 119-124. València: Universitat de València.

REVILLA, E., AND PALOMARES, F. (2002). Does local feeding specialization exist in Eurasian badgers? Canadian Journal of Zoology 80:83-93.

SCHMITT, D. N. (1995). The taphonomy of golden eagle prey accumulations at Great Basin roosts. Journal of Ethnobiology 15:237-256.

SCHMITT, D. N., AND JUELL, K. E. (1994). Toward the identification of coyote scatological faunal accumulations in archaeological contexts. Journal of Archaeological Science 21:249-262.

SERRA, A. S. (2000). Los restos de *Oryctolagus cuniculus* en las tafocenosis de *Bubo bubo* y *Vulpes vulpes* y su aplicación a la caracterización del registro faunístico arqueológico. Sagvntvm 32:31-49.

STINER, M., AND MUNRO, N. (2002). Approaches to prehistoric diet breadth, demography, and prey ranking systems in time and space. Journal of Archaeological Method and Theory 9:181-214.

VALENTE, M.-J. (2000). Arqueozoologia e Tafonomia em Contexo Paleolitico: A Gruta do Pego do Diabo (Loures). Unpublished M. A. Thesis, University of Lisbon, Lisbon.

VILLAVERDE, V., MARTINEZ-VALLE, R., GUILLEM, P., AND FUMANAL, M. (1996). Mobility and the role of small game in the Middle Paleolithic of the central region of the Spanish Mediterranean: A comparison of Cova Negra with other Paleolithic deposits. In: E. Carbonell (Ed.), The Last Neandertals, the First Anatomically Modern Humans, pp. 267-288. Cambridge: Cambridge University Press.

MUSTELID HUNTING BY RECENT FORAGERS AND THE DETECTION OF TRAPPING IN THE EUROPEAN PALEOLITHIC

Trenton W. Holliday* and Steven E. Churchill**

*Department of Anthropology, Tulane University, New Orleans, Louisiana 70118 USA
**Department of Biological Anthropology and Anatomy, Duke University, Durham, North Carolina 27708 USA

INTRODUCTION

Trapping, or the use of untended facilities in animal acquisition, plays an important role in the subsistence strategy of many groups, both foraging and agricultural, and is therefore of interest to archaeologists working in a host of different time periods and geographic regions. While the term "trapping" is often used to refer to both tended and untended facilities (Anell, 1960, 1969; Oswalt, 1976), we use it here to refer to only those devices that are left untended (i.e., "unmanned"). We recognize that this is in some respects a false dichotomy, but we retain the distinction because we have a theoretical interest in when untended facilities were first used by hominins. While other species create traps for their prey (e.g., the webs of spiders or the sand funnels of ant lions), the predatory strategy of reducing prey search costs with *untended* traps appears to be unique to humans. Therefore, the detection of the first appearance of this uniquely human behavior would be of interest to both paleolithic archaeologists and human paleontologists alike.

Discerning the earliest use of trapping in the archaeological record is made difficult by the nature of the behavior. The common use of perishable, organic materials (wood, sinew, vegetal fiber cordage, etc.) and the relative technological simplicity of many traps make the preservation of trap components in archaeological deposits unlikely. Traps are also commonly deployed well away from residential areas, further reducing the likelihood of archaeological recovery of trapping technology. Thus the direct detection of early trapping remains unlikely, and we are forced instead to rely on indirect methods to explore the emergence of this behavior. Along these lines, Klein (1973) and Straus (1985) have argued that the consistent occurrence of mustelids and other small carnivores in European late Pleistocene deposits constitutes a faunal signature of trapping (see below). Furthermore, these animals are often represented in late Upper Paleolithic sites by a preponderance of bones of the paws or by relatively complete skeletons lacking the elements of the paws – suggesting these animals were taken for their fur. Since trapping is the preferred method of acquiring fur-bearing animals in the modern world (as it does little damage to the pelt), this has been seen as further indirect support for the emergence of trapping in late glacial times.

Here we use ethnographic analogy to explore the notion that the occurrence of certain species in archaeological assemblages constitutes a faunal signature of trapping. Human groups of the recent past who used untended facilities are an invaluable source of information important to discerning the origins of trapping behavior. To explore the possibility that trapping may be recognized in the faunal record, we ask: are there animals that are rarely (if ever) hunted by recent, historically known foragers, but rather are exclusively or nearly always acquired through the use of untended facilities? If we can assume similar cost/benefit relationships surrounding hunting vs. trapping of these animals in prehistory as in the modern world, then the presence of these animals' remains in archaeological deposits might strongly suggest the presence of trapping in prehistory.

TRAPPING IN THE ETHNOGRAPHIC RECORD

In an ecological study of trapping among ethnohistorically documented hunter-gatherers, Holliday (1998) found that groups heavily reliant on trapping were more frequently found in certain ecological contexts. Specifically, in ecosystems in which prey animals are generally small, solitary and/or dispersed on the landscape, one is more likely to encounter groups more heavily dependent upon trapping in their subsistence strategy. In these contexts a trap serves as a hunter's proxy, effectively allowing the hunter to sample from multiple locations on the landscape, and therefore making it more likely he or she will encounter a greater number of animals than on his or her own[1] (Holliday, 1998). Additionally, when dealing with highly mobile prey (such as carnivores, large cervids, etc.) encounter rates can be better when one adopts a "sit-and-wait" strategy over an active search strategy. However, the choice of any given waiting location necessarily entails the loss of opportunity for success at other locations (i.e., an opportunity cost). Also, comfort concerns and other factors limit the time that a hunter can remain idle at a single location. Thus while a "sit-and-wait" strategy may

---

[1] The use of pronouns of either sex is important here. Many groups viewed at least some forms of trapping as "women's" or "children's" work (e.g., Blackfoot {Wissler, 1910}; Chugach {Birket-Smith, 1953}; G/wi {Silberbauer, 1972}; Hare {Hurlbert, 1962}; Slave {Honigmann, 1946}; Tlingit {Laguna, 1960}; and Yurok {Heizer and Mills, 1952}). We may assume the same would be true in the Paleolithic – as Stiner et al. (2000) note: "We do not know who in Paleolithic societies did the inventing, but innovations in trap, snare and net technology for hunting small prey could have been the province of women, children, and the elderly" (Stiner et al., 2000:58).

improve encounter rates for certain prey, it cannot necessarily ensure that those encounter rates will be good. Untended traps allow multiple replication of the waiting hunter, and remain "vigilant" until sprung, thus greatly reducing the costs associated with this strategy.

In the parlance of optimal foraging theory (Winterhalder, 1981; Smith, 1983), the use of traps discussed above involve efforts to reduce prey search costs in situations in which fairly large packages of animal biomass are solitary or semi-solitary and wide ranging (e.g., moose). Alternatively, traps may be used for smaller prey that is locally abundant (and thus associated with low search costs) but difficult to capture (and thus associated with high handling costs). Thus foragers and horticulturalists alike commonly set snares and other traps in the vicinity of residential sites for lagomorphs and rodents. In cases in which ecological or social factors force a group to expand their diet breadth (see below), trapping may represent an important means of managing handling costs for animals that are otherwise energetically costly to capture relative to the calories they return. Finally, trapping may play a role in situations where prey have both high search and high handling costs (and thus are undesirable as food items) but that have non-dietary attributes (such as a thick pelt) that make them desirable for the production of clothing or other technology. Small carnivores generally fall into this last category.

The conditions under which trapping is favored – involving prey that is dispersed in the environment (either large prey that is solitary and wide ranging or small prey that is more abundant and uniformly distributed) rather than patchy – tend to occur in ecosystems with low overall productivity or in which most primary productivity is locked up in non-edible plant biomass. Thus most trapping-intensive societies tend to be found in boreal forests and deserts, environments dominated by smaller and more solitary animals. Interestingly, such conditions are nearly the opposite of those in which Driver (1990) suggested one would find higher frequencies of communal hunting or drives. He posited that dispersed, solitary prey make communal hunting extremely inefficient, since the hunters as a group are less likely to encounter prey than if they had split up to hunt individually. For this reason, it appears that driving animals into traps and using untended facilities occur under very different circumstances and thus are two different phenomena with regard to subsistence.

Holliday (1998) also found (as had been predicted by Anell, 1960 and Binford, 1990) that mobility also plays a role in trapping intensity, in that highly mobile groups do not remain in an area for a sufficient length of time to periodically check and maintain traps. For this reason, trapping intensity tends to be highest among sedentary and semi-sedentary hunter-gatherers (and horticulturalists). For horticulturalists, traps serve a dual

function of providing an extra source of meat as well as ridding gardens of the animals that raid them.

As reviewed extensively in Oswalt (1976), there are a variety of trapping methods employed by humans worldwide. Globally, the most common type of trap (and technologically one of the simplest) is the snare. In a study of 43 foraging societies who trap terrestrial animals (Holliday, 1998), 38 groups, or 88%, were reported in the ethnohistoric literature to have used snares. According to Oswalt (1976), a snare may be as simple as two technounits – a line and a line holder, although more complex snares, such as those connected to spring poles, are commonly employed (Lips, 1936; Osgood, 1937; Oswalt, 1976). Spring-pole snares tend to be used for animals that can more easily break free from the noose, or chew through the snare line (Oswalt, 1976). While most animals taken by spring-pole snares are small, the Tanaina of Cook Inlet, Alaska, built a large one to capture bears, and the Tonga people of southern Zambia made one to take buffalo (Osgood, 1937; Oswalt, 1976). Perhaps not surprisingly, untended snares tend to be more complex than tended ones (Oswalt, 1976).

The second most commonly used trap is the deadfall. These traps are constructed such that a heavy weight, usually logs and/or stones, falls to crush the unlucky animal that springs the trap. Technologically, they tend to be more complicated than snares (Oswalt, 1976). Examples of deadfalls abound in the ethnohistoric literature. Both Koppert (1930) and Drucker (1951), for instance, describe the sophisticated deadfalls of varying size employed by the Nootka of Vancouver Island to trap animals ranging in size from mink and marten to larger game such as deer and bears. Other boreal forest groups such as the Chippewa (Southern Ojibwa) of Michigan's northern peninsula, the Eastern Ojibwa of the Georgian Bay area, the Kaska of the Canadian Rockies, and the Mistassini Cree of northern Québec were also known to take bears in deadfalls (Kohl, 1860; Jenness, 1935; Honigmann, 1954; Rogers, 1972). Additionally, the existence of at least one Iglulik deadfall trap built to kill polar bears has been reported (Mary-Rousselière, 1984). On a global scale, among Holliday's (1998) sample of 43 trapping hunter-gatherer groups, 27, or 63% of the groups, were reported to have used deadfalls. Interestingly, there appears to be little ecological variability in where deadfalls are used; they are found in tropical, temperate and boreal forests, temperate and tropical grasslands, circumpolar tundra, and desert contexts (Holliday, unpublished data).

A third type of trap is the pitfall, which while less commonly employed than snares or deadfalls, is nonetheless present in a variety of habitats across the globe. Pitfalls may be as simple as holes dug into the ground that, except for the simplest varieties, are subsequently covered with brush (Oswalt, 1976). Often sharpened stakes are placed upright in the bottom of the pit to incapacitate any animal that falls into it (e.g., those built by the Etolo of New Guinea; Bulmer, 1968). Of the 43 trapping hunter-gatherer groups examined by Holliday (1998), only 9, or 21%, were reported to have used pitfalls. The size of the game taken in these pitfalls is surprisingly variable – examples run from the rodents and rabbits taken by the Great Basin Western Shoshone (Steward, 1941) to the bears taken by the Tanaina (Cook Inlet, Alaska), the Tlingit (southeastern Alaska), and the Yurok of northern California (Osgood, 1937; Laguna, 1960; Heizer and Mills, 1952). Perhaps the largest animal taken in pitfalls are the 580-kg buffalo taken by the Dorobo of Kenya/Tanzania (Huntingford, 1953).

Descriptions of other, less easily categorized types of traps abound in the ethnohistoric literature, such as a rather ingenious Naskapi wolf trap in the form of a pair of concentric circles. The center circle holds the bait, which is inaccessible. The wolf enters the outer circle, and then makes its way around the center circle attempting to access the bait. In so doing, it closes an outward-swinging door that closes the trap's only entrance/exit (Lips, 1936; also described in Holliday, 1998). Another relatively common type of trap are called "spear" or "arrow" traps in which a fence guides animals to an opening that is armed with a bow and a trip line. Tripping the line releases the bowstring, firing the arrow into the hapless animal. The Ainu employed such traps equipped with poisoned arrows to kill both deer and bear (Batchelor, 1892; Watanabe, 1972). The Akamba of Kenya created a similar, albeit much larger, version of poisoned spear trap to take elephants (Oswalt, 1976). Yet another interesting "trap" is the blood knife used by both the Caribou Eskimo of the northwestern Hudson Bay region and their neighbors, the Iglulik of Baffin Island (Oswalt, 1976). For this simple trap, a bloody knife was left out in the open, blade up, with its handle buried in the ground. A passing wolf would lick the blood, cut its tongue on the knife, and continue to lap up its own blood until it bled to death.

Many other difficult-to-categorize traps exist, the discussion of which is beyond the scope of this paper. Yet as discussed above, from an archaeological perspective, all of these traps have one thing in common – none is likely to be detected in the archaeological record. According to Stiner et al. (2000), the only hints we have of trapping technology in the Paleolithic, for example, consist of possible bone triggers, cord (and potentially net) imprints in clay, and potential depictions of trapping in art. Thus we may ask if there are alternatives to detecting trapping technology in the archaeological record, ones that do not necessitate the preservation of the traps themselves?

Perhaps the archaeofaunal remains themselves could provide clues. In the European Upper Paleolithic, workers such as Klein (1973) and Straus (1985) have used the presence of fox and mustelid skeletons, in many cases represented sans paws, or, conversely, represented

solely by paws, as evidence that humans were exploiting these animals for their fur. This supposition is almost certainly correct, yet these workers also argue that the presence of these fur-bearers at the sites is *suggestive* of trapping. Additionally, in a study comparing Paleolithic archaeofaunal remains from the Italian coast and inland Israel, Stiner et al. (2000) point out that hares, rabbits and partridges are generally quite difficult to catch without the aid of some type of trap. However, as Klein (1973) and Straus (1985) both acknowledge, one cannot rule out that any of the above animals were actively hunted, as opposed to trapped. Thus the question remains: how can trapping be recognized in the archaeological record?

MATERIALS

To address this question, we combined hunting data for a sample of 96 recent hunter-gatherer groups (from Churchill, 1993), with data on the use of traps collected on a sample of 60 foraging societies (of which 17 did not use traps: from Holliday, 1998). These groups are listed in Table 1. As noted in Table 1, there is some degree of overlap between the two samples; 46 groups were studied by both authors. Our data were taken from the ethnohistoric literature; bibliographic references are available upon request. We then compiled a list of species hunted (Churchill, 1993), a list of species trapped (Holliday, unpublished data), and looked for any mammals which were present on the trapping list, yet absent on the hunting list. Were any such species found, these animals, we would argue, would be species that one could use to indicate trapping in archaeological context.

It is difficult, and not necessarily useful, to try to determine which particular *species* are most commonly trapped. Among other factors, this of course depends on geography, and the current sample of trapping groups is biased toward North America. Secondly, the actual species of trapped game are not always reported in the ethnohistoric literature. For example, some ethnographers may report that a trap was used for "rodents" (e.g., Steward, 1941). Likewise, to many hunter-gatherers, the Linnaean taxonomy is of little value – many traps (particularly unbaited ones) are designed to take animals of a given size, not a particular species. Rather than looking at the data for individual species, then, we instead looked for general trends to emerge from the ethnohistoric trapping data. After elucidating trends we examined some key archaeofaunal assemblages from Pleistocene Europe to see if we could find "faunal evidence" for trapping in any of these sites.

RESULTS

Table 2 presents the mammalian prey most frequently acquired in untended facilities and the groups ethnohistorically documented to trap them. The animals most commonly taken in traps by the recent hunter-gatherers in the sample are deer and antelope – of the 43 trapping groups investigated, 25, or 58%, of the groups

Table 1. List of recent human hunter-gatherer groups included in the study. "H" indicates that Churchill took hunting data for the group; "T" indicates that Holliday took trapping data for the group.

Arctic

Aleut (H,T)	Copper Eskimo (H,T)	Koniag (H,T)	W. Grnlnd Eskimo (H,T)
Caribou Eskimo (H,T)	Gilyak (H,T)	Netsilik (H,T)	Yukaghir (H,T)
Chugach (T)	Iglulik (H,T)	Polar Eskimo (H)	

Boreal and Northern Deciduous Forest

Ainu (H,T)	Emo Ojibwa -	Montagnais (H,T)	Tanaina (T)
Alsea (H)	(Rainy River) (H)	Naskapi (H,T)	Tlingit (H, T)
Bella Coola (H,T)	Kaska (H,T)	Nootka (H,T)	Twana (H)
Chipewyan (H)	Micmac (H,T)	Northn. Salteaux (H,T)	Upper Tanana (T)
Chippewa (H,T)[1]	Mistassini Cree (H,T)	Quileute (H)	
Eastern Ojibwa (H,T)	Modoc (H)	Slave (H,T)	

Temperate

Achomawi (H)	Crow (H,T)	Ona (H, T)	Tübatulábal (H,T)
Alacaluf (H)	Gabrieleño (H)	Patwin (H)	Wappo (H)
Arapaho (H)	Gros Ventre (H)	Plains Ojibwa (T)	Washo (H,T)
Assiniboin (H)	Hupa (H)	Pomo (H,T)	Western Mono (H, T)
Atsugewi (H)	Klamath (H,T)	Shoshoni (H)	Wintu (H)
Blackfoot-Piegan (H,T)[2]	Luiseño (H)	Sinkyone (H)	Wiyot (H)
Blood (H)	Maidu (H)	SE Salish (T)	Yahgan (H)
Chumash (H)	Miwok (H)	Tasmanians (H,T)	Yana (H)
Coast Yuki (H)	Nisenan (H)	Tehuelche (H)	Lake & N Fthil Yokut (H)
Comanche (T)	Nomlaki (H)	Tolowa (H)	Yurok (H, T)

Desert

Aranda (H)	!Kung (H,T)	Pitjandara (T)	Yavapai (T)
Cahuilla (H)	Mardudjara (H)	Seri (H,T)	Yiwara (H)
Chiricahua (T)	Northern Paiute (T)	Ute (H)	
G/wi (H,T)	Pintupi (H)	Western Shoshone (T)	

Tropical

Aché (H, T)	Bororo (H)	Kubu (H,T)	Semang (H, T)
Agta (H)	Botocudo (H)	Mbuti (T)[3]	Semaq Beri (H)
Aka (T)	Cuiva (H)	Mlabrai (H,T)	Siriono (H, T)[4]
Andaman (Onge) (H,T)	Dorobo (H, T)	Murngin (H)	Tiwi (H, T)
Aweikoma (H)	Efe (H, T)	Punan (H,T)	Waorani (H)
Bambote (T)	Hadza (H, T)	Rock Vedda (H)	

[1]Churchill (1993) referred to this group as Southern Ojibwa.
[2]Churchill (1993) considered the Blackfoot and Piegan as separate groups.
[3]Considered to be the same group as the Efe in Churchill (1993).
[4]Was excluded from Holliday's (1998) sample because the group practices horticulture.

took at least one species of deer or antelope with the aid of untended facilities. Marten, mink, fishers and other mustelids are also quite commonly trapped, especially among those groups known historically to have engaged in the fur trade. In the same sample of 43 trapping groups, 23 (or 53%) of them trapped at least one species of mustelid. Rabbits and hares are also among the most frequently targeted mammals, with 20 (or 46.5%) of the groups acquiring them with the aid of untended traps. Squirrels (18 groups, or 42%), bears (16 groups, or 37%), and foxes (15 groups, or 35%) are also commonly taken in traps. While seemingly less important (or perhaps due to their more limited ranges), wolves (10 groups, or 23%), and beavers and lynx (7 groups each, or 16%) are also frequent targets of untended facilities. We should emphasize that the above figures represent *minimum* numbers, as in some instances, ethnographers may have failed to observe the trapping of a particular animal. Likewise, for some groups (e.g., Aka, Chugach, G/wi), it was merely reported that "small mammals" or "rodents" were taken in traps; more specific data were not given (Bahuchet, 1988; Birket-Smith, 1953; Silberbauer, 1972).

It verges on self-evident that many of the above mammals, including deer, rabbits, bears, and tree squirrels are actively hunted using bow and arrow,

Table 2. List of the most commonly trapped mammals, and the groups documented to trap those mammals within the ethnohistoric sample.

Deer/Antelope

Ainu	Iglulik	Pomo	Washo
Aka	Kaska	Punan	Western Mono
Blackfoot	Kubu	Slave	Western Shoshone
Caribou Eskimo	!Kung	Southeastern Salish	Yurok
Chippewa	Micmac	Tanaina	
Dorobo	Nootka	Tlingit	
G/wi	Northern Paiute	Upper Tanana	

Rabbits and Hares

Chippewa	!Kung	Northern Salteaux	Upper Tanana
Eastern Ojibwa	Montagnais	Pomo	Western Mono
Gilyak	Naskapi	Slave	Western Shoshone
Hare	Netsilik	Southeastern Salish	Yavapai
Kaska	Northern Paiute	Tanaina	Yukaghir

Squirrels (Ground & Tree)

Gilyak	Nootka	Southeastern Salish	Western Shoshone
Hare	Northern Paiute	Tanaina	Yavapai
Kaska	Pomo	Tübatulabal	Yukaghir
Montagnais	Punan	Upper Tanana	
Netsilik	Slave	Western Mono	

Bears

Ainu	Hare	Montagnais	Southeastern Salish
Bella Coola	Iglulik	Nootka Tanaina	Tlingit
Chippewa	Kaska	Northern Salteaux	Yurok
Eastern Ojibwa	Mistassini Cree	Slave	

Foxes

Ainu	Iglulik	Naskapi	Upper Tanana
Blackfoot	Klamath	Southeastern Salish	West Greenland Eskimo
Chippewa	!Kung	Tanaina	Western Mono
Gilyak	Montagnais	Tlingit	

Wolves

Blackfoot	Gilyak	Northern Paiute	Tlingit
Caribou Eskimo	Iglulik	Southeasten Salish	
Chippewa	Naskapi	Tanaina	

Beavers

Chippewa	Micmac	Montagnais	Tlingit
Kaska	Mistassini Cree	Northern Salteaux	

Lynx

Chippewa	Mistassini Cree	Northern Salteaux	Upper Tanana
Hare	Naskapi	Tanaina	

blowgun, spear, or in many cases by driving them into traps, both natural and humanly made. However, a number of species that one might expect to be trapped are in fact frequently actively hunted. Foxes, for example, are actively hunted by a number of groups (beyond the British aristocracy!). According to Veniaminov (1840), the Aleuts would thrust a notched whalebone stick into a fox burrow, twirling it until the fox's hair was bound up, and then would drag the fox out. Among the North Foothill Yokuts in California, foxes were treed by dogs, then shot with bow and arrow (Latta, 1949). The Yurok, Lake Yokuts, and Chumash, all of California, also took fox with box and arrow (Heizer and Mills, 1952; Latta, 1949; Stuyvesant, 1978). Beavers, too, are often hunted. In North America, there are multiple reports of groups such as the Micmac of Nova Scotia, the Lake Miwok of northern California, and the Alseans of coastal Oregon breaking into beaver lodges and then either clubbing the beavers trapped inside, or dispatching them with bow and arrow or salmon harpoons (Wallis and Wallis, 1955; Beals and Hester, 1974; Drucker, 1939). The Aleuts and Montagnais are reported to have used harpoons to dispatch beaver after stalking their houses (Turner, 1889-90; Lips, 1947), and the Chippewa and Rainy River Ojibwa, Kaska, Twana, North Foothill and Lake Yokuts are said to have taken them with spears (Antropova, 1964; Kinietz, 1947; Grant, 1890; Honigmann, 1954; Elmendorf, 1960; Latta, 1949).

In like fashion, ground squirrels and marmots, commonly trapped rodents, are also actively hunted using a variety of methods. Lowie (1939) documents that among the Washo, gophers/ground squirrels were frequently taken by women, either by smoking or flooding them out of their burrows, or by inserting & twisting a forked stick into their burrows to trap them by their fur. Burrow smoke-outs were also employed by the Washo to capture field mice, moles and kangaroo rats (Lowie, 1939). Beals (1931) documents that among the Nisenan juvenile rabbits and ground squirrels were "run down". Driver (1935) documented that the Wappo would chase ground squirrels on foot, hitting them with clubs, or impaling them with sticks. Similarly, among the Yokuts, ground squirrels would be smoked or drowned out of burrows, then subsequently clubbed or strangled (Gayton, 1948)

However, there is one group of mammals that is almost exclusively trapped – members of the Mustelidae, or weasel family. These animals are prized primarily for their fur, although some groups (such as the Mistassini Cree and Tanaina) ate them, generally during lean times (Rogers, 1972; Osgood, 1937). Of the groups surveyed, there are only a few examples of the active hunting of mustelids. The Tanaina and Upper Tanana are said to have shot wolverines occasionally (Osgood, 1937; McKenna, 1959). However, the weapon used in these cases is the rifle, and it is not clear if this notoriously ferocious animal (which are known to steal prey from bears!) was ever hunted before the introduction of firearms. A similar example of active hunting of mustelids involves the Yavapai, who were reported to have shot skunks and badgers, but again using rifles (Gifford, 1937).

The only mustelids that are frequently hunted are otters. Aleuts and Koniags are reported to have taken sea otters with atlatl and dart, often by way of "spearing surrounds" where several men (as many as 15 according to Veniaminov) would surround the swimming otter with their bidarkas, or kayaks (Veniaminov, 1840; Clark, 1974). Other groups known to spear or harpoon otters include the Ainu, Chumash, Nootka, Yahgan, and Yokuts (Veniaminov, 1840; Elliot, 1886; Landberg, 1965; Gusinde, 1937; Arima, 1988; Latta, 1949). Jochelson (1933) claims the Aleuts also took otter with bow and arrow. Likewise, the Koniag are said to have shot sea

otters with "harpoon arrows" fired from a short self-bow or sinew-backed bow (Clark, 1974). Other groups reported to use bow and arrow on otters include the Nootka, Tlingit, Yahgan, and Yurok (Arima, 1988; Oberg, 1937; Gusinde, 1937; Heizer and Mill, 1952). The Tlingit may also have hunted otters with a dart fired from a whip sling (Oberg, 1937). Finally, the Aleuts, Tolowa, and Chumash are reported to have clubbed sea otters, most often while the otters were sleeping (Veniaminov, 1840; Drucker, 1937; Landberg, 1965).

All other mustelids taken by hunter-gatherers as reported in the ethnohistoric literature were acquired via trapping. This makes sense – mustelids, because of their speed, stealth, and natural burrowing ability, are notoriously difficult to hunt, and as such make excellent trapping candidates. Thus, the discovery of mustelids (other than otters) in archaeological context is as close to a faunal signature of trapping as one could hope to find. However, mustelids might be expected to occasionally occur in archaeological deposits by virtue of the fact that they are burrowing mammals. Thus caution must be exercised in interpreting the occurrence of mustelid remains, and only clearly humanly modified mustelids (i.e., cut marked) or a taxonomic abundance greater than expected from burrowing activity may serve as a faunal signature of trapping.

PLEISTOCENE ARCHAEOFAUNAL ASSEMBLAGES

To explore Pleistocene exploitation of mustelids, we used faunal data from site reports of five Paleolithic sites in Western Europe (Table 3). Only sites with quantified faunal lists and sufficient taphonomic detail to evaluate presence/absence of cut marks were evaluated, and thus the number of sites currently reported is small and the results presented here should be considered preliminary. However, based on initial consideration of a number of other sites, these sites seem to be generally representative of the small fauna picture for their time periods.

The sites from which we have drawn zooarchaeological data are, from oldest to youngest: Hoxne in England, Le Portel and Combe Grenal in France, La Riera in Spain, and Trou de Chaleux in Belgium. A brief discussion of the archaeofaunal assemblages from each of these sites follows.

Hoxne is an Acheulean site in Suffolk, England, dating to ca. 300,000 BP (Gladfelter et al., 1993). In terms of mustelid remains, the site only preserves the remains of two river otters (*Lutra lutra*; Stuart et al., 1993). While these animals may have been brought to the site by humans, one cannot rule out the possibility that they burrowed into the deposits, as there are no discernable cut marks on the bones. Also recall that otters are frequently hunted, and thus cannot be used as evidence of trapping. The other candidates for trapped game at Hoxne include *Castor fiber*, or beaver, and an extinct

Table 3. Paleolithic sites investigated and archaeofaunal data potentially suggestive of trapping.

Site	Age	Archaeological Association	Species Present	Humanly Acquired?
Hoxne	300 Kya	Acheulean	*Castor fiber*	Perhaps
			Trogontherium cuvieri	Perhaps
Le Portel	134 ± 8 Kya	Mousterian	*Vulpes vulpes*	Unlikely
			Meles meles	Unlikely
			Martes martes	No
			Mustela putorius No	
Combe Grenal	115-44 Kya	Mousterian	*Vulpes spp.*	Unlikely
			Marmota spp.	Uncertain
			Lepus spp.	Yes
La Riera	20-10 Kya	Solutrean	*Vulpes vulpes*	Perhaps
			Mustela ninvalis	Unlikely
		Magdalenian	*Vulpes vulpes*	Perhaps
			Meles meles	Unlikely
Trou de Chaleux	12.9-12.3 Kya	Magdalenian	*Lepus spp.*	Yes
			Vulpes/Alopex	Yes
			Gulo borealis	Unlikely

beaver-like rodent, *Trogontherium cuvieri* (Stuart et al., 1993). However, these remains are not clearly culturally modified, and as discussed above, beavers (like otters) are frequently hunted. Thus, there is no clear evidence for trapping in the Acheulean cultural deposits at Hoxne.

La Grotte Ouest at Le Portel is a Mousterian site in the foothills of the French Pyrenees which dates to ca. 134,000 BP (Gardeisen, 1997). According to Gardeisen (1997) the mustelids found in the western cave include *Meles meles*, or European badger, *Martes martes*, or beech marten, and *Mustela putorius*, or polecat. However, according to Gardeisen (1997) none of these mustelids, nor the remains of *Vulpes vulpes* (red fox) found there, appears likely to have been brought to the site by humans.

First, with regard to the relatively abundant *Meles meles* (badger) remains, all age classes are represented. However, there is a large proportion of fetal remains, suggesting a non-human role in the accumulations of badger bones. Also, some of the remains, especially in the upper levels, may be intrusive (due to the species' digging habits) from more recent time periods (Gardiesen, 1997). None of the material evinces any cut marks. Gardeisen (1997:57) argues that given the above observations, the badger assemblage appears to be a natural one (non-humanly introduced) – one of many "natural" occupations of the site that occurred between Neandertal ones.

With regard to the beech marten (*Martes martes*), there are precious few remains – one right mandibular canine and one right maxillary canine from Bed A, and the left half of a mandible from Bed B. Gardeisen (1997) posits that these remains could be from the same individual – this makes human agency even more unlikely in the "accumulation" of marten bones. Also, Beds A and B are the most recent beds, and hence the remains could be intrusive. Polecat (*Mustela putorius*) remains at the site are just as rare. There is only a fragment of a right half of a mandible of an adult from Bed F3, and an isolated right maxillary first molar from Bed K. These are deeper beds, making Holocene intrusion less likely, but a single mandible evincing no cut marks is not solid evidence for trapping.

The *Vulpes* remains are poorly represented and fragmentary, to the extent that Gardeisen (1997) argues it is difficult to establish age-at-death profiles for the sample – although, interestingly, only one deciduous tooth was found in Bed F2 (Gardeisen, 1997). Their numbers are relatively few, as well – the greatest MNI (9), is found in this same bed (F2). Out of the ten identified layers at the site, an MNI of 3 or fewer foxes is found in seven beds. None of the foxes evinces cut marks. One final note of interest – Gardeisen (1997) found the remains of two wolves, a cave bear, and a lion that all evince cut marks. However, she does not believe that the archaeozoological evidence from the site supports the notion that Neandertals were regularly hunting carnivores, despite pervasive, almost romantic notions of "trophy hunting" and the like, she feels that there is no evidence for such behavior at Le Portel (Gardeisen, 1997:89).

Combe Grenal, in the French Dordogne, is a rock shelter with 55 Mousterian levels spanning between ca. 115-44,000 BP (references in Mellars, 1996). Mustelid remains are absent in the Mousterian layers at Combe Grenal (Chase, 1986). Species found at the site which are commonly trapped include *Vulpes vulpes*, or red fox, species of the genus *Lepus* (hares; at least one evinces a cut mark) and *Marmota* (marmots). As discussed above, this last rodent, a burrower like the mustelids, may be smoked or flooded out of its burrow, and as such, cannot be assumed to have been trapped. Indeed, Chase (1986) points out that their status as prey animals has not been satisfactorily demonstrated. According to Chase (1986), the complete lack of mustelids and the dearth of foxes at Combe Grenal suggests that these animals evaded Neandertal hunters – we would posit that this *may* be because Neandertals lacked trapping technology (see below).

La Riera cave, in Cantabria, is an important Upper Paleolithic site with both Solutrean and Magdalenian deposits, dating to ca. 20,000-10,000 BP (Straus and Clark, 1986). While there are a number of red fox skeletons there, in terms of mustelids, the site has yielded only a single distal femur of *Mustela nivalis* (least weasel) in Solutrean deposits, and a single piece of *Meles meles* (European badger) in Magdalenian levels (Altuna, 1986). Unfortunately, Altuna (1986) does not report cut marks, but with numbers so few, it is possible that these animals burrowed into the levels, and were not brought there by humans.

Trou de Chaleux in the northwestern Ardennes of Belgium has rich Magdalenian deposits narrowly dated to between 12,900 and 12,300 BP (Charles, 1998). Mustelids are represented by 1 left scapula of *Gulo borealis* (wolverine), with inconclusive cut mark evidence, multiple remains of three species of *Mustela* (weasels) evincing marks perhaps consistent with butchery, and the remains of *Meles meles* (badger), including five femora that show clear butchery marks (Charles, 1998). In addition to the mustelids, foxes of the genera *Vulpes* and/or *Alopex* also show clear butchery marks, as do hares, while beaver remains do not.

DISCUSSION AND CONCLUSIONS

The above results suggest that the earliest unequivocal trapping of fur bearing mammals occurred in the late Upper Paleolithic, a result somewhat consistent with data from other regions. For example, West (1997) has suggested, based largely on her analysis of the fauna from the Epigravettian site of Grubgraben (Austria) that Central European Upper Paleolithic hunters acquired foxes for their furs in winter, primarily via the use of deadfalls and snares. One reason for such seasonality, according to West (1997) is that foxes are said to be quite

difficult to trap during the spring, when they eat less due to their preoccupation with mating (Pederson, 1966). She also points out that winter is when their fur is of the best quality (spring molting detracts from their value), and when their body fat is highest. An added advantage of taking them in winter, according to West (1997) would be that fresh snow would serve to conceal human scents, and when humans could most easily detect the foxes' trails. West (1997) also suggests that procuring such pelts in winter makes "economic" sense, as well, at least in terms of time. She cites a personal communication from Larry Martin (West, 1997:52) that pelts acquired during warm periods must be tanned immediately to prevent the hair from falling off of the skin. In contrast, in colder months, since the animal's body cools more rapidly, the hair is less likely to fall out, and skins can be tanned at a more convenient time. West (1997) posits that because their primary subsistence base (reindeer) provided skins which could be used for most purposes, that fox furs were a "luxury item". Likewise, she argues that neither hares nor foxes were particularly numerous in the Epigravettian levels at Grubgraben because of this primary focus on reindeer hunting.

Soffer's (1985) finding that all the fox skeletons found in Russian Plain Upper Paleolithic sites were skeletally adult supports West's argument that they were hunted in winter. West (1997) has also suggested (following the work of Dolukhanov, 1982) that fox exploitation on the Russian Plain may date back to the Mousterian, something which would make sense in such a cold, windswept environment. Yet as discussed earlier, foxes are often actively hunted, and thus their presence does not necessitate that they were trapped.

Stiner et al. (2000) discuss archaeofaunal data, broadly contemporary to that of West (1997), from the Italian coast and inland Israel that support a relatively late development (or at least recent intensification) of trapping technology. On the Italian coast, while small mammals are found throughout the Middle and Upper Paleolithic sequence at sites such as Grotte dei Moscerini, they only become a significant portion of the faunal remains in the Epipaleolithic at sites such as Riparo Mochi (Stiner et al., 2000). Likewise, in inland Israel, at the sites of Hayonim and Nahal Meged, there is a significant increase in the number of hares and other small mammals in the faunal assemblage manifested in the Natufian levels dated to ca. 13-11 kyr (Stiner et al., 2000). Stiner et al. (2000) use a diet breadth model to argue that over the course of the Middle to Upper Paleolithic, humans in the Mediterranean basin were gradually forced to acquire progressively lower and lower-ranked resources, primarily due to increasing population pressure. In other words, the increased emphasis on the capture of lagomorphs and avifauna evident in the Italian and Israeli Late Upper Paleolithic and Epipaleolithic archaeofauna is the direct result of an increase in the number of consumers leading to a decline in the number of higher-ranked resources. As they state:

"by the Upper Paleolithic, people had no choice but to pursue quicker prey to meet their need for dietary protein. Some of the radiations in Upper Paleolithic and Epipaleolithic foraging technology may have evolved on the heels of demographic increase as ways to reduce the cost of acquiring agile prey" (Stiner et al., 2000:56).

Stiner et al. (2000) argue that most groups faced with a declining resource base will simply choose to move to another location, yet by the end of the Pleistocene in the Mediterranean basin, human population densities had become too dense for this to be a viable option. Therefore, technological solutions were needed, ones to make the capture of smaller, more elusive game more efficient. As Stiner et al. (2000) note, at least some of the technological innovations of the Upper Paleolithic and Epipaleolithic would have been geared toward the capture of small mammals and birds (Stiner et al., 2000: 58).

However, it should be noted that at least some Neandertals took lagomorphs on occasion. According to Chase (1986), for example, ninety-four lagomorph bones (probably *Oryctolagus*) were found in Mousterian levels at the site of Abri Agut, and many of these bones were burned. Likewise, one lagomorph bone recovered from Mousterian levels at Combe Grenal evinced a cut mark (Chase, 1986). Chase also cites work at Pié Lombard, a rock shelter in southeastern France, which has yielded the remains of at least 25 rabbits (*Oryctolagus cuniculus*) from Mousterian levels. Of these bones, only 1.2% were from juveniles, an indication that the animals did not die naturally in their burrows (Chase, 1986). A similar situation is said to be evident at another southeastern French site, le Salpètre de Pompignan, where rabbits were found in five Mousterian levels. In these levels the percentage of juveniles was quite low (only 1.4% to 5%); by way of contrast, in non-cultural levels, young animals represented ca. 50% of the total (Chase, 1986).

Finally, in northwestern Europe, Charles (1998) has argued that trapping of mustelids is relatively rare in Late Glacial contexts, but becomes more important during the Mesolithic. She cites evidence from Starr Carr, in which a polecat skeleton shows clear evidence of butchery, as well as the late Mesolithic site of Tybrind Uig in Denmark, in which the remains of 13 pine martens, a polecat and 4 otters evince what are clearly cut marks. Thus, the trapping of mustelids, which may have begun in the Upper Paleolithic, was further intensified in the Mesolithic.

However, we cannot exclude the possibility that Lower and Middle Paleolithic people were using traps, but were not going for mustelids. Perhaps the Mousterian examples of rabbit hunting cited by Chase (1986) involved trapping – we cannot say for certain that it did not. If it is in fact the case that Early and Middle Paleolithic humans were taking non-mustelids in traps,

then the trends evident in the Upper Paleolithic zooarchaeological record reflect a change in the value of small furs rather than a change in technology. It is also quite likely that traps were independently invented multiple times in prehistory, including in the Lower and Middle Paleolithic, only to be later abandoned. Nonetheless, it does appear, given the zooarchaeological data discussed above, that there was an increased focus on smaller mammals in the Late Upper Paleolithic and Epipaleolithic in much of Europe and the Levant, and that this emphasis on small game may have been facilitated via the use of trapping technology.

REFERENCES

ALTUNA, J. 1986. The mammalian faunas from the prehistoric site of La Riera. *In* Straus, L.G. and Clark G.A. (Eds.) *La Riera Cave: Stone Age Hunter-Gatherer Adaptations in Northern Spain.* Arizona State University Anthropological Research Papers 36. Arizona State University Press. Tempe.

ANELL, B. 1960. *Hunting and Trapping Methods in Australia and Oceania.* Studia Ethnographica Upsaliensia 18.

ANELL, B. 1969. *Running down and Driving of Game in North America.* Studia Ethnographica Upsaliensia 30.

ANTROPOVA, V.V. 1964. The Aleuts. *In* M.G. Levin and L.P. Potapov (Eds.) *The People of Siberia*, pp. 884-888. Chicago University Press. Chicago.

ARIMA, E.Y. 1988. Notes on Nootkan sea mammal hunting. *Arctic Anthropology*, 25, 16-27.

BAHUCHET, S. 1988. Food supply uncertainty among the Aka Pygmies (Lobaye, Central African Republic). *In* I. deGarine and G. Harrison (Eds.) *Coping with Uncertainty in Food Supply*, pp. 118-149. Clarendon Press. Oxford.

BATCHELOR, J. 1892. *Ainu Life and Lore: Echoes of a Departing Race.* Kwobunkwan. Tokyo.

BEALS, R.L. 1931. Ethnology of the Nisenan. University of California Publications in American Archaeology and Ethnology. Vol. 31, No. 6.

BEALS, R.L. AND HESTER, J.A. JR. 1974. *California Indians VI.* Garland Publishers. New York.

BINFORD, L.R. 1990. Mobility, housing, and environment: A comparative study. *Journal of Anthropological Research*, 46, 119-152.

BIRKET-SMITH, K. 1941. *Early Collections from the Pacific Eskimo*. Ethnographical Studies Published on the Occasion of the Centenary of the Ethnographical Department, National Museum, pp. 121-163. Gy Idendalske Boghandel, Nordisk Forlag. Copenhagen.

BIRKET-SMITH, K. 1953. *The Chugach Eskimo*. Nationalmuseets Publikationsfond, Copenhagen.

BULMER, R. 1968. The strategies of hunting in New Guinea. *Oceania*, 38, 302-318.

CHARLES, R. 1998. *Late Magdalenian Chronology and Faunal Exploitation in the North-Western Ardennes*. British Archaeological Reports International Series 737.

CHASE, P.G. 1986. *The Hunters of Combe Grenal: Approaches to Middle Paleolithic Subsistence in Europe*. British Archaeological Reports International Series 286.

CHURCHILL, S.E. 1993. Weapon technology, prey size selection, and hunting methods in modern hunter-gatherers: Implications for hunting in the Palaeolithic and Mesolithic. *In* G.L. Peterkin, H.M. Bricker and P.A. Mellars (Eds.), *Hunting and Animal Exploitation in the Later Palaeolithic and Mesolithic of Eurasia*. Archeological Papers of the American Anthropological Association 4,11-24.

CLARK, D.W. 1974. *Koniag Prehistory; Archaeological Investigations of Late Prehistoric Sites on Kodiak Island, Alaska*. Verlag W. Kohlhammer. Stuttgart.

DOLUKHANOV, P. 1982. Upper Pleistocene and Holocene cultures of the Russian Plain and Caucasus: Ecology, economy, and settlement pattern. *Advances in World Archaeology*. Academic Press. New York.

DRIVER, H.E. 1935. *Wappo Ethnography*. University of California Publications in American Archaeology and Ethnology. Vol. 36, No. 3.

DRIVER, J.C. 1990. Meat in due season: The timing of communal hunts. In Davis, L. and Reeves, B. (Eds.) *Hunters of the Recent Past*. Unwin Hyman, London pp. 11-33.

DRUCKER, P. 1937. *The Tolowa and their southwest Oregon kin*. University of California Publications in American Archaeology and Ethnology; Vol. 36, no. 4. University of California Press. Berkeley.

DRUCKER, P. 1939. *Contributions to Alsea Ethnography*. University of California Publications in American Archaeology and Ethnology 35, no. 7. University of California Press. Berkeley.

DRUCKER, P. 1951. *The northern and central Nootkan tribes*. Bureau of American Ethnology. Bulletin 144. Government Printing Office. Washington, DC.

ELLIOT, H.W. 1886. *Our Arctic Province*. Charles Scribner's Sons. New York.

GARDEISON, A. 1997. La Grotte Ouest du Portel, Ariègem France: Restes fauniques et stratégies de chasses dans le Pléistocène supérieur pyrénéen. British Archaeological Reports International Series 673.

GAYTON, A.H. 1948. *Yokuts and Western Mono Ethnography II: Northern Foothills Yokuts and Western Mono*. University of California Publications in American Archaeology and Ethnology Vol. 10, No. 2.

GIFFORD, E.W. 1937. *Northeastern and Western Yavapai*. University of California Press. Berkeley.

GLADFELTER, B.G., WYMER, J.J. AND SINGER, R. 1993. Dating the deposits at Hoxne. *In* Singer, R., Gladfelter, B.G. and Wymer, J.J. (Eds.) *The Lower Paleolithic Site at Hoxne, England*. University of Chicago Press. Chicago, 207-217.

GUSINDE, M. 1937. *The Yahgan*. Modling bei Wien: Anthropos-Bibliothek.

HEIZER, R.F. & MILLS, J.E. 1952. *The Four Ages of Tsurai; A Documentary History of the Indian Village on Trinidad Bay*. University of California Press. Berkeley.

HOLLIDAY, T.W. 1998. The ecological context of trapping among recent hunter-gatherers: Implications for subsistence in terminal Pleistocene Europe. *Current Anthropology*, 39, 711-720.

HONIGMANN, J.J. 1946. *Ethnography and Acculturation of the Fort Nelson Slave*. Yale University Publications in Anthropology 33.

HONIGMANN, J.J. 1954. *The Kaska Indians: An Ethnographic Reconstruction*. Yale University Publications in Anthropology 51.

HUNTINGFORD, G.W.B. 1953. *The Southern Nilo-Hamites*. International African Institute Press. London.

HURLBERT, J. 1962. *Age as a Factor in the Social Organization of the Hare Indian of Fort Good Hope, Northwest Territories*. Northern Coordination and Research Centre, Department of Northern Affairs and National Resources. Ottawa.

JENNESS, D. 1935. *The Ojibwa Indians of Parry Island: Their Social and Religious Life.* National Museum of Canada. Bulletin 78; Anthropological Series 17.

JOCHELSON, W. 1933. *History, ethnology, and anthropology of the Aleut.* Carnegie Institution of Washington Publication 432.

KINIETZ, W.V. 1947. *Chippewa Village: The Story of Katikitegon.* Cranbrook Press. Bloomfield Hills, MI.

KOHL, J.G. 1860. *Kitchi-Gami.* Chapman and Hall. London.

KOPPERT, V.A. 1930. *Contributions to Clayoquot Ethnography.* Catholic University of America. Washington, DC.

LAGUNA, F. DE 1960. *The Story of a Tlingit Community: A Problem in the Relationship between Archeological, Ethnological, and Historical Methods.* Bulletin, Bureau of American Ethnology 172. U.S. Government Printing Office.

LANDBERG L.C.W. 1965. *The Chumash Indians of southern California.* Southwest Museum Papers 19. Los Angeles.

LATTA, F.F. 1949. *Handbook of Yokuts Indians.* Bear State Books. Oildale, CA.

LIPS, J.E. 1936. *Trap Systems among the Montagnais-Naskapi Indians of Labrador Peninsula.* Tryckeri Aktiebolaget Thule. Stockholm.

LIPS, J.E. 1947. Notes on Montagnais-Naskapi economy. *Ethnos,* 12, 1-78.

LOWIE, R.H. 1939. *Ethnographic notes on the Washo.* University of California Publications in American Archaeology and Ethnology Volume 36, No. 5.

MARY-ROUSSELIÈRE, G. 1984. Iglulik. In *Handbook of North American Indians, Vol. V, Arctic.* Smithsonian Institution. Washington, DC, 431-446.

MCKENNAN, R.A. 1959. *The Upper Tanana Indians.* Yale University Publications in Anthropology **55**. Yale University Press. New Haven.

MELLARS, P. 1996. *The Neanderthal Legacy.* Princeton University Press, Princeton.

OBERG, K. 1937. *The Social Economy of the Tlingit Indians.* Ph.D. Dissertation (Anthropology): University of Chicago. Chicago.

OSGOOD, C. 1937. *The Ethnography of the Tanaina.* Yale University Publications in Anthropology 16.

OSWALT, W.H. 1976. *An Anthropological Analysis of Food-Getting Technology.* John Wiley & Sons. New York.

PEDERSON, A. 1966. *Polar Animals.* Taplinger Publishing Company. New York.

ROGERS, E.S. 1972. The Mistassini Cree. *In* Bicchieri, M.G. (Ed.) *Hunters and Gatherers Today.* Holt, Rinehart and Winston. New York, 90-137.

SILBERBAUER, G.B. 1972. The G/wi Bushmen. *In* M.G. Bicchieri (Ed.) *Hunters and Gatherers Today,* edited by, pp. 271-326. Holt, Rinehart and Winston. New York.

SMITH, E.A. 1983. Anthropological applications of optimal foraging theory: a critical review. *Current Anthropology,* 24, 625-651.

SOFFER, O. 1985. *The Upper Paleolithic of the Central European Plain.* Academic Press. Orlando.

STEWARD, J.H. 1941. *Nevada Shoshoni.* Anthropological Records. University of California Press. Berkeley 4, 209-359.

STINER, M.C., MUNRO, N.D., AND SUROVELL, T.A. 2000. The tortoise and the hare: Small-game use, the broad-spectrum revolution, and Paleolithic demography. *Current Anthropology* 41, 39-73.

STRAUS, L.G. 1985. Stone Age prehistory of northern Spain. *Science,* 230, 501-507.

STRAUS, L.G., AND CLARK, G.A., Eds. 1986. *La Riera Cave: Stone Age Hunter-Gatherer Adaptations in Northern Spain.* Arizona State University Anthropological Research Papers 36. Arizona State University Press. Tempe, AZ.

STUART, A.J., WOLFF, R.G., LISTER, A.M., SINGER, R., AND EGGINTON, J.M. 1993. Fossil vertebrates. *In* Singer, R., Gladfelter, B.G. and Wymer, J.J. (Eds.) *The Lower Paleolithic Site at Hoxne, England.* University of Chicago Press. Chicago, 163-206.

STUYVESANT, W.C. 1978. The Chumash Indians of Southern California. *In* R.F. Heizer (Ed.) *Handbook of North American Indians.* Vol. 8: California. Smithsonian Institution. Washington, DC.

TURNER, L.M. 1889-90. *Ethnology of the Ungava District, Hudson Bay Territory.* U.S. Bureau of American Ethnology Annual Report 11, 159-350.

VENIAMINOV, I.E.P. 1840. *Zapiski ob ostorvakh unalashkinskago otdiela.* Izdano Izhidiveniem Rossiisko-amerikanshoi Kimpanii. Saint Petersburg.

WALLIS, W.D. AND WALLIS R.S. 1955. *The Micmac Indians of Eastern Canada.* University of Minnesota Press. Minneapolis.

WATANABE, H. 1972. The Ainu. In Bicchieri, M.G. (Ed.) *Hunters and Gatherers Today.* Holt, Rinehart and Winston, New York, 448-484.

WEST, D. 1997. *Hunting Strategies in Central Europe During the Last Glacial Maximum.* British Archaeological Reports International Series 672.

WINTERHALDER, B. 1981. Optimal foraging strategies and hunter-gatherer research in anthropology: theory and methods. *In* B. Winterhalder and E.A. Smith (Eds.) *Hunter-Gatherer Foraging Strategies.* University of Chicago Press, Chicago, 13-35.

WISSLER, C. 1910. *Material Culture of the Blackfoot Indians.* American Museum of Natural History Press. New York.

THE EARLY TO LATE NATUFIAN TRANSITION AT HAYONIM CAVE, ISRAEL: A FAUNAL PERSPECTIVE

Natalie D. Munro

Department of Anthropology, University of Connecticut, Storrs, CT USA

THE EARLY TO LATE NATUFIAN TRANSITION IN THE SOUTHERN LEVANT

In the southern Levant, the Natufian cultural period (ca. 12,800–10,200 B.P.) has particular importance because it directly precedes the advent of agriculture. Topics such as human demography, settlement, and subsistence are of key interest in current research on the Natufian period, as each of these themes has been promoted as a significant factor in models of agricultural origins (Bar-Yosef and Belfer-Cohen 1989, 1991; Bar-Yosef and Meadow 1995; Belfer-Cohen and Bar-Yosef 2000; Binford 1968; Boserup 1965; Braidwood 1960; Childe 1951; Cohen 1977; Flannery 1969; Gebauer and Price 1992; Henry 1989; Hillman 1996; Kaufman 1992; Keeley 1995; McCorriston and Hole 1991; Redding 1988; Tchernov 1991, 1994). The actual significance or relative importance of these factors has, however, proven difficult to test, and none of them have been examined with the temporal resolution required to isolate the specific conditions that directly preceded agricultural origins at the very end of the Natufian period. Instead, the Natufian culture has largely been treated as a single temporal unit—although increasingly dynamic interpretations are emerging as research expands and diachronic change is identified both within and beyond the core region of the Natufian adaptation (see Bar-Yosef and Valla 1979; Belfer-Cohen 1991; Belfer-Cohen and Bar-Yosef 2000; Goring-Morris 1987; Goring-Morris and Belfer-Cohen 1998; Horwitz and Tchernov 2001; Moore and Hillman 1992; Valla 1987, 1998). Refining our understanding of diachronic change within the Natufian period—which spanned about 2500 years—is particularly crucial if we expect our data to bear on the question of agricultural origins. Although the major episode of cultural florescence in the Natufian seems to have taken place in the Early phase (12,800–11,000 B.P.), the less well known Late Natufian phase (ca. 11,000–10,200 B.P.) is more likely to reveal conditions relevant to the origins of agriculture in southwest As☐a in general. This paper thus seeks to reconstruct diachronic change in human adaptations during the Natufian period, and in the Late phase in particular.

In Natufian research demographic and economic conditions are often reconstructed according to the presence or absence of various classes of material remains (e.g., architectural features, ground stone tools, artwork, and ornaments; Bar-Yosef and Belfer-Cohen 1989, 1992; Byrd 1989; Henry 1989; Kaufman 1992), and particularly the occurrence of certain biological markers (e.g., commensal species, migratory birds;

Lieberman 1991, 1993; Pichon 1984, 1991; Tchernov 1984, 1991). Although the presence of these items does signal important changes in Natufian strategies, we are left with an essentially qualitative understanding of these transformations. This paper offers a more rigorous method for measuring human demographic and economic change: the interpretation of faunal data within an optimal foraging framework. The intensity with which humans hunt and use animal prey is directly linked to the balance between human population size and available resources. Using principles rooted in foraging theory (following Charnov 1976; Emlen 1966; Krebs et al. 1983; MacArthur and Pianka 1966; Perry and Pianka 1997; Pyke et al. 1977; Schoener 1986; Stephens and Krebs 1986), it is possible to predict the impact of varying intensities of human use on the relative availability of prey taxa, prey age structures, and butchering patterns. These predictions can then be compared to archaeofaunal data in an effort to reconstruct the demographic and economic conditions under which the archaeological record was formed.

Hayonim Cave presents a unique opportunity to examine the details of the Early to Late Natufian transition with precise geographic control. The site, one of few that bridge the Early and Late Natufian phases, provides a well-preserved faunal assemblage and detailed contextual information from a rich, quantified database (for details see Bar-Yosef 1991; Belfer-Cohen 1988). By quantifying and comparing multiple lines of taphonomic and economic evidence from the Early and Late Natufian faunas of Hayonim Cave, this study seeks to pinpoint changes in Natufian economic strategies that are relevant to questions surrounding the transition to agriculture.

HAYONIM CAVE

Hayonim Cave is a multicomponent site that sits 230 meters above sea level in the Mediterranean foothills of the western Galilee region of Israel (Figure 1). The site is located 13 kilometers east of the Mediterranean Sea in the Wadi Meged, close to the juncture between the Mediterranean foothills and the coastal plain. The Natufian layer at Hayonim Cave was extensively excavated during the 1970s under the direction of O. Bar-Yosef, and again on a smaller scale in the 1990s, when Bar-Yosef's team returned to expose the underlying Middle Paleolithic layers. Since its inception, the project has maintained high standards of recovery, and as a result it has amassed a faunal assemblage that represents the full size spectrum of animals deposited in the site via both natural and cultural processes.

Spatially, the Natufian layer at Hayonim Cave is divided into *Loci*, *Graves*, and *Areas*, each with its own stratigraphic sequence (Figure 2). Loci are bounded by

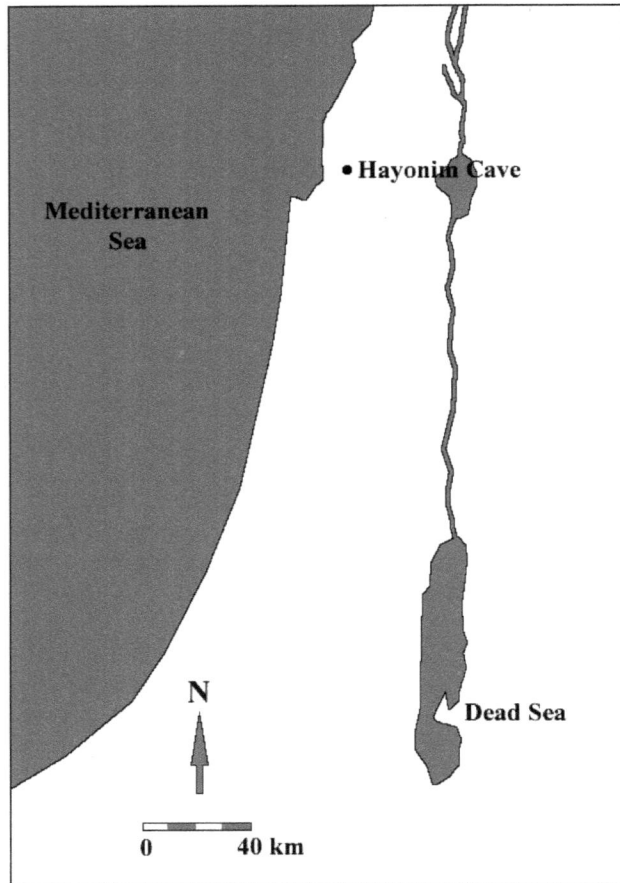

Figure 1. Map of the southern Levant, showing the location of HayonimCave in the western Galilee region of Israel.

low circular walls that are composed of undressed limestone manuports from the surrounding hillside. Nine loci (3–11) have been identified just inside the dripline of the cave, but three of these have not yet been fully excavated. The structures comprise the main occupation area of the Natufian layer, which ranges in thickness from a few centimeters to one meter near the entrance of the cave (Bar-Yosef 1991; Bar-Yosef and Belfer-Cohen n.d.). Open spaces, designated Areas 201–206, are situated between and on top of the loci. Though areas lack the spatial integrity and distinct architecture of loci, they are characterized by independent depositional sequences. Most but not all of the areas cap deposits in the loci, and most represent later stages of Natufian occupation in the cave. Seventeen graves were also excavated, but because several graves were dug into earlier layers (Mousterian, Aurignacian, and Kebaran), those graves with potentially mixed fills were excluded from the sample (that is, only fauna from Graves X–XII and XIV–XVII are included here).

Two lupine seeds from the Natufian layer have been dated by AMS, yielding dates of 12,010±180 B.P. and 12,360±160 B.P. (Bar-Yosef 1991; Hopf and Bar-Yosef 1987). Despite the paucity of absolute dates, a five phase relative chronology of the Natufian layer has been defined within each locus, area, and grave (Bar-Yosef 1991; Bar-Yosef and Belfer-Cohen n.d; Belfer-Cohen 1988). The phases, which correspond to a chronological sequence of building and occupation events, link deposits from spatially segregated areas in the cave. The detailed temporal sequence provides a rare opportunity to observe diachronic change across the duration of occupation at a single site. Phase assignments are based solely on the stratigraphic relationships between archaeological layers, and are independent of cultural markers recovered from the fill. Cultural markers were only used to assign the phases to the Early or Late Natufian after the relative chronology of the deposits had already been established. The phases are numbered from I to V, with Phases I–III representing the Early Natufian occupation in the cave (ca. 12,800–11,000 B.P.) and Phases IV and V the Late Natufian (ca. 11,000–10,200 B.P).

An important caveat must also be mentioned. The stratigraphy of Locus 10 and that of Grave XVII, two features excavated during the 1990s, have not yet been linked with deposits uncovered during the original excavations. Although they certainly belong to the Early Natufian occupation of the cave, to which of the first three phases is unclear. The layers from these two areas are thus excluded from the phase-by-phase analysis presented in this study, but they are combined with data from the Early Natufian phases of occupation for subsequent Early-to-Late Natufian comparisons.

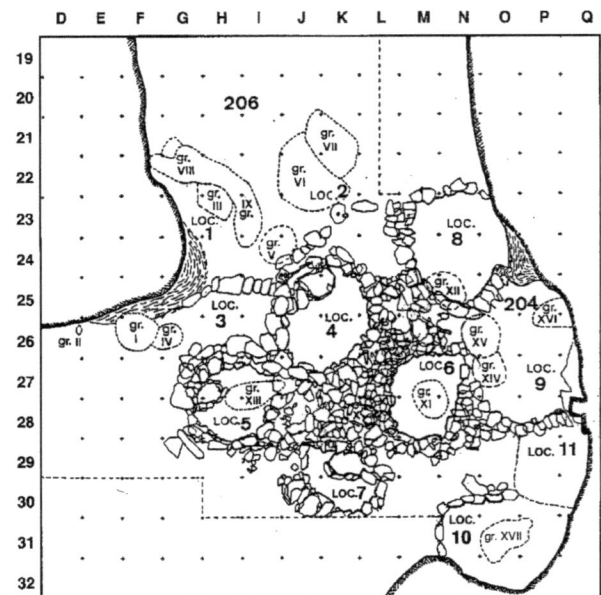

Figure 2. Plan of the Natufian layer at Hayonim Cave showing position of loci (Loc.) and graves (gr.).

FAUNAL VARIABLE	EARLY NATUFIAN	LATE NATUFIAN
Descriptive Characters		
Total NISP	8096	7948
Volume Excavated Sediment	21.8 m^3	25.4 m^3
Bone Density	269/m^3	253/m^3
Prey Relative Abundance		
Ungulates in Assemblage	2804 (34.6%)	1645 (30.1%)
Carnivores in Assemblage	305 (3.8%)	316 (5.8%)
Small Game in Assemblage	4987 (61.6%)	3512 (64.2%)
Gazelle in Ungulate Assemblage	2520 (89.1%)	1457 (89.2%)
Tortoises in Small Game Assemblage	1777 (35.8%)	2542 (72.5%)
Birds (non-passerine) in Small Game Assemblage	1628 (32.8%)	545 (15.6%)
Hares in Small Game Assemblage	1559 (31.4%)	417 (11.9%)
Gazelle Age Structures		
Juvenile Gazelle (Epiphyses Data)	255 (34.3%)	194 (35.5%)
Gazelle Carcass Butchery		
Cut Marks (All Gazelles)	38 (1.5%)	18 (1.2%)
Cone Fractures (Gazelle Long Bone Shafts)	17 (4.3%)	15 (4.8%)
Spiral Breaks (Gazelle Long Bone Shafts)	295 (58.6%)	309 (63.1%)
Burned (All Gazelles)	277 (11.0%)	370 (25.4%)
Average Fragment Length (cm) (All Gazelles)	2.6✕2.0	2.7✕2.2
Complete Gazelle Elements	626 (24.8%)	306 (21.0%)
Natural Damage (For Entire Assemblage)		
Root Etch	170 (1.8%)	264 (3.3%)
Weathering	182 (2.0%)	259 (3.3%)
Carnivore Tooth Marks	13 (<1.0%)	7 (<1.0%)
Possible Digestion	2 (<1.0%)	2 (<1.0%)

Table 1. Summary data from Early and Late Natufian faunal assemblages from Hayonim Cave. Numbers outside of parentheses are NISP values, while those in parentheses are percentages.

Several researchers with a variety of research goals have studied portions of the Hayonim fauna (Bar-El and Tchernov 2001; Bar-Yosef and Tchernov 1967; Cope 1991a, 1991b; Davis 1978; Lieberman 1991, 1993; Pichon 1984). Most of these studies focused on specific taxonomic groups, including ungulates (Cope 1991a, 1991b; Davis 1978; Lieberman 1991, 1993), hares (Bar-El and Tchernov 2001), and birds (Pichon 1983, 1984, 1991). Thus, despite intense research attention, the Hayonim Cave faunal assemblage has never been examined in its entirety, and has been treated only as a single component. This has precluded any comparative analyses between taxonomic groups, and has prevented researchers from detecting temporal and spatial variation within the Natufian period itself.

To explore temporal variation within the Natufian layer at Hayonim Cave, this study takes advantage of Bar-Yosef and Belfer-Cohen's stratigraphic work. It examines the entire Hayonim Cave faunal assemblage, with the exception of the microfauna and bones from potentially mixed contexts or unknown proveniences. Potentially mixed contexts are those that, though stratigraphically assigned to the Natufian, are more likely to contain intrusive materials because of their proximity to deposits from neighboring layers. Areas with potentially mixed deposits have been excluded from the following analysis to ensure that the patterns reported below are as clean and accurate as possible. With an NISP of 15,000, the remaining sample from the secure contexts is more than ample for the selected analyses.

Overall the quality of preservation of the Natufian layer from Hayonim Cave is very good. Bones representing a full range of structural densities (*sensu* Lyman 1984, 1994), sizes, and forms have been recovered intact from the deposits (Munro 2001). The bone assemblages are extensively fractured and most complete elements are naturally small and compact. The exceptional quality of preservation permits the identification of even the smallest fragments, provided they retain anatomically diagnostic features.

METHODS

The Hayonim Cave bone specimens were identified to the most specific taxonomic level possible. If a bone could not be identified to genus or species, it was assigned to a broader group, defined according to general taxonomic and body size criteria (e.g., small ungulate, large mammal). Articulated elements were rare in the assemblage, but, when present, were recorded as separate units, with physical associations noted. This includes mandibles and maxillae with teeth intact. Specimens were only identified if they could be assigned to element, and portion of element according to the presence of diagnostic characteristics on bone shafts and articular ends. Side, age, sex, and gross length were recorded for each specimen when possible. Breakage and a range of surface damage categories were also described when present and permitted the reconstruction of the taphonomic history of each taxonomic group (see Munro 2001).

All frequencies and proportions presented here are NISP counts, since this measure is believed to be the most accurate for tracking broad trends in relative abundance (Grayson 1984; Lyman 1994). To facilitate comparisons of taxonomic abundance between the Early and Late Natufian at Hayonim Cave, assemblages are first grouped into three broad categories: ungulate, carnivores, and small game. Although carnivores and predatory birds may not be "prey" *senso stricto* they were caught and used by humans. The small game fraction includes reptiles, birds, and small mammal species weighing no more than 2 kilograms. Only prey types demonstrably modified by humans, as evidenced by cut marks, burning, body part representation, fragmentation, and other taphonomic criteria, are included in this comparison (see Munro 2001 for details). The relative abundance of small game was determined by subdividing the small game fraction into small mammal (hares), bird (game birds and waterfowl), and reptile (tortoise) categories (see Munro 2001 for complete species list with NISP values). Microfauna, including most rodents, small passerine birds, and the majority of small reptiles and amphibians have been shown to be intrusive (Munro 2001) and are not included here.

Comparison of the Early and Late Natufian occupations at Hayonim Cave proceeds by way of a summary of numerous taphonomic and economic aspects of the faunal assemblages. This strategy allows rapid identification of disparities between assemblages as well as reconstruction of cultural change. Twenty-one taphonomic and economic variables are grouped into analytical categories (i.e., descriptive characters, prey relative abundance, gazelle age structures, gazelle carcass butchery, and natural damage) and summarized in Table 1. Interesting patterns in the data are subsequently highlighted and explored. Thanks to the detailed work of Belfer-Cohen 1988), complimentary data on architectural features, settlement organization, lithics, ground stone, bone tools, ornaments, artwork, and burials from the Early and Late Natufian of Hayonim Cave are also available. These data provide a means of independently assessing the reliability of faunal trends identified in this study.

PREY RELATIVE ABUNDANCE

In sheer numbers (NISP), small game taxa dominate both the Early and Late Natufian faunas from Hayonim Cave (61.6% NISP in Early Natufian, 64.2% NISP in Late Natufian; see Figure 3). Although the small size of these prey precluded them from replacing ungulates as the primary meat source, their high relative abundance indicates an undeniable increase in human dependence on lower-ranked, small-bodied resources from habitats immediately surrounding Hayonim Cave. The florescence of a diverse array of small reptile, bird, and mammal species in faunal assemblages has long been considered an Epipaleolithic phenomenon (cf. Bar-Yosef and Belfer-Cohen 1989; Binford 1968; Braidwood 1960; Byrd 1989; Davis et al. 1994; Hayden 1981; Tchernov 1993a, 1993b), and is generally consistent with the predictions of Flannery's (1969) Broad Spectrum Revolution (BSR) hypothesis. Several researchers have recently questioned the value of the BSR hypothesis, arguing that prey diversity changes little from the Middle Paleolithic to the Natufian period (Bar-Oz et al. 1999; Neely and Clark 1993; Edwards 1989); nonetheless, the high proportions of small game quantified in both the Early and Late Natufian layers at Hayonim Cave far exceed proportions in all earlier Paleolithic assemblages (Munro 1999; 2001; Stiner et al. 1999, 2000). Despite the dominance of small game in absolute numbers, there is no question that the ungulate fraction is the most important source of meat throughout the Natufian occupation. As is typical of Mediterranean Natufian sites in general (Bar-Oz 2001; Davis et al. 1994; Edwards 1991; Garrod and Bate 1937; Henry et al. 1981; Munro 2001; Noy et al. 1973), gazelle is the most common ungulate species in both the Early and Late Natufian faunal assemblages from Hayonim Cave (Early = 89.1%, Late = 89.2% of ungulate taxa).

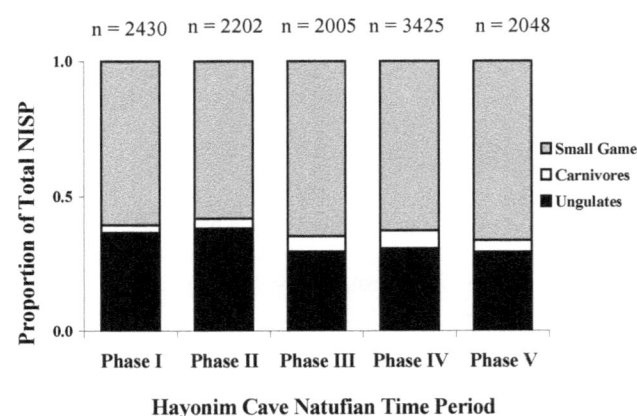

Figure 3. Proportion of broad taxonomic groups in five phases of occupation at Hayonim Cave. Phases I-III represent the Early Natufian, Phases IV and V, the Late Natufian.

According to the principles of optimization theory, humans should preferentially hunt high-ranked species—those that provide the highest returns for the energy invested—over low-ranked species (Emlen 1966; Charnov 1976; Kelly 1995; Stephens and Krebs 1986; Winterhalder 1986). Only when the rate of energy acquisition of high-ranked species drops below that of low-ranked prey are humans expected to add the latter to their diets. The introduction of small animals (e.g., tortoises, hares, and partridges) to Epipaleolithic assemblages previously dominated by high-ranked ungulates (Stiner et al. 1999, 2000) thus likely reflects the failure of large animal species to meet human demands for animal products. This may have resulted from an increase in human demand or a reduction in the availability of large game—or both—during the Natufian period. A greater dependence on small animals also implies the increased use of local habitats surrounding Hayonim Cave. Overall, the abundance of small game in Natufian diets points to intensive human use of the immediate environment of Hayonim Cave beginning in the Early and continuing into the Late Natufian phase.

RELATIVE ABUNDANCE OF SMALL GAME PREY TYPES

While the relative abundance of broad taxonomic groups including ungulates, carnivores, and small game have much to tell us about the intensity of human resource use at a regional level, the small game better reflects the intensity of site occupation on a local scale. Unlike their ungulate counterparts, small game animals differ greatly in their escape strategies and, by extension, their cost of capture (see Stiner et al. 1999, 2000). Cost of capture affects the energy returned from a given prey species and has the potential to alter the relative ranking of animals with similar body size. Traditionally, rankings were based on prey body-size (Broughton 1994; Griffiths 1975; Simms 1987; Szuter and Bayham 1989) and, until fairly recently, the cost of capture was largely ignored (Stiner 2001; Stiner et al. 1999, 2000). Escape strategies do vary dramatically among the common Mediterranean small game types hunted by the Paleolithic occupants of Hayonim, namely, tortoise, partridge, and hare. The notoriously slow-moving tortoise has virtually no capture costs and provides essentially pure energetic gains; thus tortoises should not have been refused upon encounter, and should have been highly ranked. Fast, small animals like partridges and hares, on the other hand, use rapid flight or cursorial strategies to flee from predators, and are quite difficult to capture. With or without special technology the capture of fast, small game requires a greater energy investment to obtain similar returns as compared to slow, small prey. Fast, small game are thus ranked below slow, small game. The ratio of small, slow game to fast, small game hunted by human foragers and deposited in the archaeological record thus provides an excellent gauge of human occupation intensity: when occupation intensity was low, hunters should have

primarily captured tortoises, but as site occupation intensified, they should have taken progressively greater proportions of low-ranked fast, small animals.

The consistency of the relative proportions of all other taxonomic groups from the Early and Late Natufian phases at Hayonim Cave (shown previously in Figure 3) makes the changes revealed by the often-ignored small game fraction all the more surprising (Figure 4, Table 1). In the Early Natufian (Phases I–III), the representation of tortoises, partridges, and hares is fairly even. Together fast-moving birds and hares outnumber the high-ranked tortoises. Beginning with the onset of the Late Natufian in Phase IV, there is an abrupt reversal in the proportion of high-ranked tortoises in relation to their low-ranked counterparts (partridges and hares). The proportion of tortoise increases substantially and continues to rise to a peak in Phase V, the final period of occupation at Hayonim Cave.

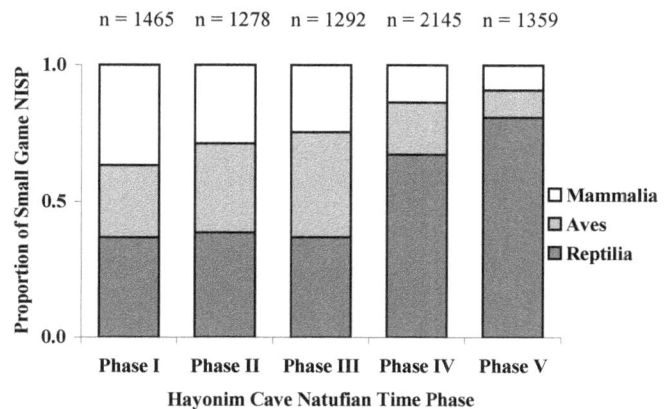

Figure 4. Relative abundance of small Game fauna across five phases of Natufian occupation at Hayonim Cave. Phases I–III date to the Early Natufian and Phases IV and V to the Late Natufian. Small mammals include Lepus, aves include game birds, waterfowl and Falconiformes, and Reptilia is composed of tortoises. n is the sample size for each column.

The sudden increase in the proportion of tortoise remains in the Late Natufian assemblage from Hayonim Cave indicates an increase in human foraging efficiency. During the first three phases of Natufian occupation, high proportions of fast, expensive game animals were selected, suggesting that there was a substantial need for small animals that clearly exceeded the availability of higher-ranked tortoises. Instead, humans were forced to invest in the capture of small, agile animals whose procurement provided reduced returns for the energy invested as compared to slow, easy-to-capture animals. Significant increases in the proportions of slow, small game in the Late Natufian deposits at Hayonim Cave further suggest that these animals were sufficiently abundant in the ecosystem to meet human demands. This in turn implies that the intensity of occupation—the number of people-hours the site was occupied—must have been greatly reduced at the site in the Late Natufian in comparison to the Early Natufian phase. This may have resulted from a reduction in group size, the number of consecutive days of occupation, the frequency of visits to the site each year, or any combination of these.

GAZELLE MORTALITY PROFILES

Gazelle bone fusion data from the Early and Late Natufian occupations at Hayonim Cave are presented and compared in Table 1. The fusion data were calculated from a combined sample of bone elements—distal tibia, tuber calcis of the calcaneum, distal metapodial, distal femur, and distal radius—that fuse between 10 and 18 months of age (following Davis 1983). Unfused gazelle elements from the combined sample are evenly represented in the Early (34.3%) and Late Natufian (35.5%) deposits. Each of the five elements is also examined independently to check for subtler variation within the sample. In Figure 5 the gazelle elements from the combined sample are arranged from youngest to oldest in the sequence in which they fuse. The graph reveals high proportions of unfused epiphyses for all five elements (between 25.0 and 57.0%) from both Early and Late Natufian deposits at Hayonim Cave. In general, elements that fuse at older ages are represented by higher proportions of unfused specimens, with the exception of the metapodial. Results for the metapodial may be inflated as a result of the greater risk of multiple counting, which can occur because there are four distal metapodial condyles for every distal radius, femur, tibia, or calcaneus epiphysis in a complete gazelle skeleton. The Hayonim Cave fusion data clearly show that a high percentage of gazelles were culled before they reached 18
months of age in both the Early and Late Natufian phases.

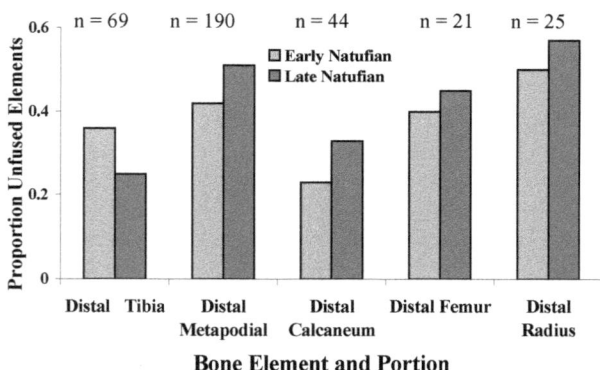

Figure 5. Proportion of unfused gazelle epiphyses in the combined sample of (cf. Davis 1983) from Early and Late Natufian assemblages from Hayonim Cave. Elements are listed from left to right in the order in which they fuse.

The consistency of the results from the element-by-element analysis supports the broader pattern identified above for the combined sample, despite small sample sizes for individual bones. Although, some differences between the two Natufian phases exist—for example, there are slightly higher proportions of juveniles in the Late Natufian phase—these differences range between only 5 and 10%. The results suggest similar or slightly greater hunting pressure during the Late Natufian period.

Comparative gazelle tooth wear and eruption data from the Mousterian and Kebaran layers at Hayonim Cave and from the Early Kebaran deposit at nearby Meged Rockshelter were generously provided by M. Stiner (Figure 6). In this comparison, small samples sizes required the gazelle tooth eruption data from the Early and Late Natufian layers to be collapsed into a single unit. Figure 6 shows a stark contrast between the proportion of juveniles represented in the earlier Paleolithic layers from Hayonim Cave and Meged Rockshelter and those represented in the Natufian period. Fifty percent of the Natufian gazelles were killed before they attained adult dentitions (less than ca. 18 months old), compared to a maximum of 26.0% in all earlier assemblages. Davis (1983) was the first to observe unusually high proportions of juvenile gazelles in Natufian assemblages, and subsequent excavations of Paleolithic faunas have supported this pattern. Moreover, it has become clear that this pattern is widespread across the Mediterranean Hills of the Levant (see Davis 1983; Munro 2001 for details).

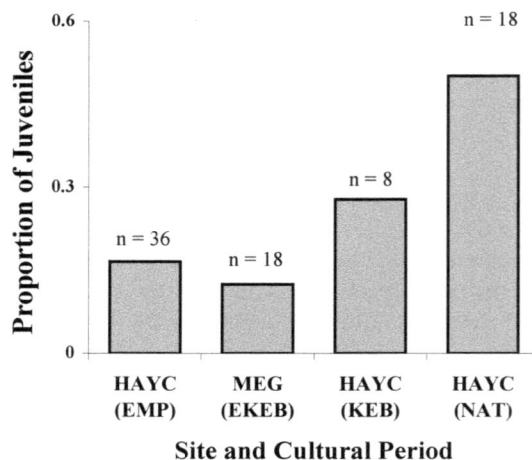

Figure 6. Relative proportion of juvenile gazelles based on tooth wear and eruption data of the lower deciduous third premolar and the lower permanent third molar. Samples are from Paleolithic occupations in the Wadi Meged, Israel. HAYC is Hayonim Cave and MEG is Meged Rockshelter. Abbreviations in parentheses refer to cultural period: E. MP is the Early Middle Paleolithic, E.KEB is the Early Kebaran, KEB is the Kebaran and NAT is the Natufian period.

The proportion of juvenile gazelles in the Hayonim Cave Natufian assemblage shows a marked departure from earlier hunted assemblages at the site and at Meged Rockshelter. This must reflect a dramatic change in procurement strategy or in the natural composition of gazelle populations available to human hunters, or both. Examples of human selectivity for juvenile animals are extremely rare in the ethnographic record (but see Binford 1978; Stiner 1990 on Nunamiut skin-hunting in spring). Nonetheless, inflated proportions of juveniles in prey living structures may occur either at certain times of year for animals with seasonal births or as the result of sustained hunting pressure population (Broughton 1994; Davis 1983; Elder 1965; Lyman 1987; Koike and Ohtaishi 1985, 1987; Munro 2001; Stiner 1990, 1994; Wolverton 2001). Hunting increases the mortality rate of prey populations, forcing them to grow and inflating the proportion of juveniles in the population. Although seasonal hunting is also a viable explanation, in the Natufian case a juvenile bias occurs across the Mediterranean zone throughout the entire period, indicating sweeping changes in predator-prey relationships (Davis 1983; Munro 2001). This exploitation pattern, though insufficient to have driven gazelles to extinction, strongly suggests that the Natufians intensified and maintained heavy hunting pressure on gazelle throughout their occupation of Hayonim Cave.

BUTCHERY OF GAZELLE CARCASSES

Natufian hunters harvested gazelle skeletons for a wide variety of materials, most importantly food products. Evidence for human processing activities are preserved on gazelle elements in the form of cutmarks, cone fractures, spiral fractures, burning, and fragmentation. Human-inflicted damage is prevalent on ungulate remains from both Early and Late Natufian assemblages. Cutmarks were identified on 1.5% of Early and 1.2% of Late Natufian gazelle elements, a direct testament to human butchering activities. Cone fractures (4.3% of Early and 4.81% of Late Natufian gazelle long bone shafts) and ubiquitous spiral breaks (58.6% of Early and 63.1% of Late Natufian breaks on gazelle long bone shafts) indicate that much of the assemblage was broken by humans while fresh, likely with the aid of a hammerstone.

Early and Late Natufian gazelle specimens were frequently burned (11.0 % of Early and 25.4% Late Natufian gazelle), and often intensively, especially in the Late phase. Though striking, this difference is attributable to the presence of one large burned area (squares Q26, P26, and P27) packed with ash, burned slabs, and bone in the Late Natufian deposits. Very high percentages of gazelle bones recovered from these units were burned (42.0%) and of the burned bones many specimens were calcined (56.0% of burned bones), thus exaggerating the total proportion of burned bones in the

Late Natufian assemblage. Although, the frequency of burning on Late Natufian gazelle drops to 20.9% if these squares are eliminated, the Late Natufian gazelle assemblage is still substantially more burned than its Early Natufian predecessor.

Although non-economic human factors such as trampling undoubtedly also contributed to assemblage formation, the rarity of dry fractures and surface abrasion on bone specimens suggests that the impact of these processes was secondary to human processing activities. Likewise, evidence of non-human carnivore activity is virtually non-existent in both Natufian assemblages: fewer than eight gazelle bones were punctured or scored, and only four showed even questionable evidence for digestion. Though it is not possible to reconstruct the life history of every bone in the Natufian assemblage, the combined evidence from cultural and natural indicators unequivocally points to human processing activities as the dominant taphonomic force behind both the Early and Late Natufian gazelle assemblages.

Several indicators suggest that Natufian use of gazelle assemblages went well beyond the transport and consumption of carcasses for meat. Fragmentation indices derived from the Hayonim Cave gazelles suggest intense processing in both the Early and Late Natufian phases; simply put, the skeletons are bashed to pieces. The average size of a gazelle fragment measures 2.6 centimeters in the Early and 2.7 centimeters in the Late Natufian phase. Complete gazelle elements were rarely discarded (24.8% and 21.0% in the Early and Late Natufian respectively), and those that were are nearly exclusively (96.0% of Early and 95.3% of Late Natufian complete gazelle elements) small, compact elements such as teeth, carpals, tarsals, and toes that yield little or no marrow. Once again this evidence points to intensive resource use by the Natufians throughout both the Early and Late phases.

FREQUENCY OF NATURAL DAMAGE

The frequency of natural damage types is similar for both the Early and Late Natufian assemblages, suggesting comparable depositional histories. This is not surprising, given that the assemblages were created in the same general time period and were recovered from the same geographic location. Most categories of natural damage occur in such low frequencies (i.e., a few percentages or less) that the differences between assemblages appear insignificant. Still, a difference of only one or two percentage points can be important in certain damage categories. For example, notable differences between the Early and Late Natufian layers exist in the proportions of bones damaged by weathering and root etching. During the Early Natufian 2.0% of the Hayonim Cave assemblage displays evidence for weathering, and 1.8% of bones were corroded by root activity. The frequency of both types of damage increases by approximately twofold during the Late Natufian (3.3% weathered, 3.3% root etched).

Differences in the frequencies of non-anthropogenic damage categories, such as *in situ* weathering and root etching may provide coarse-grained evidence of the intensity of site use. The frequencies of weathering and root etching roughly double during the Late Natufian at Hayonim Cave. Because weathering occurs after deposition but prior to burial (Behrensmeyer 1978; Lyman 1994), its intensity should vary directly with the amount of time a bone spends on the surface. Rapid accumulation of debris, in tandem with anthropogenic activity, reduces the length of a bone's exposure to the elements and, by extension, its chance of becoming weathered. Bones should be buried more rapidly during periods of human occupation, especially when rebuilding takes place. Likewise, root etching occurs to lightly buried bones when plant growth is not checked by space clearing and human traffic. Some roots penetrate deeply into the soil, but in general, as the depth of burial increases, the chance of rootlet damage declines. Root etching is more likely to happen during periods when sites are not intensively occupied, because human activity causes disturbances that repress plant re-colonization. Weathering and root etching are thus more likely to occur when occupational hiatuses (i.e., periods of reduced occupation intensity) are common. Of course, some damage may also be much more recent, as the site was abandoned long ago.

SUMMARY OF FAUNAL TRENDS

Similar proportions of ungulates to small game taxa in the Early and Late Natufian faunal assemblages point to stability in the primary hunting strategy throughout the Natufian period at Hayonim Cave. Ungulates were the main source of meat, but small game played a consistent and significant supplementary role. Inflated proportions of juvenile gazelles are also constant across the Natufian phases, and well above their frequencies in all earlier Paleolithic occupations at Hayonim Cave (M. Stiner, personal communication 2001). Intensive hunting pressure on the part of the Natufians may have forced gazelle populations into growth mode, leading to both region-wide age depression and an increased availability of youngsters to hunters. Consistent intensities of gazelle butchery throughout the occupation indicate that the Natufians followed long-term traditions of hunting, butchery, and carcass preparation. Furthermore, fragmentation indices and the frequency of human-derived damage to gazelle elements demonstrate that carcasses were intensively butchered throughout the entire Natufian period.

The ungulate data from the Hayonim Cave Natufian point to two general conclusions. First, much of the faunal data indicates remarkable consistency in hunting and butchering strategies throughout the Natufian period

at Hayonim Cave. The Natufians continued to hunt the same spectrum of animals, and butchered their carcasses with the same intensity and the same techniques in both the Early and Late phases. Second, despite the stability in the Natufian fauna itself, aspects of the assemblage differ significantly from earlier Paleolithic occupations in the cave. Increases in the abundance of small game and juvenile gazelles are particularly noteworthy, and indicate unprecedented hunting pressure in the surrounding region as compared to earlier Paleolithic periods.

Against the similarity in nearly all aspects of the Early and Late Natufian ungulate remains from Hayonim Cave, the dramatic increase in the frequency of tortoises versus quick-moving small prey in Late Natufian assemblages is all the more significant. Because the Natufians reverted from prey types that require more technological sophistication to capture (i.e., birds and hares) in the Early phase to those that can be captured easily by hand in the Late phase, technological innovation could not have been a factor in this economic shift. I contend that this shift, along with Late Natufian increases in the proportion of root etching and weathering, reflects a significant reduction in site occupation intensity at Hayonim Cave during the Late Natufian phase.

The small game fraction points to decreased site use intensity during the Late Natufian at Hayonim Cave, yet the results from all other faunal tests point to sustained hunting pressure on high-ranked large game (gazelle) across the Natufian period. Although these results may at first appear contradictory, they are not—different prey types simply highlight different scales of human hunting pressure. Localized effects can be distinguished from regional pressures by reference to the home range of prey species. Small game such as tortoises, hares, and partridges have small territories, thrive at high densities in the absence of predator pressure, and are expected to be captured close to home because they provide limited caloric returns and are thus unworthy of search and transport over long distances. As a result, the relative proportions of different small game animals captured by humans record the local impact of human populations. In contrast, gazelle and other high-ranked ungulate populations occupy large home ranges that are more likely to intersect with the seasonal rounds of multiple groups of human foragers. Changes in the intensity of gazelle hunting by humans are therefore expected to better reflect regional pressure on animal resources; this is detectable in the relative proportions of gazelle to small game, and in the age profiles and butchering intensity of gazelle and other ungulate species.

SUPPORTING ARCHAEOLOGICAL DATA

Independent material cultural evidence from Hayonim Cave supports the conclusions drawn from the faunal data. The frequency and density of major material

MATERIAL CLASS	ARTIFACT OR FEATURE	EARLY NATUFIAN	LATE NATUFIAN
	Volume Excavated (m³)	21.8	25.4
Architecture	Rooms (Loci)	9	0
	Built Hearths	6	0
	Slab-lined Floors	5	0
	Slab-lined Graves	2	2
Graves	Total Graves	8	8
	Human Burials (MNI)	29 + 2 fetuses	18+1 fetus
Modified Bone	Bone Tools	202 (9.3/m³)	284 (11.2/m³)
Ornaments/Art	Decorated Bone	1 (<1.0/m³)	3 (<1.0/m³)
	Bone Beads in Graves	123 (5.6/m³)	2 (<1.0/m³)
	Bone Beads outside Graves	45	41
	Dentalium	837 (38.4/m³)	1437 (56.7/m³)
	Engraved limestone	4 (<1.0/m³)	1 (<1.0/m³)
Ground Stone	Groundstone	78 (3.6/m³)	121 (4.8/m³)
Stone Tools	Stone Tools	2110 (96.8/m³)	2042 (80.6/m³)
	Lunates	226 (10.4/m³)	424 (16.7/m³)
	Burins	794 (36.4 /m³)	663 (26.2/m³)
	Sickle Blades	32 (1.5/m³)	91 (3.6/m³)
	Bifaces	27 (1.2/m³	31 (1.2/m³)

Table 2. The frequency and density of features and major artifact classes from the Early and Late Natufian of Hayonim Cave. Numbers outside of parentheses are frequencies, and numbers in parentheses are density values (m³). Data is compiled from Belfer-Cohen (1988), and does not include material from the 1990s excavations.

datasets recorded by Belfer-Cohen (1988) are summarized in Table 2. On the basis of the archaeological data, Bar-Yosef and Belfer-Cohen (n.d.; Bar-Yosef 1991; Belfer-Cohen 1988) outline three major stages of construction and occupation during the Hayonim Cave Natufian (Bar-Yosef and Belfer-Cohen n.d.). The first two stages correspond to the Early Natufian occupation at the site (Phases I–III) and the final stage to the Late Natufian phase (Phase IV–V). The first of the stages (most of Phase I) is the shortest of the three, and marks the return of humans to Hayonim Cave after a long hiatus that spanned the Late Kebaran and Geometric Kebaran periods. This stage is defined by the construction of Locus 3, the first of the circular structures at the site. Hereafter, the first stage of Natufian occupation at Hayonim Cave is combined with the second stage and referred to as the Early Natufian.

The second stage of occupation (the remainder of Phase I and Phases II–III) is marked by an intensive sequence of construction and rebuilding at the site (Bar-Yosef and Belfer-Cohen n.d.). With the exception of Locus 3, and two slab-lined graves constructed in the Late Natufian, all built features at Hayonim Cave—including eight loci, six built hearths, five slab-lined floors, and one small kiln—were constructed during this stage (Bar-Yosef 1991). Cultural debris from this stage indicates that domestic activities were concentrated in the loci near the cave's entrance, and the dead were buried behind the structures and primary living area. Although sample sizes are small (eight graves with a maximum of twenty-

nine interments), most Early Natufians were recovered in primary position (75.0% of individuals) in group graves (75.0% of graves). Moreover, decorated burials (13.8% of individuals) and extended burial positions (33.3% of individuals) are restricted to Early Natufian contexts. Finally, plant processing equipment including ground stone (mortars, pestles, and grinding stones) and sickle blades provides good secondary evidence for cereal exploitation (Unger-Hamilton 1989; Wright 1994). Both ground stone and sickle blades are regular features of Early Natufian assemblages (ground stone NISP = 78, 3.6/m³, and sickle blade NISP = 32, 1.5/m³), attesting to the importance of plant processing activities at the site.

The final stage of occupation at Hayonim Cave corresponds directly to the Late Natufian phase. The Late Natufian is characterized by the emergence of a large, continuous activity area along the eastern wall of the cave. Although the activities that took place in this area cannot be specified due to the intrusion of a Byzantine glass furnace into the Natufian deposits, it appears that domestic activities shifted from the loci to this eastern area. The open area wall lacks formal features, but is home to several unusual caches. The caches, which include complete gazelle horns, ground stone pestles, *Dentalium,* and bovid ribs—some worked into tool preforms— appear to have been stockpiled for future use. Loci 1 and 2, situated at the back of the cave, are also assigned a Late Natufian age. Although these two loci do not have walls, they are delimited by packed living floors and ash concentrations.

During this final phase of occupation human interments were concentrated in the fill of abandoned loci. By the end of the occupation (Phase V), the activity area along the east side of the cave was filled with new graves (e.g., XIV, XV, XVI); however, faunal, lithic, and other debris continued to accumulate in this area on a small scale. All Late Natufian burials are flexed or semi-flexed, and the proportion of secondary burials increases slightly to 32.5% from 25.0% in the Early Natufian. Although group burials remain the norm (62.5%) as in the Early Natufian (75.0%), the frequency of individual burials rises to 37.5% from 25.0% in the preceding period. None of the Late Natufian burials are decorated, but some individuals (three out of five primary burials) were recovered without the cranium. In these cases the mandible was left intact. This pattern antecedes the more ubiquitous practice of skull removal that flourished in the Neolithic period.

Finally, the abundance of specialized plant processing tools, including sickle blades (NISP = 91, $3.6/m^3$) and ground stone mortars and pestles (NISP = 121, $4.8/m^3$), increased during the Late Natufian. Plant processing equipment was concentrated along the eastern wall of the cave, the primary activity area during the formation of the Late Natufian deposits. Pestles were most often recovered in small groups and caches, and sickle blades are at least two to three times more abundant than they were in any of the first three phases of occupation at the site.

DISCUSSION OF EARLY TO LATE NATUFIAN CHANGES IN MATERIAL CULTURE

The material remains from Hayonim Cave depcit a contrast in energy investment between the Early and Late Natufian occupations. Architectural features were constructed almost exclusively in the Early phase. The permanence of shelter and other features such as hearths and floors are expected to correlate inversely with the degree of occupation intensity (e.g., Binford 1990; Kelly 1995). Mobile foragers who make frequent residential moves must make and break camp each time they move. The energy required for construction activities is thus better expended on other, more immediate demands during short occupations. Though architectural investment can result in certain kinds of long-term gains, this is likely only if reoccupation for a significant amount of time is reasonably certain. Not surprisingly, the major episode of building at Hayonim Cave is interpreted as the most intensive phase of occupation at the site (Bar-Yosef and Belfer-Cohen n.d.). Conversely, the Late Natufian features suggest a more ephemeral and sporadic occupation. The termination of major construction during the Late Natufian implies that it was no longer worthwhile to invest significantly in the site, likely because of a decrease in site occupation intensity.

Increases in the number of secondary inhumations and the absence of decorated burials in Late Natufian graves

may also indicate a decrease in site occupation intensity and associated increases in residential mobility during this later phase (Belfer-Cohen et al. 1991). Secondary burials are interpreted as the skeletal remains of individuals who died elsewhere and were later transported to Hayonim Cave for burial (cf. Belfer-Cohen 1988, 1991; Belfer-Cohen and Bar-Yosef 2000). The absence of decorations in Late Natufian burials supports the interpretation that individuals were already skeletonized at the time of burial, as ornaments are most likely to be associated with clothing or fully fleshed bodies (Belfer-Cohen 1991; Belfer-Cohen et al. 1991). The few primary burials recovered from Late Natufian contexts suggest that the Natufians continued to occupy Hayonim Cave, and that some individuals died while in residence at the site or nearby, but not to the extent seen in the Early Natufian.

Finally, secondary evidence for plant processing, including the frequency of ground stone implements and sickle blades (Belfer-Cohen 1988), and the attrition of human teeth (Smith 1991) indicate that the Natufians at Hayonim Cave invested heavily in the collection and processing of small, labor-intensive plant remains. An increase in the density of ground stone and sickle blades in Late Natufian deposits points to sustained if not more intensive plant exploitation in this phase. Despite changes in mobility, the Natufians continued to utilize the same basic strategy to procure plant resources.

CONCLUSION: THE EARLY TO LATE NATUFIAN TRANSITION AT HAYONIM CAVE

The faunal record and supporting archaeological data from Hayonim Cave provide good evidence for two major trends at the end of the Pleistocene. First, there was a significant drop in the intensity of human occupation at Hayonim Cave that is in turn associated with an increase in human mobility at the regional scale (see also Bar-Yosef and Belfer-Cohen n.d.; Belfer-Cohen 1995; Goring-Morris and Belfer-Cohen 1988; Valla 1998). This shift began at the onset of the Late Natufian, with occupation becoming increasingly more ephemeral by the final stage of Natufian habitation in the cave. Late Natufian visits to the site were either of shorter duration and/or less frequent than they had been in the past (see also Bar-Yosef and Belfer-Cohen n.d.; Belfer-Cohen and Bar-Yosef 2001). During the Late Natufian phase, people continued to use Hayonim Cave as a cemetery that had clear social and ritual significance for local populations (Bar-Yosef and Belfer-Cohen n.d.). Secondary evidence for plant exploitation and the faunal data also indicate that the site continued as a base for the extraction of plant and animal resources, though some of these activities may have shifted to Hayonim Terrace.

Second, the intensity of use of both plant and animal resources remained high throughout the duration of the Natufian period, and was not reduced or intensified in response to greater population mobility during the Late Natufian phase. Pressure was exerted to the point of resource depression in high-ranked game species, and secondary evidence suggests that the Natufians invested significant amounts of energy to collect and prepare small, energy-rich foods such as grains and nuts for consumption. Of particular interest in the case of both plant and animal resources is the tenacity of the subsistence system in face of strong climatic fluctuations (i.e., the Younger Dryas ca. 11,000 B.P.) and settlement changes from the beginning to the end of the Natufian occupation at Hayonim Cave. These observations have important implications for understanding the nature of the Natufian occupation at Hayonim Cave.

Increased mobility of the Hayonim Cave population in the Late Natufian corresponds to the onset of the Younger Dryas, a major cooling and drying event that began around 11,000 B.P. A contraction of the Mediterranean belt associated with the Younger Dryas (Baruch and Bottema 1991) required that humans adjust their strategies to combat shrinking resource abundance. The Late Natufians from Hayonim Cave did not, as far as we know, turn to agriculture at this point, but they did increase mobility and decrease site occupation intensity in order to mitigate pressures as they developed. This strategy could not have been successful under Late Natufian conditions without a concomitant drop in human population density, likely caused by reduced population growth rates and some population emigration to surrounding arid zones. In sum, the data suggest that intensive occupation at Hayonim Cave in the Early Natufian was followed by a significant decline in the intensity of site use in the Late Natufian and was most likely accompanied by a partial depopulation of the western Galilee ca. 11,000 B.P. This trend continued throughout the duration of the Late Natufian phase, until the onset of the Holocene and agricultural transition ca. 10,000 B.P.

ACKNOWLEDGEMENTS

This research was supported by grants from the National Science Foundation (SBR-9815083), the University of Arizona Final Project Fund, the Levi Sala CARE Foundation, and Doctoral Fellowships from the Social Sciences and Humanities Council of Canada (SSHRC), and the Department of Anthropology of the University of Arizona. Special thanks to Mary C. Stiner who was instrumental at all stages of this research, to Ofer Bar-Yosef for granting permission to study the collections and participate in the Hayonim Cave Archaeological Project, and to Eitan Tchernov for providing space for my analysis in his lab at the Hebrew University in Jerusalem. Thanks also to Guy Bar-Oz for illuminating discussions on this research and to Kate Sarther for editing the manuscript under time constraints.

REFERENCES

BAR-EL, T. AND E. TCHERNOV. 2001. Lagomorph remains at prehistoric sites in Israel and southern Sinai. *Paléorient* 26, 93-109.

BAR-OZ, G. 2001. Cultural and ecological changes at the end of the last glacial in the northern coastal plain of Israel. Unpublished Ph.D. Dissertation. Tel Aviv University, Tel Aviv, Israel.

BAR-OZ, G., T. DAYAN, AND D. KAUFMAN. 1999. The Epipaleolithic faunal sequence of Israel: a view from Neve David. *Journal of Archaeological Science* 26, 67-82.

BARUCH, U. AND S. BOTTEMA. 1991. Palynological evidence for climatic changes in the Levant ca. 17,000-9,000 B.P. In *The Natufian Culture in the Levant*, ed. O. Bar-Yosef and F. R. Valla. Ann Arbor: International Monographs in Prehistory, pp. 11-20.

BAR-YOSEF, O. 1991. The archaeology of the Natufian layer at Hayonim Cave. In *The Natufian Culture in the Levant*, ed. O. Bar-Yosef and F. R. Valla. Ann Arbor: International Monographs in Prehistory, pp. 81-92

BAR-YOSEF, O. AND A. BELFER-COHEN. 1989. The origins of sedentism and farming communities in the Levant. *Journal of World Prehistory* 3: 447-498.

BAR-YOSEF, O. AND A. BELFER-COHEN. 1991. From sedentary hunter-gatherers to territorial farmers in the Levant. In *Between Bands and States*, ed. S. A. Gregg. Center for Archaeological Investigations, Occasional Paper No. 9. Carbondale, IL: Southern Illinois University, pp. 181- 202.

BAR-YOSEF, O. AND A. BELFER-COHEN. n.d. The Natufian in Hayonim Cave and the Natufian of the Terrace. Prepared for volume on Hayonim Terrace, ed. F. R. Valla.

BAR-YOSEF, O. AND R. H. MEADOW. 1995. The origins of agriculture in the Near East. In *Last Hunters—First Farmers: New Perspectives on the Prehistoric Transition to Agriculture*, ed. T. D. Price and A. B. Gebauer. Santa Fe: School of American Research Press, pp. 39-94

BAR-YOSEF, O. AND E. TCHERNOV. 1967. The Natufian bone industry of Ha-yonim Cave. *Israel Exploration Journal* 20, 141-150.

BAR-YOSEF, O. AND F. R. VALLA. 1979. L'évolution du Natoufien nouvelles suggestions. *Paléorient* 5, 145-151.

BEHRENSMEYER, A. K. 1978. Taphonomic and ecological information from bone weathering. *Paleobiology* 4, 150-162.

BELFER-COHEN, A. 1988. *The Natufian Settlement at Hayonim Cave: A Hunter-gatherer Band on the Threshold of Agriculture.* Unpublished Ph.D. Dissertation. Institute of Archaeology, The Hebrew University, Jerusalem.

BELFER-COHEN, A. 1991. The Natufian in the Levant. *Annual Review of Anthropology* 20, 167-186

BELFER-COHEN, A. 1995. Rethinking social stratification in the Natufian culture: the evidence from the burials. In The *Archaeology of Death in the Near East*, ed. S. Campbell and A. Green. Oxbow Monograph 51. Oxford: Oxbow, pp. 9-16.

BELFER-COHEN, A. AND O. BAR-YOSEF. 2000. Early sedentism in the Near East: A bumpy road to village life. In *Life in Neolithic Farming Communities: Social Organization, Identity and Differentiation*, ed. I. Kuijt. New York: Plenum Publishers, pp.19-37.

BELFER-COHEN, A., S. L. SCHEPARTZ, AND B. ARENSBURG. 1991. New biological data for the Natufian populations in Israel. In The *Natufian Culture in the Levant*, ed. O. Bar-Yosef and F. R. Valla. Ann Arbor: International Monographs in Prehistory, pp. 411-424.

BINFORD, L. R. 1968. Post-Pleistocene adaptations. In *New Perspectives in Archaeology*, ed. S. R. Binford and L. R. Binford. Chicago: Aldine Publishing Company, pp. 313-341.

BINFORD, L. R. 1978. *Nunamiut Ethnoarchaeology.* New York: Academic Press.

BOSERUP, E. 1965. *The Conditions of Agricultural Growth.* Chicago: Aldine.

BRAIDWOOD, R. J. 1960. The agricultural revolution. *Scientific American* 203, 130-141.

BROUGHTON, J. M. 1994. Declines in mammalian foraging efficiency during the Late Holocene, San Francisco Bay, California. *Journal of Anthropological Archaeology* 13, 371-401.

BYRD, B. F. 1989. The Natufian: settlement variability and economic adaptations in the Levant at the end of the Pleistocene. *Journal of World Prehistory* 3(2), 159-197.

CHARNOV, E. L. 1976. Optimal foraging: the marginal value theorem. *Theoretical Population Biology* 9, 129-136.

CHILDE, V. G. 1951. *Man Makes Himself.* New York: Mentor.

COHEN, M. N. 1977. *The Food Crisis in Prehistory: Overpopulation and the Origins of Agriculture.* New Haven: Yale University Press.

COPE, C. R. 1991a. The Evolution of Natufian Megafaunal Communities. Unpublished Ph.D. Dissertation. Department of Ecology, Systematics and Evolution, Hebrew University, Jerusalem.

COPE, C. R. 1991b. Gazelle hunting strategies in the southern Levant. In The *Natufian Culture in the Levant*, ed. O. Bar-Yosef and F. R. Valla. Ann Arbor: International Monographs in Prehistory, pp. 341-358.

DAVIS, S. J. 1978. The Large Mammals of the Upper Pleistocene-Holocene in Israel. Unpublished Ph.D. dissertation. Department of Ecology, Systematics and Evolution, Hebrew University, Jerusalem.

DAVIS, S. J. 1983. The age profiles of gazelles predated by ancient man in Israel: Possible evidence for a shift from seasonality to sedentism in the Natufian. *Paléorient* 9, 55-62.

DAVIS, S. J., O. LERNAU, AND J. PICHON. 1994. Chapitre VII, The animal remains: new light on the origin of animal husbandry. In *Le site de Hatoula en Judée occidentale, Israel*, ed. M. Lechevallier and A. Ronen. Mémoires et Travaux du Centre de Recherche Français de Jérusalem. Paris: Association Paléorient, pp. 83-100.

EDWARDS, P. C. 1989. Revising the Broad Spectrum Revolution: its role in the origins of southwest Asian food production. *Antiquity* 63, 225-246.

ELDER, W. H. 1965. Primeval deer hunting pressures revealed by remains from American Indian middens. *Journal of Wildlife Management* 29(2), 366-371.

EMLEN, J. 1966. The role of time and energy in food preference. *The American Naturalist* 100, 611–617.

FLANNERY, K. V. 1969. Origins and ecological effects of early domestication in Iran and the Near East. In *The Domestication and Exploitation of Plants and Animals*, ed. P. J. Ucko and G. W. Dimbleby. Chicago: Aldine Publishing Company, pp. 73-100.

GARROD, D. A. AND D. M. BATE. 1937. *The Stone Age of Mount Carmel: Excavations at the Wady El-Mughara,* Volume 1. Oxford: Clarendon Press.

GEBAUER, A. B. AND T. D. PRICE. 1992. Foragers to farmers: an introduction. In *Transitions to Agriculture in Prehistory*, ed. A. B. Gebauer and T. D. Price, Monographs in World Archeology No. 4. Madison: Prehistory Press, pp. 1-10.

GORING-MORRIS, N. 1987. *At the Edge: Terminal Hunter-Gatherers in the Negev and Sinai.* BAR International Series 361. Oxford: British Archaeological Reports.

GORING-MORRIS, N. AND A. BELFER-COHEN. 1998. The articulation of cultural processes and Late Quaternary environmental changes in Cisjordan. *Paléorient* 23, 107-119.

GRAYSON, D. K. 1984. *Quantitative Zooarchaeology: Topics in the Analysis of Archaeological Faunas.* Orlando: Academic Press.

GRIFFITHS, D. 1975. Prey availability and the food of predators. *Ecology* 56, 1209-1214.

HAYDEN, B. 1981. Research and development in the Stone Age: technological transitions among hunter-gatherers. *Current Anthropology* 22, 519-548.

HENRY, D. O. 1989. *From Foraging to Agriculture: The Levant at the End of the Ice Age.* Philadelphia: University of Pennsylvania Press.

HENRY, D. O., A. LEROI-GOURHAN, AND S. DAVIS. 1981. The excavation of Hayonim Terrace: an examination of Terminal Pleistocene climatic and adaptive changes. *Journal of Archaeological Science* 8, 33-58.

HILLMAN, G. C. 1996. Late Pleistocene changes in wild plant-foods available to hunter-gatherers of the northern Fertile Crescent: possible preludes to cereal cultivation. In *The Origins and Spread of Agriculture and Pastoralism in Eurasia*, ed. D. R. Harris. Washington, DC: Smithsonian Institution Press, pp. 159-203

HOPF, M. AND O. BAR-YOSEF. 1987. Plant remains from Hayonim Cave, western Galilee *Paléorient* 10, 49-60.

HORWITZ, L. K. AND E. TCHERNOV. 2001. Climate change and faunal diversity in Epipaleolithic and Early Neolithic sites from the lower Jordan Valley. In *Archaeozoology of the Near East IV A*, ed. M. Mashkour, A. M. Coyke, H. Buitenhuis, and F. Poplin. Proceedings of the fourth international symposium on the archaeozoology of southwestern Asia and adjacent areas. Groningen, Netherlands: ARC Publicatie 32, pp. 49-66.

KAUFMAN, D. 1992. Hunter-gatherers of the Levantine Epipaleolithic: the sociological origins of sedentism. *Journal of Mediterranean Archaeology* 5, 165-201.

KEELEY, L. H. 1995. Protoagricultural practices among hunter-gatherers a cross-cultural survey. In *Last Hunters First Farmers*, ed. T. D. Price and A. B. Gebauer. Santa Fe: School of American Research Press, pp. 243-272

KELLY, R. 1995. *The Foraging Spectrum: Diversity in Hunter-Gatherer Lifeways.* Washington, DC: Smithsonian Institution Press.

KOIKE, H. AND N. OHTAISHI. 1985. Prehistoric hunting pressure estimated by the age composition of excavated sika deer (*Cervus nippon*) using the annual layer of tooth cement. *Journal of Archaeological Science* 12, 443-456.

KOIKE, H. AND N. OHTAISHI. 1987. Estimation of prehistoric hunting rates based on the composition of sika deer. *Journal of Archaeological Science* 14, 251-269.

KREBS, J. R., D. E. STEPHENS, AND W. F. SOUTHLAND. 1983. Perspectives in optimal foraging. In *Perspectives in Ornithology: Essays presented for the Centennial of the American Ornithologists Union*, ed. A. C. Brush and G. A. Clark. Cambridge: Cambridge University Press, pp. 165-221

LIEBERMAN, D. E. 1991. Seasonality and gazelle hunting at Hayonim Cave: New evidence for "sedentism" during the Natufian. *Paléorient* 17, 47-57.

LIEBERMAN, D. E. 1993. The rise and fall of seasonal mobility among hunter-gatherers: The case of the southern Levant. *Current Anthropology* 34, 599-631.

LYMAN, R. L. 1984. Bone density and differential survivorship of fossil classes. *Journal of Anthropological Archaeology* 3, 259-299.

LYMAN, R. L. 1987. On the analysis of vertebrate mortality profiles: sample size, mortality type, and hunting pressure. *American Antiquity* 52(1), 125-142.

LYMAN, R. L. 1994. *Vertebrate Taphonomy*. Cambridge: Cambridge University Press.

MACARTHUR, R. H. AND E. PIANKA. 1966. On optimal use of a patchy environment. *The American Naturalist* 100, 603-609.

MCCORRISTON, J. AND F. HOLE. 1991. The ecology of seasonal stress and the origins of agriculture in the Near East. *American Anthropologist* 93(1), 46-69.

MOORE, A. M. AND G. C. HILLMAN. 1992. The Pleistocene to Holocene transition and human economy in Southwest Asia: the impact of the Younger Dryas. *American Antiquity* 57, 482-94.

MUNRO, N. D. 1999. Small game as indicators of sedentization during the Natufian period at Hayonim Cave in Israel. In *Zooarchaeology of the Pleistocene/Holocene Boundary*, ed. J. D. Driver. Oxford: BAR International Series 800, pp. 37-45.

MUNRO, N. D. 2001. A Prelude to Agriculture: Game Use and Occupation Intensity during the Natufian Period in the Southern Levant. Unpublished Ph.D. Dissertation. Department of Anthropology, University of Arizona.

NEELEY, M. P. AND G. A. CLARK. 1993. The human food niche in the Levant over the past 150,000 years. In *Hunting and Animal Exploitation in the Later Palaeolithic and Mesolithic of Eurasia*, ed. G. L. Peterkin, H. Bricker, and P. Mellars. Archaeological Papers of the American Anthropological Association, Vol. 4, pp. 221-240.

NOY, T., A. J. LEGGE, AND E. S. HIGGS. 1973. Recent excavations at Nahal Oren, Israel. *Proceedings of the Prehistoric Society* 39, 75-99.

PERRY, G. AND E. R. PIANKA. 1997. Animal foraging: past, present and future. *TREE* 12(9), 360-364.

PICHON, J. 1983. Parures natoufiennes en os de perdrix. *Paléorient* 9, 91-98.

PICHON, J. 1984. L'avifaune natoufienne du Levant. These de 3e cycle, Université Pierre et Marie-Curie (Paris VI).

PICHON, J. 1987. L'avifaune de Mallaha. In *La Faune du Gisement Natufien de Mallaha (Eynan) Israel*, ed. J. Bouchud. Mémoires et Travaux du Centre de Recherche Français de Jérusalem. Paris: Association Paléorient, pp. 115-150.

PYKE, G. H., H. R. PULLIAM, AND E. L. CHARNOV. 1977. Optimal foraging: a selective review of theory and tests. *Quarterly Review of Biology* 52, 137-154.

REDDING, R. W. 1988. A general explanation of subsistence change: from hunting and gathering to food production. *Journal of Anthropological Archaeology* 7, 59-97.

SCHOENER, T. W. 1986. A brief history of optimal foraging theory. In *Foraging Behavior*, ed. A. C. Kamil, J. R. Krebs, and H. R. Pulliam. New York: Plenum Press, pp. 5-67.

SIMMS, S. R. 1987. *Behavioral ecology and hunter-gatherer foraging: an example from the Great Basin*. BAR International Series 381. Oxford: British Archaeological Reports.

SMITH, E. A. AND B. WINTERHALDER. 1992. *Evolutionary Ecology and Human Behavior*. Hawthorne, NY: Aldine de Gruyter.

SMITH, P. 1991. The dental evidence for nutritional status in the Natufians. In *The Natufian Culture in the Levant*, ed. O. Bar-Yosef and F. R. Valla. Ann Arbor: International Monographs in Prehistory, pp. 425-432

STEPHENS, D. W. AND J. R. KREBS. 1986. *Foraging Theory*. Princeton, NJ: Princeton University Press.

STINER, M. C. 1990. The use of mortality patterns in archaeological studies of hominid predatory adaptations. *Journal of Anthropological Archaeology* 9, 305-351.

STINER, M. C. 1994. *Honor Among Thieves: A Zooarchaeological Study of Neandertal Ecology*. Princeton: Princeton University Press.

STINER, M.C. 2001. Thirty years on the "Broad Spectrum Revolution" and Paleolithic Demography. *PNAS* 98, 6993-6996.

STINER, M. C., N. D. MUNRO, AND T. A. SUROVELL. 2000. The tortoise and the hare: small game use, the Broad Spectrum Revolution, and Paleolithic demography. *Current Anthropology* 41, 39-73.

STINER, M. C., N. D. MUNRO, T. A. SUROVELL, E. TCHERNOV, AND O. BAR-YOSEF. 1999.

Paleolithic population growth pulses evidenced by small animal exploitation. *Science* 283 (8 January issue), 190-194.

SZUTER, C. R. AND F. E. BAYHAM. 1989. Sedentism and prehistoric animal procurement among desert horticulturalists of the North American Southwest. In *Farmers as Hunters: the Implications of Sedentism*, ed S. Kent. Cambridge: Cambridge University Press, pp. 80-95.

TCHERNOV, E. 1984. Commensal animals and human sedentism in the Middle East. In *Animals and Archaeology*, ed. J. Clutton-Brock and C. Grigson. BAR International Series 202. Oxford: British Archaeological Reports, pp. 91-115

TCHERNOV, E. 1991. Biological evidence for human sedentism in southwest Asia during the Natufian. In *The Natufian Culture in the Levant*, ed. O. Bar-Yosef and F. R. Valla. Ann Arbor: International Monographs in Prehistory, pp. 315-340.

TCHERNOV, E. 1993a. Exploitation of birds during the Natufian and early Neolithic of the southern Levant. *Archaeofauna* 2, 121-143.

TCHERNOV, E. 1993b. The impact of sedentism on animal exploitation in the southern Levant. In *Archaeozoology of the Near East*, ed. H. Buitenhuis and A. T. Clason. Leiden: Universal Book Services, pp. 10-26.

UNGER-HAMILTON, R. 1989. Epi-Palaeolithic Palestine and the beginning of plant cultivation—the evidence from harvesting experiments and microwear studies of flint sickle blades. *Current Anthropology* 30(1), 88-103.

VALLA, F. R. 1987. Chronologie absolue et chronolgies relatives dans le Natoufien. In *Chronologies in the Near East*, ed. O. Aurenche, J. Evin, and F. Hours. BAR International Series 379. Oxford: British Archaeological Reports, pp. 267-294

VALLA, F. R. 1998. Natufian seasonality: a guess. In *Seasonality and Sedentism Archaeological Perspectives from Old and New World Sites*, ed. T. R. Rocek and O. Bar-Yosef. Cambridge, MA: Peabody Museum of Archaeology and Ethnology.

WINTERHALDER, B. 1986. Diet choice, risk, and food sharing in a stochastic environment. *Journal of Anthropological Archaeology* 5, 369-392.

WOLVERTON, S. 2001. Environmental Implications of Zooarchaeological Measures of Resource Depression. Unpublished Ph.D. Dissertation, Department of Anthropology, University of Missouri, Columbia.

WRIGHT, K. I. 1994. Ground-stone tools and hunter-gatherer subsistence in southwest Asia: implications for the transition to farming. *American Antiquity* 59, 238-263.

THE ROLE OF WOOLLY RHINOCEROS AND WOOLLY MAMMOTH IN PALAEOLITHIC ECONOMIES AT VOGELHERD CAVE, GERMANY

Laura B. Niven

Institut für Ur- und Frühgeschichte, Universität Tübingen

The Swabian Jura region of southern Germany contains a series of cave sites located in the vast karst systems of the Lone and Ach Valleys (Figure 1) that were occupied throughout the Middle and Upper Palaeolithic. Archaeological research has been conducted in this region since the mid-late 1800s and has contributed a great deal to our understanding of the Palaeolithic. The scientific significance of this region comes not only from the number of sites with dense Paleolithic deposits but from especially rich artefact and faunal assemblages. For example, many small figurines carved from mammoth ivory were recovered from Aurignacian deposits at Vogelherd, Geissenklösterle, and Hohlenstein-Stadel representing the earliest artwork in Europe. These sites also yielded extensive stone and organic tool inventories as well as large archaeofaunas. Other notable finds include remains of early *Homo sapiens sapiens* from Vogelherd known as the Stetten fossils (Czarnetski 1983; Churchill and Smith 2000); and early dates of 35-40 ka BP for Aurignacian deposits from Geissenklösterle (Richter et al. 2000; Conard and Bolus, in press).

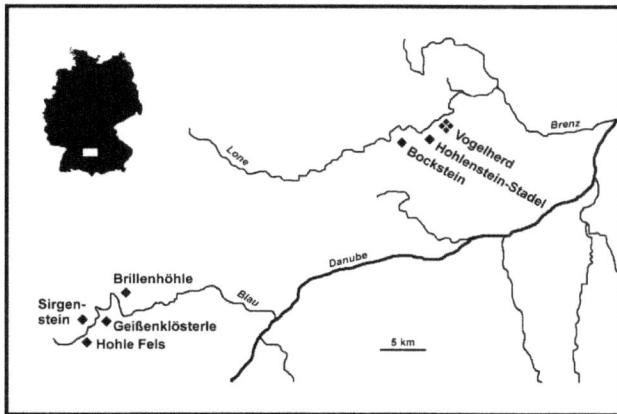

Figure 1: Map of sites mentioned in the text.

Vogelherd is also notable for a large archaeofauna, particularly in the Aurignacian deposit. This paper will focus on the megaherbivore remains from the Middle Palaeolithic and Aurignacian horizons at Vogelherd, which include woolly rhinoceros and woolly mammoth. These taxa are common in Palaeolithic deposits from cave sites in southern Germany but are especially abundant in Vogelherd, a detail that might be a factor of human economic choices, ecology of the taxa, or site taphonomy. A minimum number of 28 individual mammoths in the Aurignacian horizon distinguish Vogelherd not only in the region but as one of the key mammoth localities in Eurasia (Niven 2001). Age profiles and skeletal element representation suggest that multiple factors were involved in the acquisition and

transport of both megaherbivore species at Vogelherd. The exceptional assemblages of rhinoceros and mammoth at the site provide a unique opportunity to evaluate the role of these species in prehistoric economies.

VOGELHERD CAVE

Vogelherd is situated 18 m above the Lone Valley floor and contains entrances to the south, southwest, and north. Passages in the cave run from 15 m – 25 m in length and are at most seven meters wide. Excavations conducted by Gustav Riek in 1931 (Riek 1934) documented seven cultural horizons spanning the Neolithic to the Middle Palaeolithic. The horizons most relevant to this discussion are the Middle Palaeolithic (Riek's Layer VII) and the Aurignacian (Riek's Layers IV and V). Although Riek designated two separate Aurignacian layers, refitting of lithics and bones between Layers IV and V suggests that mixing occurred between them and therefore the faunal remains from both are discussed as one assemblage here. No absolute dates are available for the Middle Palaeolithic deposit but the Aurignacian layers have yielded dates ranging from 29-36 ka BP (Hahn 1993; Conard and Bolus, in press). The wealth of material in the Aurignacian deposit in particular suggests that the site was used intensively during this period, probably in the contexts of multiple occupations.

A large archaeofauna was recovered from Vogelherd, most of which comes from the dense Aurignacian deposit. The Aurignacian faunal assemblage is still being analysed at the time of this writing but consists of ~ 17,000 pieces and is to date the largest of the Swabian Jura cave site faunas from this time period. Provenience information is primarily limited to find horizon only, except for some descriptions of "bone piles" (mammoth) in the Aurignacian. Bone preservation in this deposit ranges from good to substantially weathered. Exact numbers of each taxon are not yet available since this archaeofauna is still being analyzed, but species representation in the Aurignacian includes *Lepus* sp., *Vulpes* sp., *Meles meles, Gulo gulo, Canis lupus, Crocuta spelaea, Felis spelaea, Felis silvestris, Ursus spelaeus, Mammuthus primigenius, Equus ferus, Coelodonta antiquitatis, Bos/Bison, Rupicapra rupicapra, Megaloceros giganteus, Cervus elaphus, Rangifer tarandus,* and *Sus scrofa.*

In the Middle Palaeolithic Layer VII, 518 specimens were recovered from a limited area in the south cave entrance. Represented taxa include *Vulpes* sp., *Canis lupus, Crocuta spelaea, Felis spelaea, Mammuthus*

Table 1. Skeletal element representation for woolly rhinoceros (*Coelodonta antiquitatis*) in the Middle Palaeolithic and Aurignacian deposits at Vogelherd.

Element	VII - Middle Palaeolithic			IV-V - Aurignacian		
	NISP	MNE	MNI	NISP	MNE	MNI
Cranium						
- occipital cond.	-	-	-	2	2	1
- max molars	22	18	10	18	16	7
Mandible						
- mand molars	8	6	3	29	28	12
Tooth fragments	5	-	-	-	-	-
Hyoid	-	-	-	-	-	-
Scapula	1	1	1	4	1	1
Humerus	5	2	2	1	1	1
Radius	2	2	1	1	1	1
Ulna	3	3	3	3	3	3
Carpals	-	-	-	3	3	3
Metacarpal I - III	-	-	-	3	2	2
Os Coxae	-	-	-	-	-	-
Femur	1	1	1	-	-	-
Tibia	4	3	3	3	3	2
Fibula	-	-	-	-	-	-
Astragalus	1	1	1	-	-	-
Calcaneous	2	2	1	3	3	3
Tarsals	-	-	-	2	2	1
Metatarsal I - III	-	-	-	3	3	3
Longbone Fragment	3	-	-	-	-	-
Sesamoid	-	-	-	3	3	1
Phalanx I	-	-	-	2	2	1
Phalanx II	-	-	-	3	3	1
Phalanx III	-	-	-	1	1	1
Vertebrae	-	-	-	-	-	-
Ribs	-	-	-	2	2	1
Sacrum	-	-	-	-	-	-
	57	39	**10**	86	79	**12**

primigenius, *Equus ferus*, *Coelodonta antiquitatis*, *Bos/Bison*, *Megaloceros giganteus*, *Cervus elaphus*, and *Rangifer tarandus*. Much of this archaeofauna is substantially weathered or rolled, probably through geological processes. In addition to the fauna, a small lithic assemblage was also recovered from this layer.

Thorough collection of most if not all faunal material during excavation is indicated by the amount of small or unidentifiable bone fragments, specimens that were often discarded in early archaeological fieldwork. However, considering that the excavation of Vogelherd was conducted in just three months without sediment screening, it is possible that some smaller material was not collected by Riek and his team. Despite the rich archaeofauna having been recovered from Vogelherd, analysis of the bone assemblage is limited to one paleontological study by Ullrich Lehmann (1954). Therefore, an archaeozoological study of the faunal

material is currently being conducted by the author in an attempt to elucidate patterns of faunal exploitation by prehistoric humans in the Swabian Jura.

THE WOOLLY RHINOCEROS ASSEMBLAGES

All Vogelherd rhinoceros specimens were identified to *Coelodonta antiquitatis* based on the distinctive tooth morphology of this species (Guérin 1980). The assemblages are predominated by molars but bone is also present (Table 1). The teeth were aged using a combination of tooth eruption, wear patterns, and crown heights, which were then compared to published data from both known-age samples of African black rhinoceros (Goddard 1970; Hitchins 1978; du Toit 1986). Absolute ages were not the goal, instead this methodology was applied in order to estimate the age of the individuals with appropriately wide age ranges to allow for differences among the genera. Numerous studies of both modern and fossil rhinoceros show similar tooth development among the genera, with tooth eruption subject to less variation than tooth wear. Fortunately, a large proportion of the Vogelherd rhinoceros molars from both deposits are not yet in wear and could be aged with more confidence than older individuals. Similar methodologies were applied to other Pleistocene rhinoceros assemblages including Hofstade, Belgium (Germonpré 1993), Taubach, Germany (Bratlund 1999a), Biache-Saint-Vaast, France (Auguste 1992), and Le Cotte de Saint-Brelade, Jersey Islands (Scott 1986).

The ageing study and interpretations of age distributions of the Vogelherd rhinoceroses are based on both biology and behavior of modern African rhinoceros. Age profiles are divided into five age groups; these groups are not all of equal year amounts, since several major life changes occur in the first three to four years of life. Incorporating life histories and behavior specific to rhinoceros seemed most appropriate to understanding the age distributions of the archaeological assemblage. Group I (0 – 3 years) consists of infancy to the weaning period (~24 months) and independence of calves from their mothers at ca. 2.0 – 3.5 years (Owen-Smith 1988:136-139); Group II (4 – 11 years) includes these newly independent juveniles, subadults (4 – 11 years, depending on sex), and individuals reaching sexual maturity at ca. seven years (females) (Owen-Smith 1988:143-144); Groups III – V are of seven-year increments and include fully adult animals until estimated age of death at ~35 years.

Layer VII: Middle Palaeolithic. A total of 57 rhinoceros specimens come from Layer VII. The entire archaeofauna from this layer is characterized as severely damaged by carnivores. Extensive carnivore gnawing is exhibited on all the rhinoceros bone, with every long bone shaft reduced to a midshaft cylinder and showing scooping of cancellous bone, deep tooth scoring, and ragged break edges typical of hyaena damage (Zapfe 1939; Sutcliffe 1970). Considering the thickness of rhinoceros cortical bone (up to 2 cm), it is clear that hyaenas were the only creature powerful enough to cause such damage and presence of hyaena remains in the deposit (NISP = 7, MNI = 4) speaks to their involvement in the entire bone assemblage (Stiner 1994). Remains of wolf (NISP = 9, MNI = 4) and lion (NISP = 2, MNI = 1) also suggest these animals' participation and some of the gnawing damage appears to have been caused by other bone chewers than hyaenas. The extent of gnawing on much of the Layer VII bone (all taxa) implies a "kennel pattern" (Haynes 1982) by either wolves and/or hyaenas, although the absence of juvenile teeth from either of these carnivores does not support this argument. Seventy-nine percent (91% of rhinoceros bone NISP) of the Layer VII bone exhibits carnivore gnawing, suggesting that the assemblage was accumulated primarily by these animals as opposed to hominids, however it is worth briefly discussing other criteria in this argument.

The Middle Palaeolithic archaeofauna from Vogelherd is comprised of 20% (MNI) carnivores and 80% herbivores. One criterion for carnivore accumulated assemblages is that ≥20% of the total MNI is carnivores (Cruz-Uribe 1991; Pickering 2002), a factor derived from studies of modern hyaena assemblages. A lack of anthropogenic modifications on the rhinoceros and other Layer VII bone also argues against hominid accumulation, however it is possible that hominids were responsible for some of the spiral breakage on horse and bovid long bones. Weathering of the bone might also account for a lack of surface modifications such as cut marks. If the absence of anthropomorphic modifications is not just a taphonomic factor, then overall the rhinoceros assemblage does not fit Blumenschine's (1988) suggested criteria for a hominid accumulation; the lack of modifications also prohibits recognition of whether hominids had first access to the bones, which they subsequently discarded and were subjected to carnivore ravaging later (Blumenschine 1988, 1995). The amount and location of gnawing marks is usually used to distinguish the sequence of carnivores and hominid access to a carcass (Blumenschine 1988, 1995; Selvaggio 1994, 1998; Capaldo 1998) but this is often a more complicated issue than we think (see Lupo and O'Connell 2002). For example, marrow in rhinoceros long bones is distributed throughout trabecular and cancellous bone as opposed to being concentrated in cavities. This factor might have made these elements unattractive for marrow exploitation by hominids and therefore we should not expect breakage of these elements nor rule out hominid activity based solely on presence or absence of breakage typical of marrow extraction. Whether or not hominids did accumulate the rhinoceros bone, the spongy nature of the long bones would have made them appealing to carnivores even if they had been earlier defleshed by hominids and the extensive tooth marks on this assemblage might obscure first access by hominids. In general, the spongy nature of rhinoceros limb bones (note: as well as proboscidean) must be taken into account before assuming that hominids did not utilize them for food but overall, the taphonomic evidence points to carnivores as the primary bone collectors in the Vogelherd Middle Palaeolithic layer.

The post-cranial rhinoceros bone assemblage is small in this layer and is represented solely by limb elements. Excluding the astragalus and calcaneous, tarsals, carpals, foot, and axial bone are not present, elements that would certainly have been destroyed through carnivore feeding and/or diagenesis. According to surveys of Pleistocene hyaena dens and mixed bone assemblages (hominids and hyaenas), such bone frequencies of rhinoceros are found at both types of sites (Brugal et al. 1997; Fosse 1999). In addition, tooth NISPs for rhinoceros are often >50% in both site types; Vogelherd Layer VII teeth make up 61% of rhinoceros NISP. In other words, the skeletal element frequency from the small Middle Palaeolithic assemblage at Vogelherd offers no clarification of hominid role in this accumulation and no meaningful conclusions can be

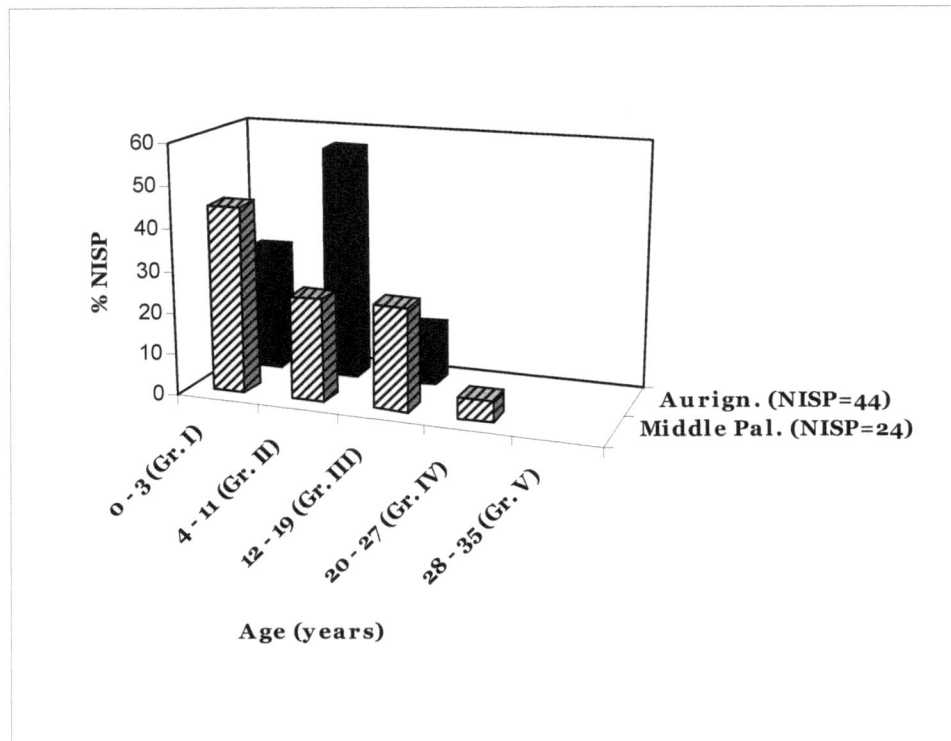

Figure 2. Age representation for woolly rhinoceros in the Middle Palaeolithic and Aurignacian deposits at Vogelherd.

made about skeletal element representation of rhinoceros in this layer except that bone is underrepresented in comparison to the teeth, with the highest bone MNI estimate being three (ulna, tibia).

Age profiles should not be used to identify the cause of death (e.g., Kurtén 1953; Stiner 1994) and often raise more questions than they answer, but they can be used in conjunction with other lines of evidence to recognize patterns of predation by various agents. The age profile for rhinoceros in Layer VII (Figure 2) is based on a molar assemblage consisting of 24 isolated specimens, representing a minimum of 10 individuals (MNI). The highest proportion of individuals is found in Group I with smaller numbers in Groups II-IV and no individuals in Group V. Based on the archaeological and taphonomic evidence, this age profile might reflect predation by carnivores, scavenging by carnivores of natural or hominid-procured rhinoceros, or hunting by hominids.

There is no doubt that large carnivores chewed on the rhinoceros bone in this deposit and it is quite possible they were the cause of death for at least some of the individuals. This proposition is based on published data on the hunting behavior of modern counterparts of the three large carnivores represented at Vogelherd: cave hyaena (*Crocuta spelaea*), wolf (*Canis lupus*),

and cave lion (*Felis spelaea*). Cave bears (*Ursus spelaeus*) could have gnawed on the bone similar to

extant ursids (Haynes 1980, 1982) but are not candidates as predators of rhinoceros.

The infantile rhinoceroses (Group I) would be vulnerable to predation by large carnivores, as this age class of both rhinoceros and other large herbivores is often preyed upon by extant hyaena (Kruuk 1972; Kingdon 1979; Owen-Smith 1988; Berger and Cunningham 1994), lion (Owen-Smith 1988; Kingdon 1979; Brain et al. 1999) and wolf (Mech 1970; Haynes 1980; Carbyn et al. 1993). Fossil assemblages of large herbivores also show a similar pattern of prey choice by large carnivores and the proportion of juveniles goes up according to body weight (e.g., Rawn-Schatzinger 1992; Daeschler 1996; Palmqvist et al. 1996; Navarro and Palmqvist 1999; Lister 2001). Group II individuals would have been newly independent from their mothers and also vulnerable to predation, alone or in pairs (Owen-Smith 1988). Groups III and IV would have been less likely to fall prey to carnivores or die from illness or injury but could have perished from any one of these factors. The big carnivores (fossil and extant) did/do occasionally prey on unencumbered and healthy adult large game, for example from solitary species or single animals excluded from a herd (Schaller 1972; Kingdon 1979; Guthrie 1990). If Pleistocene rhinoceroses were similar to modern ones in terms of herd structure, the young adult and adult age groups would have included solitary animals and small groups or pairs (Owen-Smith 1988; Kingdon 1979). In addition to predation, adults would also have

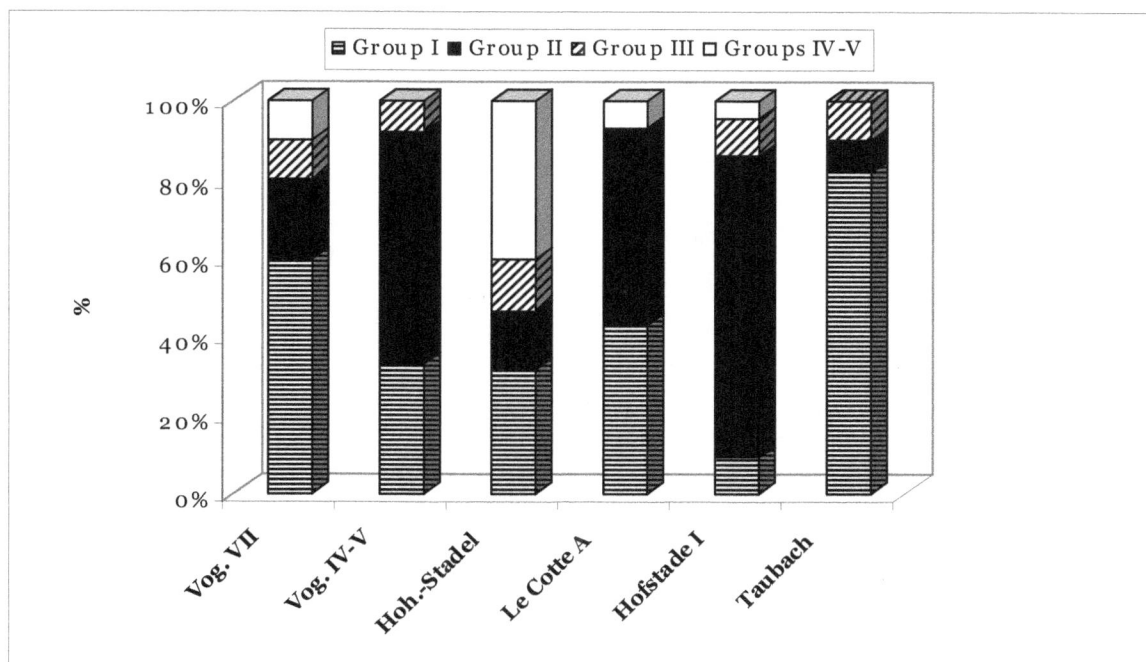

Figure 3. Comparison of rhinoceros age representation from selected Pleistocene assemblages as expressed in %MNI (except Hohlenstein-Stadel %NISP). Data from Gamble (1999:314, Table 7 - Hohlenstein-Stadel), Scott (1986:133, Figure 13.15 - Le Cotte A), Germonpré (1993:290, Table 13 - Hofstade I), and Bratlund (1999a:100, Table 13 - Taubach).

been vulnerable to death from severe ecological conditions such as drought or cold as well as natural causes. Adult rhinoceroses are reflected in the age profile from the paleontological locality of Hofstade I, Belgium (Figure 3), which was interpreted by Germonpré (1993) as showing death from extreme winters and/or drought. Modern studies of African rhinoceros that died from drought also show substantial frequencies of young adult and adult individuals (Goddard 1970; Dunham 1985). Scavenging of carcass parts from such death events of adult rhinoceroses is also possible, as any of the large carnivores would have been capable of transporting these parts into the cave.

It is also probable that large carnivores scavenged rhinoceros bones on the landscape and/or those left by hominid predators. The very young and solitary young adult/adult rhinoceros reflected in the Vogelherd age profile would have been vulnerable to predation by hominids as well as carnivores, as these age groups would pose less of a hunting challenge than adults. Perhaps they were targeted around a source of water or minerals, a scenario suggested by Bratlund (1999a) for some of the rhinoceros procurement at Taubach. In some cases, adult prey might have been hunted by hominids as an adaptation to their predator competition (large carnivores), who singled out infantile and very old animals (Stiner 1994; Gamble 1999). It is plausible that hominids hunted a range of age groups depending on the situation.

A similar rhinoceros age profile is seen at the Swabian Jura site of Hohlenstein-Stadel, which also shows what looks to be an overlap of hominid and large carnivore use of the cave during the Middle Palaeolithic (Gamble 1979, 1999). The woolly rhinoceros age representation at Hohlenstein-Stadel is similar to Vogelherd, with a higher proportion of infantile animals but quite different in its nearly equal number of the next three age groups (Figure 3). Like Vogelherd Layer VII, the Hohlenstein-Stadel age representation could reflect a combination of activities and the presence Group III and IV individuals at the two sites does not necessarily reflect hunting of these age classes by hominids. However Stiner (1994) and Gamble's (1999) suggestions that adult game made up the hominid niche deserves consideration and is also supported by other rhinoceros assemblages with strong evidence for hominid procurement.

Despite a great deal of skepticism over the hunting abilities of Neandertals, there is ample evidence of these hominids hunting rhinoceros. Using modern rhinoceros as an analog, it could be proposed that Pleistocene rhinoceroses were often found solitary or in small groups and pairs, which would have presented less of a hunting challenge than a herd species such as proboscideans. Although some extant rhinoceros can be aggressive towards predators (see review in Bratlund 1999a), it has poor long-distance eyesight (Kingdon 1979) and would therefore be vulnerable when alone.

The best example of Neandertal rhinoceros hunting is seen at the interglacial site of Taubach, Germany (Bratlund 1999a, 1999b), where it looks as if most of the 76 woodland rhinoceroses (*Stephanorhinus kirchbergensis*) were procured by Neandertals. The age profile shows predominantly Group I and Group II animals with a few individuals from Group III+ (Bratlund 1999a:100). Cutmarked bone is common and carnivore modification present but not extensive. Interglacial rhinoceros (*Stephanorhinus kirchbergensis, Stephanorhinus hemitoechus*) assemblages from Biache-Saint-Vaast, France (Auguste 1992) also suggest Neandertal hunting but of adult animals (MNI = 8). Cut marks were documented on some of the bone (Auguste 1992:64, Table 12). The woolly rhinoceros and woolly mammoth bonebeds at Le Cotte de Saint-Brelade, Jersey Islands were deposited in a glacial phase before the last Interglacial presumably as the result of hominid activity (Scott 1986). Most of the rhinoceroses fall into age Groups I and II with a few individuals from Group IV (Scott 1986:133, Figure 13.15). Although we have no carcass with embedded weapon such as the straight-tusked elephant and spear at Lehringen, Germany (Thieme and Veil 1985), the argument for Neandertal hunting of rhinoceros is supported by butchery traces on multiple rhinoceros assemblages. It is beyond the scope of this paper to discuss whether or not Neandertals were capable of hunting large mammals regularly, however a large body of research on Middle Palaeolithic stone artifacts as projectiles (Shea 1993; Shea et al. 2001) and archaeofaunas (e.g., Jaubert et al. 1990; Hoffecker et al. 1991; Gaudzinski 1995; Gaudzinski and Turner 1999; Gaudzinski and Roebroeks 2000) has shown the answer to be "yes". Additionally, isotopic signatures reflecting highly carnivorous Neandertal diets (Bocherens et al. 1999, 2001; Richards et al. 2000) are adequate support to put this debate to rest.

Layers IV-V: Aurignacian. A total of 86 rhinoceros specimens was recovered from Layers IV-V (Table 1). Isolated teeth are the most frequent element but a small bone assemblage is present. An MNI of 12 is based on mandibular molars. In contrast to the Middle Palaeolithic rhinoceros remains, carnivore gnawing is minimal on the Aurignacian rhinoceros assemblage, exhibited on just 17% of the specimens. No modifications attributed to humans were documented. Skeletal elements are more equally represented in this assemblage although bone counts are still low when compared to teeth. The Aurignacian archaeofauna is large and association with hearth features and rich artefact assemblage points to accumulation primarily by humans, probably in the contexts of repeated occupations. Large carnivores were present as well and no doubt contributed to this assemblage, but they were clearly not as major players in the Aurignacian deposit as they were in the Middle Palaeolithic. Nonetheless, the role of humans in the rhinoceros assemblage is ambiguous considering the lack of butchery traces.

Skeletal bone is similarly lacking in the Aurignacian deposit, representing a maximum bone MNI of three from several elements. The small sample size and probable palimpsest nature of this deposit demand cautious interpretations of element frequency and carcass utilization. One such cautious proposal is that complete carcasses or carcass portions were transported to the site. Presence of carpals, tarsals, and sesamoids attest to transport of limb segments, a pattern that was also detected in the equid and bovid assemblages from the Aurignacian deposit in Vogelherd. Bone frequency from Layers IV-V fits both hyaena and mixed hyaena-hominid assemblages (Brugal el al. 1997; Fosse 1999) but is also similar to the probable hunted assemblage from Taubach (Bratlund 1999a). Overall, some hints of interesting patterns can be discerned from the small Aurignacian rhinoceros assemblage but they must be regarded tentatively, considering the complicated formational history of the deposit.

The age profile for the Aurignacian rhinoceros remains reflects individuals from age groups I-III and no animals from the older adult groups (Figure 2). As discussed in the above summary of the Middle Palaeolithic rhinoceros age profile from Vogelherd, the Group II and III individuals would have been susceptible to predation by carnivores or humans. The best-represented age group in the Aurignacian assemblage is Group II (4-11 years), which includes newly solitary or small groups and paired rhinoceroses. It is possible that Aurignacian groups opportunistically procured single rhinoceroses of this age group or cow-calf pairs of Groups I and II.

To summarize, the woolly rhinoceros assemblages from the Middle Palaeolithic and Aurignacian deposits at Vogelherd provide interesting information yet ambiguous pictures of the role of this species in the site. The heavily carnivore modified nature of the Middle Palaeolithic rhinoceros remains clearly shows the role of large carnivores in the assemblage but prohibits any conclusions regarding the role of hominids. Alternating use of the cave by carnivores and hominids might be reflected in the assemblage, similar to other Middle Palaeolithic caves in Eurasia (e.g., Gamble 1999; Enloe et al. 2000; and see Table 1 in Fosse 1999:74). The slightly larger Aurignacian rhinoceros assemblage offers more insights on skeletal element frequencies and reflects a higher proportion of Group II individuals, the age class most likely to be preyed upon by human groups. Although carnivore modification is minimal on the Aurignacian assemblage, a dearth of anthropogenic modifications and the complicated formational history of the deposit prohibit making any confident conclusions regarding human contribution to the rhinoceros assemblage. In spite of studies of extant hyaenas and their food remains as well as descriptions of Pleistocene hyaena dens (Villa and Bartram 1996; Brugal et al. 1997; Bartram and Villa 1998; Fosse 1999; Tournepiche and Couture 1999) that have contributed vastly to our understanding of this bone collector, defining the roles of

Table 2. Skeletal element representation for woolly mammoth (*Mammuthus primigenius*) in the Middle Palaeolithic and Aurignacian at Vogelherd.

Element	VII - Middle Palaeolithic			IV-V - Aurignacian		
	NISP	MNE	MNI	NISP	MNE	MNI
Cranium						
- *petrous portion*	-	-	-	17	17	8
- *occipital cond.*	-	-	-	9	9	7
- *max molars*	4	4		57	41	28
- *other*	-	-	-	319	-	-
Mandible						
- *bone*	-	-	-	13	4	3
- *mand molars*	1	1	1	32	30	14
Unid. Molars	4	-	-	50	-	-
Hyoid	-	-	-	-	-	-
Scapula	-	-	-	54	8	8
Humerus	-	-	-	14	6	3
Radius	-	-	-	1	1	1
Ulna	-	-	-	9	2	2
Carpals	-	-	-	4	4	2
Os Coxae	-	-	-	19	2	1
Femur	-	-	-	13	6	4
Tibia	-	-	-	4	2	2
Fibula	-	-	-	-	-	-
Tarsals	-	-	-	2	2	1
Metapodials	-	-	-	-	-	-
Longbone Fragment	2	-	-	41	-	-
Sesamoid	-	-	-	-	-	-
Phalanges	-	-	-	5	4	2
Vertebrae	-	-	-	12	8	1
Ribs	1	1	1	45	8	1
Sacrum	-	-	-	1	1	1
	12	6	**3**	721	155	**28**

carnivores and hominids in bone accumulations, especially in caves, remains a complicated task (Gaudzinski and Turner 1999).

THE WOOLLY MAMMOTH ASSEMBLAGES

Mammoth remains are found in 90% of cave localities in the Swabian Jura of southern Germany (Gamble 1986:313, Table 7.4) although indisputable evidence of mammoth hunting has not yet been found at sites in this region. The specimens from these caves are primarily limited to fragments of teeth, ivory, and bone or in the case of Geissenklösterle, selectively chosen long bone fragments and ribs to be used in tool production (Münzel 2001). Vogelherd is an exception to this pattern and contains a large mammoth assemblage in the Aurignacian deposit. These differences among sites pose intriguing questions about the paleoecology of mammoths as well as their use at these sites.

All mammoth specimens from the Middle Palaeolithic and Aurignacian deposits at Vogelherd were identified as woolly mammoth (*Mammuthus primigenius*) based on tooth morphology (Maglio 1973). Molars make up a large proportion of the mammoth assemblages from Vogelherd and were analyzed in detail for age information. Molars and deciduous tusks were aged using published African and Asian elephant and Siberian mammoth molar data (Laws 1966; Haynes 1991; Kuzmina and Maschenko 1999) and are listed here in equivalent African Elephant Years (AEY; Laws 1966).

Layer VII: Middle Palaeolithic. A total of 13 mammoth specimens were recovered from this layer (Table 2). The ageable tooth sample (NISP = 6, MNI = 3) is too small to be meaningfully illustrated in an age profile but is described briefly: five specimens fall into age Group I (0 – 12 AEY), including three specimens aged at < 1 year; and one molar belongs to Group II or III. Similar to the rhinoceros sample from this layer, juvenile individuals

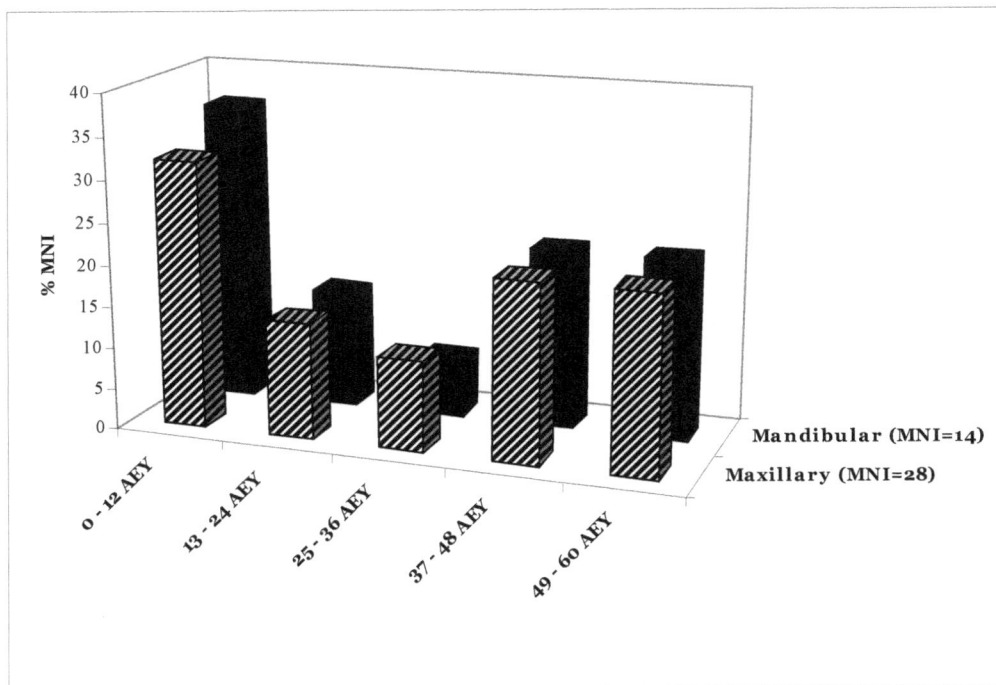

Figure 4. Age representation of woolly mammoth from the Aurignacian deposit at Vogelherd.

are most frequent and could have been the prey of both large carnivores and hominids.

Layers IV-V: Aurignacian. The Aurignacian deposit at Vogelherd contains an extensive mammoth assemblage made up of molars from a minimum of 28 individuals as well as the bone from 12 animals (Table 2). The question of whether mammoths were hunted or collected remains unanswered but age, skeletal element data, and bone preservation suggest a combination of these activities.

All but two molars were isolated; therefore upper and lower molar sets were analyzed separately and respective MNIs were tabulated. The age profile reflects selective deaths of individuals from all age groups, most likely the result of time-averaged, cumulative single mortalities as opposed to one, catastrophic kill (Figure 4). A high proportion of subadults is common in nearly all types of proboscidean death assemblages, as these age groups are more vulnerable to death by predation or natural causes (Haynes 1987). Presence but not predominance of the young adult and adult age groups as seen at Vogelherd is characteristic of selective or non-selective proboscidean death assemblages. Similar to juveniles, old animals are more susceptible to death by predation, disease, and nutritional stress and an age profile showing similar proportions of these age groups might reflect repeated, single mortalities by these causes. The Vogelherd age profile might also reflect opportunistic predation by humans of single animals or small groups from all age classes at sources of water, vegetation, or minerals. Periods of drought or extreme cold would have forced

mammoths to concentrate near water and patches of vegetation and proboscideans' dietary dependence on sodium and calcium is known to drive them to isolated sources (Redmond 1982). Hunting of proboscideans or scavenging of carcasses from natural mortalities at such locations have been proposed at several prehistoric sites in both Eurasia and North America (Abraczinskas 1994; Haynes 1999; Derevianko *et al.* 2000), and such scenarios may be reflected at Vogelherd.

The mammoth bone assemblage is dominated by cranial portions, which in addition to the molars, points to complete or nearly complete heads being transported to the cave. Tusk portions, scapulae and innominates

are also well-represented, followed by smaller numbers of limb elements. Differential weathering on much of the bone might reflect collecting of already weathered bone on the landscape, similar to what has been proposed at many of the mammoth bone "dwellings" and bone pile sites in central Europe and Russia (Soffer 1993). In the Aurignacian deposit at Vogelherd, a mammoth bone pile containing several tusks, molars, scapulae, one mandible, a "smashed" cranium, and other unidentified bone was documented in the south entrance of the cave (Riek 1934:53-54). According to the excavator Riek (1934:53), the pile was carefully constructed and quite sturdy, which suggests a special use of these elements or the bone pile as a whole. Considering that the cave has three entrances, Aurignacian groups might have used bulky elements such as the crania, mandibles, innominates, and scapulae to construct some sort of barricade or closure. Similar skeletal element frequencies between Vogelherd and the "dwelling" sites supports the hypothesis that mammoth bone could have been used as a building material at Vogelherd. The bone pile might also have been a store of fuel, as wood would have been scarce on the landscape.

Neither certain evidence of mammoth hunting nor butchery has been found at Vogelherd but mammoth as a source of food cannot be ruled out. Crania might have been an important source of nutrition for human groups in addition to their utilitarian use. Consumption of fat-rich cranial tissues from medium-sized ungulates has been discussed for modern hunter-gatherer groups (Binford 1978, 1984; O'Connell et al. 1988) and proposed for Neandertals as well (Stiner 1994). Reports of modern elephant butchery (Crader 1983; Fisher 1992, 1993) note that crania are usually not transported or extensively butchered, but the number of mammoth crania at Vogelherd requires exploration of possible reasons of their frequency, including their utilization as a nutritional source. Limb portions, also present in the Vogelherd assemblage, would have been a rich source of meat.

There is no question that mammoths were used extensively for other purposes by Upper Palaeolithic groups in the Swabian Jura. The most elegant examples are the small ivory figurines depicting animals (mammoth, horse, lion, bear, bovid) and anthropomorphs from Vogelherd (Aurignacian), Geissenklösterle (Aurignacian, Gravettian), Hohlenstein-Stadel (Aurignacian), and Hohle Fels (Gravettian). Ivory was also used to fashion ornaments, tools, and other objects, while mammoth ribs and long bone flakes served as raw materials for bone points and various tools. Vogelherd is the only regional cave that contained a pile of mammoth remains and vast amounts of bone and complete molars, which possibly reflect a special use for the material. The significantly larger mammoth assemblage at Vogelherd is just one aspect of an exceptionally rich Aurignacian deposit that points to an intensive use of this cave. The Vogelherd mammoths also suggest that fluctuating environmental conditions could have influenced the location and number of mammoths in the local area, provided natural death sites to collect bone, possibilities for opportunistic hunting by Aurignacian groups, or both. Mammoths are represented in various amounts and forms in the Swabian Jura cave sites and in turn provide insight into several aspects of Upper Palaeolithic life in the region.

CONCLUSIONS

Vogelherd cave offers a unique opportunity to evaluate the role of woolly rhinoceros and woolly mammoth in Palaeolithic economies with its large sample of both megaherbivores preserved in the Middle Palaeolithic and Aurignacian deposits. Taphonomic analysis of the rhinoceros and mammoth assemblages indicates that a combination of factors were involved in their acquisition

and transport and that the role of these taxa in the economies of hominid occupants of the cave is not always clear.

Two important questions are raised by these data: 1) why are rhinoceros and mammoth so much more frequent at Vogelherd (especially in the Aurignacian) than at other Swabian Jura sites? and 2) despite their abundance, why is the role of rhinoceros and mammoth in the Palaeolithic economies at Vogelherd much less clear than other well-represented taxa in the assemblages, such as horse and reindeer? To address the first question, the frequency of these taxa might say more about the life histories of the species and paleoecology of the local area than any decisions of human groups, for example periods of higher populations concentrated locally as the result of favorable or unfavorable environmental conditions. This issue is being explored further in the ongoing analysis of the Vogelherd archaeofauna. The mammoth bone pile also points to specific use(s) of the large skeletal elements that could have been related to a number of economic decisions. Excluding the bone pile, the amount of time in which the other mammoth bone or rhinoceros bone was introduced to the cave is not clear and therefore the numbers of these taxa might be in part slightly inflated due to time-averaging. Taphonomic analysis suggests that the rhinoceros and mammoth in this deposit were not always human prey but instead reflect a combination of occasional, opportunistic procurement, collecting of bone on the landscape, and contributions of large carnivores, all of which most likely transpired over time. If some of the animals were indeed human prey, the lack of anthropogenic modifications might be due to several factors, including weathering of bone surfaces and minimal (if any) butchering of carcasses. Spongy rhinoceros and mammoth long bones were probably not worth exploiting for within-bone nutrients, unlike horse and reindeer long bones. In addition, if these megaherbivores were subsistence species, it appears that this was an occasional occurrence at best and were supplemental to more abundant prey such as horse and reindeer. Overall, the Vogelherd data suggest that woolly rhinoceros and woolly mammoth present research challenges unique to their ecology, behavior, and body size but they also raise many intriguing questions about the role of these animals at Vogelherd, especially during the Aurignacian, and the place of the site in the regional settlement system.

ACKNOWLEDGEMENTS

The Vogelherd analysis was partly supported by the Sondersforschungsbereich 275 under the Deutsche Forschungsgemeinschaft; and the Landesgraduierten-förderungsgesetz, Baden-Württemburg. Thanks to the symposium organizers Dr. Bryan Hockett and Jonathan Haws for including me in their session at the 66th Meeting of the Society for American Archaeology (2001). I am very grateful to Dr. Reinhard Ziegler for help identifying the mammoth and rhinoceros molars;

Drs. Bodil Bratlund and Sabine Gaudzinski for providing references; and to Drs. Nicholas Conard, Gary Haynes, Susanne Münzel, Hans-Peter Uerpmann, and Piotr Wojtal for their contributions to this study.

REFERENCES CITED

ABRACZINSKAS, L. M. 1994. The Distribution of Pleistocene Proboscidean Sites in Michigan: A Cooccurence Analysis of Their Relation to Surface Saline Water. *Michigan Academician* 17: 65-80.

AUGUSTE, P. 1992. Étude Archéozoologique des Grands Mammifères du Site Pléistocène Moyen de Biache-Saint-Vaast (Pas-De-Calais, France): Apports Bio-stratigraphiques et Paleoethnographiques. *L'Anthropologie* 96: 49-70.

BARTRAM, L. E. AND P. VILLA. 1998. The Archaeological Excavation of Prehistoric Hyena Dens: Why Bother? In *Économie Préhistorique: Les Comportements De Subsistance Au Paléolithique*, edited by J.-P. Brugal, L. Meignen and M. Patou-Mathis, pp. 15-29. Editions APDCA, Antibes.

BERGER, J. AND C. CUNNINGHAM. 1994. Active Intervention and Conservation: Africa's Pachyderm Problem. *Science* 263: 1241-1242.

BINFORD, L. R. 1978. *Nunamiut Ethnoarchaeology*. Academic Press, New York.

BINFORD, L.R. 1984. *Faunal Remains from Klasies River Mouth*. Academic Press, New York.

BLUMENSCHINE, R. J. 1988. An Experimental Model of the Timing of Hominid and Carnivore Influence on Archaeological Bone Assemblages. *Journal of Archaeological Science* 15: 483-502.

BLUMENSCHINE, R. 1995. Percussion Marks, Tooth Marks, and Experimental Determinations of the Timing of Hominid and Carnivore Access to Long Bones at FLK *Zinjanthropus*, Olduvai Gorge, Tanzania. *Journal of Human Evolution* 29: 21-51.

BOCHERENS, H., D. BILLIOU, A. MARIOTTI, M. PATOU-MATHIS, M. OTTE, D. BONJEAN, AND M. TOUSSAINT. 1999. Palaeoenvironmental and Palaeodietary Implications of Isotopic Biogeochemistry of Last Interglacial Neanderthal and Mammal Bones in Scladina Cave (Belgium). *Journal of Archaeological Science* 26: 599-607.

BOCHERENS, H., D. BILLIOU, A. MARIOTTI, M. TOUSSAINT, M. PATOU-MATHIS, D. BONJEAN, AND M. OTTE. 2001. New Isotopic Evidence for Dietary Habits of Neanderthals from Belgium. *Journal of Human Evolution* 40: 497-505.

BRAIN, C. K., O. FORGE, AND P. ERB. 1999. Lion Predation on Black Rhinoceros (*Diceros Bicornis*) in Etosha National Park. *African Journal of Ecology* 37: 107-109.

BRATLUND, B. 1999a. Taubach Revisited. *Jahrbuch des Römisch-Germanischen Zentralmuseums Mainz* 46: 67-174.

BRATLUND, B. 1999b. Anthropogenic Factors in the Thanatocoenose of the Last Interglacial Travertines at Taubach (Germany). In *The Role of Humans in the Accumulation of European Lower and Middle Palaeolithic Bone Assemblages*, edited by S. Gaudzinski and E. Turner, pp. 255-262. Habelt, Bonn.

BRUGAL, J.-P., P. FOSSE, AND J.-L. GUADELLI. 1997. Comparative Study of Bone Assemblages Made by Recent and Pleistocene Hyenids. In *Proceedings of the 1993 Bone Modification Conference, Hot Springs, South Dakota*, edited by L. A. Hannus, L. Rossum and R. P. Winham, pp. 158-187. Occasional Publication No. 1, Archaeology Laboratory, Augustana College, Sioux Falls.

CAPALDO, S. 1998. Simulating the Formation of Dual-Patterned Archaeofaunal Assemblages with Experimental Control Samples. *Journal of Archaeological Science* 25: 311-330.

CARBYN, L. N., S. OOSENBRUG, AND D. W. ANIONS 1993. *Wolves, Bison and the Dynamics Related to the Peace-Athabasca Delta in Canada's Wood Buffalo National Park*. Canadian Circumpolar Institute, Edmonton.

CHURCHILL, S. E. AND F. SMITH. 2000. A Modern Human Humerus from the Early Aurignacian of Vogelherdhöhle (Stetten, Germany). *American Journal of Physical Anthropology* 112: 251-273.

CONARD, N. J. AND M. BOLUS. 2003. Dating the Appearance of Modern Humans and Timing of Cultural Innovations in Europe. *Journal of Human Evolution,* 44: 331-371.

CRADER, D. C. 1983. Recent Single-Carcass Bone Scatters and the Problem of "Butchery" Sites in the Archaeological Record. In *Animals and Archaeology: Hunters and Their Prey (I)*, edited by J. Clutton-Brock and C. Grigson, pp. 107-141. British Archaeological Reports Series 163.

CRUZ-URIBE, K. 1991. Distinguishing Hyena from Hominid Bone Accumulations. *Journal of Field Archaeology* 18: 467-486.

CZARNETSKI, A. 1983. Zur Entwicklung Der Menschen in Südwestdeutschland. In *Urgeschichte in Baden-Württemberg*, edited by H.-J. Müller-Beck, pp. 217-240. Konrad Theiss Verlag, Stuttgart.

DAESCHLER, E. B. 1996. Selective Mortality of Mastodons (*Mammut americanum*) from the Port Kennedy Cave (Pleistocene; Irvingtonian), Montgomery County, Pennsylvania. In *Palaeoecology and Palaeo-environments of Late Cenozoic Mammals: Tributes to the Career of C.S. (Rufus) Churcher*, edited by K. M. Stewart and K. L. Seymour, pp. 83-96. University of Toronto Press, Toronto.

DEREVIANKO, A. P., V. ZENIN, S. V. LESHCHINSKIY, AND E. N. MASHCHENKO. 2000. Peculiarities of Mammoth Accumulation at Shestakovo Site in West Siberia. *Archaeology, Ethnology and Anthropology of Eurasia* 3: 42-45.

DU TOIT, R. 1986. Re-Appraisal of Black Rhinoceros Subspecies. *Pachyderm* 6: 5-9.

DUNHAM, K. 1985. Ages of Black Rhinos Killed by Drought and Poaching in Zimbabwe. *Pachyderm* 5: 12-13.

ENLOE, J. G., F. DAVID, AND G. BARYSHNIKOV 2000. Hyenas and Hunters: Zooarchaeological Investigations at Prolom II Cave, Crimea. *International Journal of Osteoarchaeology* 10: 310-324.

FISHER, J. W. 1992. Observations on the Late Pleistocene Bone Assemblage from the Lamb Spring Site, Colorado. In *Ice Age Hunters of the Rockies*, edited by D. J. Stanford and J. S. Day, pp. 51-81. Denver Museum of Natural History and University Press of Colorado, Boulder.

FISHER, J.W. 1993. Foragers and Farmers: Material Expressions of Interaction at Elephant Processing Sites in the Ituri Forest, Zaire. In *From Bones to Behavior: Ethnoarchaeological and Experimental Contributions to the Interpretation of Faunal Remains*, edited by J. Hudson, pp. 247-262. Southern Illinois University at Carbondale Occasional Paper 21, Carbondale.

FOSSE, P. 1999. Cave Occupation During Palaeolithic Times: Man and/or Hyena? In *The Role of Humans in the Accumulation of European Lower and Middle Palaeolithic Bone Assemblages*, edited by S. Gaudzinski and E. Turner, pp. 73-88. Habelt, Bonn.

GAMBLE, C. 1979. Hunting Strategies in the Central European Palaeolithic. *Proceedings of the Prehistoric Society* 45: 35-52.

GAMBLE, C. 1986. *The Palaeolithic Settlement of Europe*. Cambridge University Press, Cambridge.

GAMBLE, C. 1999. The Hohlenstein-Stadel Revisited. In *The Role of Humans in the Accumulation of European Lower and Middle Palaeolithic Bone Assemblages*, edited by S. Gaudzinski and E. Turner, pp. 305-324. Habelt, Bonn.

GAUDZINSKI, S. 1995. Wallertheim Revisited: A Re-Analysis of the Fauna from the Middle Palaeolithic Site of Wallertheim (Rheinessen/Germany). *Journal of Archaeological Science* 22: 51-66.

GAUDZINSKI, S. AND W. ROEBROEKS. 1999. Adults Only: Reindeer Hunting at the Middle Palaeolithic Site Salzgitter-Lebenstedt, Northern Germany. *Journal of Human Evolution* 38: 497-521.

GAUDZINSKI, S. AND E. TURNER. 1999. Summarizing the Role of Early Humans in the Accumulation of European Lower and Middle Palaeolithic Bone Assemblages. In *The Role of Humans in the Accumulation of European Lower and Middle Palaeolithic Bone Assemblages*, edited by S. Gaudzinski and E. Turner, pp. 381-393. Habelt, Bonn.

GERMONPRÉ, M. 1993. Taphonomy of Pleistocene Mammal Assemblages in the Flemish Valley, Belgium. *Bulletin de l'Institut Royal des Sciences Naturelles de Belgique* 63: 271-309.

GODDARD, J. 1970. Age Criteria and Vital Statistics of a Black Rhinoceros Population. *East African Wildlife Journal* 8: 105-121.

GUÉRIN, C. 1980. Les Rhinocéros (Mammalia, Perissodactyla) du Miocène Terminal au Pléistocène Supérieur en Europe Occidentale. *Documents des Laboratoires de Gèologie* 79: 1-1185.

GUTHRIE, R. D. 1990. *Frozen Fauna of the Mammoth Steppe: The Story of Blue Babe*. University of Chicago Press, Chicago.

HAHN, J. 1993. Urgeschichtliche Forschung der Ostalb. *Karst und Höhle* 1993: 213-224.

HAYNES, G. 1980. Evidence of Carnivore Gnawing on Pleistocene and Recent Mammalian Bones. *Paleobiology* 6 (3): 341-351.

G. HAYNES. 1982. Utilization and Skeletal Disturbances of North American Prey Carcasses. *Arctic* 35 (2): 266-281.

G. HAYNES. 1987. Proboscidean Die-Offs and Die-Outs: Age Profiles of Fossil Collections. *Journal of Archaeological Science* 14: 659-668.

G. HAYNES. 1991. *Mammoths, Mastodonts, and Elephants: Biology, Behavior, and the Fossil Record.* Cambridge University Press, Cambridge.

G. HAYNES. 1999. The Role of Mammoths in Rapid Clovis Dispersal. In *Mammoths and the Mammoth Fauna: Studies of an Extinct Ecosystem*, edited by G. Haynes, J. Klimowicz and J. W. F. Reumer, pp. 9-38. Deinsea, Rotterdam.

HITCHINS, P. M. 1978. Age Determination of the Black Rhinoceros (*Diceros Bicornis* Linn.) in Zululand. *South African Journal of Wildlife Research* 8 (2): 71-80.

HOFFECKER, J., G. BARYSHNIKOV, AND O. POTOPOVA. 1991. Vertebrate Remains from the Mousterian Site of Il'skaya I (Northern Caucasus, USSR): New Analysis and Interpretation. *Journal of Archaeological Science* 18: 113-147.

JAUBERT, J., M. LORBLANCHET, H. LAVILLE, R. SLOTT-MOLLER, A. TURQ, AND J.-P. BRUGAL. 1990. *Les Chasseurs d'aurochs de La Borde : Un Site du Paléolithique Moyen (Livernon, Lot).* Maison des Sciences de l'Homme, DAF No. 27, Paris.

KINGDON, J. 1979. *East African Mammals: An Atlas of Evolution in Africa.* University of Chicago Press, Chicago.

KRUUK, H. 1972. *The Spotted Hyena: A Study of Predation and Social Behavior.* University of Chicago Press, Chicago.

KURTÉN, B. 1953. *On the Variation and Population Dynamics of Fossil and Recent Mammal Populations.* Acta Zoologica Fennica 76. Helsingforsiae.

KUZMINA, I. E. AND E. N. MASCHENKO. 1999. Age Morphological Changes in the Skull and Skeleton of Mammoth Calves of the Russian Plain. In *Mammoth Calves Mammuthus Primigenius*, edited by I. E. Kuzmina, pp. 51-120. Proceedings of the Zoological Institute of the Russian Academy of Sciences, St. Petersburg.

LAWS, R. M. 1966. Age Criteria for the African Elephant *Loxodonta A. Africana. East African Wildlife Journal* 4: 1-37.

LEHMANN, U. 1954. Die Fauna des "Vogelherds" bei Stetten ob Lontal (Württemberg). *Neues Jahrbuch für Geologie und Paläontologie* 99: 33-146.

LISTER, A. 2001. Age Profile of Mammoths in a Late Pleistocene Hyaena Den at Kent's Cavern, Devon, England. In *Proceedings of the International Conference on Mammoth Site Studies*, edited by D. West, pp. 35-43. University of Kansas Publications in Anthropology Vol. 22, Lawrence.

LUPO, K. D. AND J. F. O'CONNELL. 2002. Cut and Tooth Mark Distributions on Large Animal Bones: Ethnoarchaeological Data from the Hadza and Their Implications for Current Ideas About Early Human Carnivory. *Journal of Archaeological Science* 29: 85-109.

MAGLIO, V. J. 1973. *Origin and Evolution of the Elephantidae.* American Philosophical Society, Philadelphia.

MECH, L. D. 1970. *The Wolf: The Ecology and Behavior of an Endangered Species.*

MÜNZEL, S. 2001. The Production of Upper Palaeolithic Mammoth Bone Artifacts from Southwestern Germany. In *Le Terra Degli Elefanti - the World of Elephants: Proceedings of the 1st International Congress*, edited by G. Cavarretta, P. Gioia, M. Mussi and M. Palombo, pp. 448-454. CNR, Rome.

NAVARRO, B. M. AND P. PALMQVIST. 1999. Venta Micena (Orce, Granada, Spain): Human Activity in a Hyena Den During the Lower Pleistocene. In *The Role of Humans in the Accumulation of European Lower and Middle Palaeolithic Bone Assemblages*, edited by S. Gaudzinski and E. Turner, pp. 57-71. Habelt, Bonn.

NIVEN, L. 2001. The Role of Mammoths in Upper Palaeolithic Economies of Southern Germany. In *Le Terra Degli Elefanti - the World of Elephants: Proceedings of the 1st International Congress*, edited by G. Cavarretta, P. Gioia, M. Mussi and M. Palombo, pp. 323-327. CNR, Rome.

O'CONNELL, J. F., K. HAWKES, AND N. BLURTON JONES. 1988. Hadza Hunting, Butchering, and Bone Transport and Their Archaeological Implications. *Journal of Anthropological Research* 44 (2): 113-161.

OWEN-SMITH, R. N. 1988. *Megaherbivores : The Influence of Very Large Body Size on Ecology.* Cambridge University Press, Cambridge.

PALMQVIST, P., B. MARTINEZ-NAVARRO, AND A. ARRIBAS. 1996. Prey Selection by Terrestrial Carnivores in a Lower Pleistocene Community. *Paleobiology* 22 (4): 514-534.

PICKERING, T. R. 2002. Reconsideration of Criteria for Differentiating Faunal Assemblages Accumulated by Hyenas and Hominids. *International Journal of Osteoarchaeology* 12: 127-141.

RAWN-SCHATZINGER, V. 1992. *The Scimitar Cat Homotherium Serum Cope: Osteology, Functional Morphology, and Predatory Behavior.* Illinois State Museum Reports of Investigations, Springfield.

REDMOND, I. 1982. Salt Mining Elephants of Mount Elgon. *Swara* 5: 28-31.

RICHARDS, M., P. PETTIT, E. TRINKAUS, F. SMITH, M. PAUNOVIC, AND I. KARAVANIC 2000. Neanderthal Diet at Vindija and Neanderthal Predation: The Evidence from Stable Isotopes. *Proceedings of the National Academy of Sciences* 97 (13): 7663-7666.

RICHTER, D., J. WAIBLINGER, W. J. RINK, AND G. A. WAGNER. 2000. Thermoluminescence, Electron Spin Resonance and ^{14}C-Dating of the Late Middle and Early Upper Palaeolithic Site of Geißenklösterle Cave in Southern Germany. *Journal of Archaeological Science* 27: 71-89.

RIEK, G. 1934. *Die Eiszeitjägerstation am Vogelherd im Lontal.* Akademische Verlagsbuchhandlung, Tübingen.

SCHALLER, G. B. 1972. *The Serengeti Lion: a Study of Predator-Prey Relations.* University of Chicago Press, Chicago.

SCOTT, K. 1986. The Large Mammal Fauna. In *Le Cotte St. Brelade, 1961-1978*, edited by P. Callow and J. M. Cornford, pp. 109-137. Geo Books, Norwich.

SELVAGGIO, M. M. 1994. Carnivore Tooth Marks and Stone Tool Butchery Marks on Scavenged Bones: Archaeological Implications. *Journal of Human Evolution* 27: 215-228.

SELVAGGIO, M.M. 1998. Evidence for a Three-Stage Sequence of Hominid and Carnivore Involvement with Long Bones at FLK *Zinjanthropus*, Olduvai Gorge, Tanzania. *Journal of Archaeological Science* 25: 191-202.

SHEA, J. 1993. Lithic Use-Wear Evidence for Hunting by Neandertals and Early Modern Humans from the Levantine Mousterian. In *Hunting and Animal Exploitation in the Later Palaeolithic and Mesolithic of Eurasia*, edited by G. L. Peterkin, H. M. Bricker and P. Mellars, pp. 189-187. Archeological Papers of the American Anthropological Association No. 4. American Anthropological Association, Washington, D.C.

SHEA, J., Z. DAVIS, AND K. BROWN. 2001. Experimental Tests of Middle Palaeolithic Spear Points Using a Calibrated Crossbow. *Journal of Archaeological Science* 28: 807-816.

SOFFER, O. 1993. Upper Paleolithic Adaptations in Central and Eastern Europe and Man-Mammoth Interactions. In *From Kostenki to Clovis: Upper Paleolithic-Paleo-Indian Adaptations*, edited by O. Soffer and N. Praslov, pp. 31-49. Plenum Publishers, New York.

STINER, M. 1994. *Honor among Thieves: A Zooarchaeological Study of Neandertal Ecology.* Princeton University Press, Princeton.

SUTCLIFFE, A. J. 1970. Spotted Hyaena: Crusher, Gnawer, Digester and Collector of Bones. *Nature* 227: 1110-1113.

THIEME, H. AND S. VEIL. 1985. Neue Untersuchungen zum Eemzeitlichen Elefanten-Jagdplatz Lehringen, Ldkr. Verden. *Die Kunde* 36: 11-58.

TOURNEPICHE, J.-F. AND C. COUTURE. 1999. The Hyena Den of Rochelot Cave (Charente, France). In *The Role of Humans in the Accumulation of European Lower and Middle Palaeolithic Bone Assemblages*, edited by S. Gaudzinski and E. Turner, pp. 89-101. Habelt, Bonn.

VILLA, P. AND L. E. BARTRAM. 1996. Flaked Bone from a Hyena Den. *Paleo* No 8: 143-159.

ZAPFE, H. 1939. Die Lebensspuren der eiszeitlichen Höhlenhyäne. Die Urgeschichtliche Bedeutung der Lebensspuren knochenfressender Raubtiere. *Palaeobiologica* 7: 111-146.

THE LARGE MAMMALIAN FOSSIL FAUNA OF THE GEELBEK DUNES, WESTERN CAPE, SOUTH AFRICA

Timothy J. Prindiville & Nicholas J. Conard

Institut für Ur- und Frühgeschichte, Und Archäologie des Mittelalters, Ältere Abteilung Urgeschichte und Quartärökologie, Universität Tübingen, Schloss Hohentübingen, D-72070 Tübingen GERMANY, tim.prindiville@uni-tuebingen.de, nicholas.conard@uni-tuebingen.de

INTRODUCTION

The Geelbek Dunes (33°66'S, 18°56'E) located approximately 90 km north of Cape Town in the West Coast National Park are known for their fossil and archaeological occurrences dating to the Pleistocene and Holocene (du Toit 1 et al. 998). Fieldwork funded by a research grant from the Deutsche Forschungsgemeinschaft (DFG) in this ca. 4 km² dune field represents the first attempt to systematically document and interpret the fossils from the calcrete formations, consolidated and unconsolidated sands (Conard et al. 1999). The context of the dunes provides a unique situation in which to study the large-scale spatial distribution of archaeological and non-archaeological occurrences in order to reconstruct past environments.

Currently available absolute dates in Table 1 suggest that at least two fossiliferous, calcretized sand bodies, dating to the late Middle Pleistocene and Late Pleistocene, respectively, are superficially exposed in the deflation hollows, which is overlain by sand dunes, probably of Late Pleistocene or Holocene age. The same calcrete, which is exposed in the deflation hollows of the dunes has a much larger distribution throughout the sandveld. The fossil fauna represented in the dunes suggests a more open environment in which grass was more common than it is today in the fynbos bushveld. In this contribution, we focus on the fossilized large mammal remains, their age, use as environmental indicators, taphonomy, distribution, find-density and importance in the reconstruction of the occupational history of the site.

AGE, GEOLOGICAL CONTEXT AND TAPHONOMY

Fragmentary, highly mineralized bone has been documented in nearly all of the 113 deflation hollows of the Geelbek Dunes. Over 2,800 fossilized bone fragments have been recovered from the 22 deflation hollows, which were subject to detailed investigation. Eleven of these find localities produced significant amounts of identifiable material and the faunal remains of Stella and Rhino, discussed below, have yielded the largest samples.

Faunal elements are clearly associated with the calcretes at Geelbek but the precise stratigraphic relationship is not always certain. Fossil bone has been documented in three locations: (1) embedded in, (2) cemented to the top of calcrete formations, and (3) on 'pavements' where a former calcrete has weathered. Bones clearly eroding from hard-pan calcretes are rare and generally difficult to recover. More common are fossilized bones cemented to the top of calcrete formations, which appear to have been subject to dissolution, and recementation. These occurrences have provided some of the largest, most complete fossil specimens from the dunes. The undersides of these bones are typically coated with a hard calciumcarbonate concretion, where this substance preferentially precipitates.

Five seasons of observation and survey in the dunes have shown that the recent erosion and deposition associated with the deflation hollows occurs rapidly). Many fossil occurrences in the dunes had appeared and were reburied within the course of twelve months. Daily wetting and drying and heating and cooling of mineralized faunal remains occurs, leading to the rapid destruction of the fossils. Often only relatively stable skeletal elements of large animals (e.g. equid and bovid carpal and tarsal bones) can be identified among the many small fragments in these contexts, but in some contexts low density axial skeletal parts of large mammals are particularly well represented. This observation contradicts the expectations that these elements are especially prone to rapid destruction by a variety of taphonomic processes (Lyman 1984, 1994).

The distribution of the fossil occurrences in the dunefield is not uniform and dependent upon numerous factors including, but not limited to: the ancient distribution of animals in the environment, differential weathering and erosion, local soil chemistry and the visibility at the time of investigation. Geological investigations demonstrate that lateral changes in calcrete morphology occur rapidly, often over several tens of meters. Mapping of the dunes reveals that fossil-bearing calcretes exposed in the dunes may be seen as single formations, which follow an ancient, undulating landscape.

Clusters of fossils are present in several locations throughout the dunefield and may be preserved due to their relatively low position in the landscape. Impermeable calcrete transfers precipitation along its top surface, from higher to lower areas. At these locations, laminar structures on the tops of calcretes, iron staining and 'organ pipe' solution cavity structures have been documented and attest to the presence of significant amounts of water. Standing water would have been attractive to animals dependant upon it and the soft, moist substrate may explain the better bone preservation at these localities. However, it must be noted, the timing, number and frequency of these wetter periods and the potential connection to the occurrence of animals remain unknown. The fossil fauna of Geelbek probably represents several chronologically distinct assemblages, which are internally contemporaneous and not random associations of bones from numerous, temporally distinct periods (Prindiville et al. 2001; Felix-Henningsen et al. 2001). Many of the specimens impress us as having been subjected to the same taphonomic processes.

Artifacts associated with calcretes and fossilized bones are rare at Geelbek. Despite this, the artifacts present do offer some information useful in bracketing the age of the fossils. The lack of handaxes in the Geelbek Dunes suggests that the fauna derives from deposits younger than 200 ka, the time at which these cease to occur in Southern African (Volman 1984). Artifacts associated with the fossil fauna at Geelbek are often found on pavement surfaces and include radial cores, grinders and flakes. Formal tools and artifacts attributable to the MSA are very rare. The fragment of one bifacial rough-out found in association with fossils in the locality Homo is noteworthy and may indicate an early glacial date. Also rare are ostrich eggshell beads in association with fossil bones. At the locality Equus, over 1,200 fragments of at least seven perforated ostrich egg-shells were recovered eroding from the same calcrete as the highly mineralized remains of Equus capensis, Taurotragus oryx and Pelorovis antiquus, species which became extinct at the end of the Pleistocene. The age of these finds lies beyond the range of radiocarbon dating, and at present an extensive project using OSL and U-series dating is underway in the Geelbek Dunes to determine the ages of the geological formations and fossil bone assemblages (Felix-Henningsen et al. 2001). The morphology of these perforations fall within the range of artifically modified eggshells and as well as those modified by captive hyenas in experiments (Andrew Kandel, pers. comm. 2002). Further work is needed to determine the agent of these modifications.

Bone preservation is often poor and hinders identification. Most fragments are smaller than four cm in size and weigh less than 10 g each. The identified fauna, shown in Table 2, include almost exclusively 'large-medium', 'large' and 'very large' animals (Klein et al. 1999b). The size distribution of the indeterminate component of the assemblages is essentially identical to that of the identified fauna: unidentifiable pieces consist of indeterminate compact bone fragments from vertebrae, innominates and the lower limbs of large and very large species. Particularly noteworthy is the presence of low-density bones such as innominates and vertebrae at many localities. Here the observation of taphonimic processes, which deviate from those documented as destroying low-density bones (Lyman 1984, 1994). In our view these low-density skeletal elements survive because there

porous structure is less susceptible to destruction as a result of repeated wetting and drying and heating and cooling in the dunes. Similar observations have been made in Texas dune fields (Byerly, pers. comm. 2002). Clearly bone density is not the only factor affecting preservation in these settings.

Another important observation relates to the near absence of skeletal material from smaller mammals in the pre-Holocene assemblages from Geelbek. Although there are no clear explanations for this phenomenon, based on ecological arguments, a wide array of smaller animals must have been present in the environment occupied by the lager Pleistocene mammals. It is noteworthy that all species documented at Elandsfontein Main, which became extinct before the Late Quaternary, are small- and medium-sized animals (Klein & Cruz-Uribe 1991). The absence of these species at Geelbek may be caused by taphonomic biases. Their presence would significantly affect current interpretations of the age of the fauna.

DISCUSSION

Taxa

The identified larger mammals and their relative abundance are listed in Table 2. Following Klein and Cruz-Uribe (1991) we have attributed all large buffalo remains to Pelorovis antiquus. This species, identified mostly on metapodials, is predominantly a grazer, which preferred more open settings (Klein 1980) and, like its modern counterparts, probably had to drink daily (Klein & Cruz-Uribe 1991). A maxillary fragment with two molars could be identified to the greater kudu (Tragelaphus strepsiceros), an adaptive browser, which occurs today in savanna woodlands where a source of drinking water is present (Smithers 1983:666-8). The blue antelope (Hippotragus leucophaeus) is represented by one fragmentary horn core. This predominant grazer, which became extinct historically, probably preferred open habitats (Klein 1974). The eland, Taurotragus oryx, has been identified on metapodials, isolated teeth and more rarely on horn cores. Eland are mixed feeders (Klein & Cruz-Uribe 1991), considered very versatile in their habitat requirements (Smithers 1983:680). They will drink when water is available, but are not dependent on it, obtaining moisture from their food (Smithers 1983:681). Two adjacent mandibular molars are attributable to either the black wildebeest (Connochaetes gnou) or the red (or Cape) hartebeest (Alcelaphus buselaphus). Both the wildebeest and the hartebeest are grazers, which prefer open settings. However, while the wildebeest is dependent on water, the hartebeest is not (Smithers 1983:601-3, 611-2). As is common in Pleistocene contexts, we have assigned all large equid remains to Equus capensis. At Geelbek, the 'giant' zebra is well-represented by isolated teeth, carpals, tarsals and metapodials. E. capensis was a grazer, and, like all zebra, dependent on water (Smithers 1983:569-77). While postcranial remains of rhinoceros are very common at Geelbek, only the two nearly complete crania from the

Analysis No.	Sample No.	Material	Method	Resulting Date
C6556/U639	RH1245	calcrete	U-series	83.0 ± 3.2 ka BP (f=0); 67.1 ± 3.2 ka BP (f=1)
GBRH1170	RH1170	sand	IRSL	61 ± 5 ka BP
C6432/U638	ST1913	calcrete	U-series	161.8 ± 10.1 ka BP (f=0); 146.4 ± 10.7 ka BP (f=1)
GBSB 2	ST1912	sand	IRSL	147 ± 12 ka BP

Table 1. Absolute dates

Taxon	Common Name	Size-Class	Localities	Frequency
Diceros bicornis	Black Rhinoceros	very large	RH, ST	Very common
Equus capensis	Giant Cape Zebra	large	AL, B35, EDM, EQ, HO, RH, ST	Very common
Taurotragus oryx	Eland	very large	AL, EQ, RH, LO, ST	Common
Tragelaphus strepsiceros	Greater Kudu	large	ST	Very rare
Pelorovis antiquus	Long-Horned Buffalo	very large	Al, EDM, EQ, LO, RH, SN, ST	Common
Megalotragus priscus	Giant Hartebeest	very large	RH	Very rare
Hippotragus leucophaeus	Blue Antelope	large-medium	HO	Very rare
Connochaetes gnou	Black wildebeest	large-medium	ST	Very rare
Loxodonta africana	Elephant	very large	CR, HO, LO, RH, ST	Common

Table 2. Identified fossil taxa from the Geelbek Dunes.

Locality	area (m2)	bone count	stone count	stone/ m2	bone/ m2	bone : stone
Rhino	1179	122	142	0,12	0,10	0.86:1
Stella	9805	1120	790	0,08	0,11	1.42:1
Loop	3194	285	827	0,26	0,09	0.34:1
Equus	10943	640	84	0,01	0,06	76.2:1
EDM	3695	170	83	0,02	0,05	0.25:1
Homo/Bay35	3120	525	271	0,09	0,17	1.94:1
Alice	5310	61	114	0,02	0,01	0.54:1
Crow	1696	45	69	0,04	0,03	0.65:1
Cutting 10	240	456	260	1,10	1,90	17.5:1
Death Site	119	376	36	0,30	3,20	10.4:1
Hyena Den 2	33	386	16	0,50	11,70	24.1:1

Table 3. Area, bone and stone counts, densities and ratios for several localities at Geelbek with comparative data from Avery (1989).

localities Stella and Rhino could be identified to *Diceros bicornis*, the black rhinoceros. Black rhinoceros are browsers, which are dependent on water, but can abstain from drinking for up to three days (Smithers 1983:565).

The fossil fauna at Geelbek has preserved no marine or avian species. While this may indicate a greater distance between the sea and the site during the period of deposition, this situation may also arise as a result of unfavorable or biased bone preservation discussed above. Large, fresh water-loving species (i.e. Hippopotamus), which have been documented at Elandfontein Main (Klein & Cruz-Uribe 1991) and Duinefontein 2 (Klein et al. 1999a), do not occur at Geelbek. Despite evidence for ponds and standing water, we assume that no permanent body of fresh water was available for species dependent on it. Carnivores' presence has been documented through tooth scores and punctures on large herbivore bones, but carnivore remains are not present in the assemblage. This may be due to the poor preservation of small- and medium-sized animals, but also on the thin ungulate populations from which some larger carnivores live. Tortoise, hare and microfauna are present, but extremely rare among fossilized remains. In Holocene assemblages, these species are at times extremely abundant. The rarity of these species in the earlier fossil assemblages is consistent with the rarity of other smaller animals at Geelbek, and almost certainly results from a taphonimic bias against these species.

The large mammalian fauna suggests an open environment around Geelbek in which grasses were more predominant than they are today. Of the identified species from Geelbek, none clearly date to the Middle Pleistocene, although fauna from this period has been documented at other neighboring fossil sites in the Southwestern Cape (Klein 1980, Klein et al. 1999a, Klein & Cruz-Uribe 1991). The general faunal composition of Geelbek is similar to the faunas of Swartklip (Klein 1975), Elandfontein 'Bone Circle' (Inskeep & Hendey 1966, Klein & Cruz-Uribe 1991), Duinefontein 1 (Melkbos) (Hendey 1968, Klein & Cruz-Uribe 1991), all of which date roughly to the last glacial (Klein 1980) at a time when sea levels were lower than today (Klein et al. 1999a). At Elandsfontein 'Bone Circle', bones have been documented on – and not in - the ferrunginous crust, making comparisons and correlation with the fossil fauna at Geelbek tempting, and may suggest that these assemblages share similar formation processes. However, while Elandsfontein 'Bone Circle' has been interpreted as a hyena nursery site (Avery 1989), the formation processes at Geelbek may be more complicated, as is discussed below.

PRESERVATION

Bone fragments do not appear water-rolled nor do they show signs of either sand-polish or desert patina, suggesting that the fossils are autochthonous and were rapidly buried. Although fragments of older calcretes

have been observed as clasts in younger calcretes (Netterberg 1978; Felix-Henningsen et al. 2001), this has not been documented for bone. Given the harsh environment at Geelbek, it is not anticipated that older fossils could withstand erosion in such a way that they would be regularly incorporated into younger deposits. Generally, the internal bone structure is mineralized and glassy, in contrast to the poorly preserved, generally exfoliated bone surfaces. This contrast also suggests that burial and subsequent fossilization through the surrounding carbonate-rich matrix took place relatively quickly and that surface weathering occurred only after fossilization and reexposure. Visits to the neighboring fossil locality Elandsfontein and casual observations of the material from this locality at the South African Museum reveal that these fossils, in contrast to those of Geelbek, are well preserved. The specimens are highly mineralized with generally good surface preservation (Klein & Cruz-Uribe 1991).

The contrast between the fossil assemblages from Geelbek and Elandsfontein may be due to differences in the fossilization process (Butzer 1973), but also indicates that the fossils of Geelbek have been subject to longer periods of exposure. While the deflation bays at Elandsfontein are a historical phenomenon (Klein & Cruz-Uribe 1991), the Geelbek dunes and the entire Ysterfontein-Geelbek dune plume to which it belongs may be of Middle Holocene (Compton, in prep.) or Late Pleistocene (Rogers 1980; Tinley 1985) age, and thus the Geelbek fauna has been subject to more prolonged periods of weathering.

The poor preservation of the fossil fauna at Geelbek is apparent in the pattern of represented skeletal elements, in which vertebrae, innominates, metapodials, tarsal and carpal bones dominate. Complete bones, upper limb bones, cranial elements including horn cores and teeth are rare. Equid teeth appear more commonly preserved than those of bovids, suggesting that the specific morphological and structural characteristics of these teeth served to withstand destruction.

Geological investigations indicate that the bushveld was subject to complex cycle of aeolian sand deposition, calcrete formation, sand erosion, calcrete dissolution and reprecipitation during the Pleistocene and Holocene. Taphonomic experiments with modern bone in the Geelbek Dunes have produced results similar to those of Behrensmeyer in East Africa (Behrensmeyer 1978). Surface bone is subject to substantial weathering and shows significant destruction after one year. The majority of the Geelbek fossils can be attributed to Behrensmeyer's weathering stage 3, although many are more poorly preserved and examples of better preservation (1 and 2) occur, but are rare. This classification implies that burial took place in less than 10 years after death (Behrensmeyer 1978), however, exposure through wind erosion as well as cycles of wetting and drying and heating and cooling of already fossilized bone must also be taken into account. While the absence of certain skeletal elements at Geelbek including long bone fragments from the upper limbs, may be due to the differential resistance of these elements to fluctuations in moisture and temperature on account of their morphology and structure, it could also, in theory, be due to removal of these elements from the investigated area before burial.

MODIFICATIONS

In the localities Stella and Rhino the relatively well-preserved remains of semi-articulated axial elements of black rhinoceros were documented. These features can be seen as analogies for the bulk of the fauna at Geelbek. The skeletal elements include the cranium, mandible, vertebral column, pelvis, carpal and tarsal bones, and - rarely- the articular ends of long bones. Often, segments of vertebrae were found articulated, demonstrating that the carcass was not greatly moved after death. Tooth crowns were shattered, presumably from frequent, wetting and drying and heating and cooling of the remains before discovery. The majority of the vertebrae carry damage attributable to a large, indeterminate carnivore: many vertebral spines and occasionally the corpus have been punctured. Light gnawing marks from porcupine are also common on a quarter of the remains. Also common among these well-preserved fossils are burrows and pupa cases from sphecid of 'digger' wasps. These appear to have been formed after the bones were buried, but before the final phase of calcium-carbonate precipitation.

Klein and Cruz-Uribe (1991) describe burrows of digger wasps on specimens from Elandsfontein Main. These are a common feature of the well-preserved fossil specimens at Geelbek and provide important information for the ecological reconstruction of the localities. The environmental requirements of digger wasps are quite particular: they choose to make their shallow borrows into loose, damp sand slopes near standing water (Smit 1964:354-6). At Elandsfontein Main, Klein and Cruz-Uribe report only 1% of (88/7267) bovid bones having these borrows. At Stella 20% (4/20) and at Rhino 63% (19/30) mineralized specimens (mostly black rhinoceros or 'very large' size-class) have at least one insect burrow. This implies different local ecological conditions at these localities and Elandsfontein.

Occasional stone artifacts found spatially associated with fossils indicate that hominids were present throughout the time of bone deposition. Demonstrating a causal relationship between faunal remains and hominid activities is difficult and only possible through the presence of anthropogenically modified bone. No fossil faunal remains appear burned, nor are any unambiguously cutmarked bones present in the fossil assemblage at Geelbek. However, poor preservation of bone surfaces at Geelbek limits our ability to observe any cutmarks, which may have existed. A single radius shaft of eland documented in the Rhino locality may have an impact fracture, but this may also be the result of trampling.

DISTRIBUTIONS AND DENSITY

While most fossils at Geelbek do not occur in clear scatters, many localities contain clearly defined concentrations, which represent the remains of individual animals. Avery (1989) has used both bone density per square meter and bone to stone ratios to define site types. Attempts to apply this interpretive tool to Geelbek demand the assumption that inflated bone counts due to fragmentation and inflated stone counts due to deflation from younger layers do not radically distort the archaeological record. This assumption will require more scrutiny in the future.

In no one instance in Avery's study does the area investigated meet that of the deflation hollows at Geelbek, as seen in Table 3. Likewise, no bone or stone count per square meter at Geelbek meets or exceeds the counts in Avery's study, despite the potential for artificially inflated counts mentioned above. Accepting these differences, bone to stone ratios from Geelbek may be interpretable using Avery's classifications. Different results are obtained at different locations, suggesting that a combination of different agents is responsible for the resulting assemblages. According to the site classifications put forth by Avery, many fossil occurrences at Geelbek would represent either 'Kill and Butchery Sites', in which hominids were a main contributor or 'Death Sites', locations from which animal resources were removed by carnivores and/or hominids (Avery 1989).

Although the scatters of fossil fauna occur in areas with low artifact density, sites do occur where evidence for animals and hominids are present in areas, which were probably attractive for both. Here, the interaction of the two cannot be ruled out. While the general low density of artifacts and absence of clearly anthropogenic modifications to bone is indicative of a low occupation intensity by hominids during the period in which the fossils accumulated, the lack of carnivore remains at Geelbek alternatively speak in favor of a larger anthropogenic component to the assemblages. However, the scarcity of carnivore remains may also be affected by a taphonomic bias against small- and medium-sized animals. Hominid activity at Geelbek during the time of fossil deposition must be seen as ephemeral. While Geelbek represents an area from which hominids may have occasionally obtained animal resources, hominids do not appear to have spent long periods of time here.

We interpret the majority of the fossil fauna from Geelbek as a combination of carnivore kills and hominid predation and/or scavenging during the first half of the last glacial. The presence of standing water at certain times of the year would have been attractive to ungulate species. The congregation of animals at these foci would have been equally attractive to large carnivores and hominids. Represented skeletal elements suggest that upper limb bones may have been removed from the investigated areas by either carnivores, hominids or both.

It is noteworthy that visits to the dunes about three kilometers south of Geelbek in the same dune plume have fossil and archaeological similar to that of Geelbek, thus implying that the patterns in the Geelbek Dunes are typical for these Pleistocene deposits in this portion of the coastal plain. The fossil assemblages at Geelbek are can make an important contribution to the open-air, Later Quaternary record not only because they demonstrate the complexity and importance of taphonomic study at open-air, archaeological sites but also because they provide ecological framework in which hominid occupation of the region took place.

ACKNOWLEDGEMENTS

The research in Geelbek was funded by the Deutsche Forschungsgemeinschaft and the University of Tübingen. Many people have made important contributions to the work in Geelbek. These include Graham Avery, John Compton, Janette Deacon, Mary Leslie, John Parkington, Dave Roberts, and Stephan Woodborne. We are particularly indebted to Peter Felix-Henninsen, Andrew Kandel, Maria Malina and the many students who have contributed to the field and laboratory work at Geelbek. We also grateful for the institutional support provided by the Iziko - South African Museum, the South African Heritage Resources Agency, the University of Cape Town, and the South African National Parks Board.

REFERENCES

AVERY, G. A. 1989. Some features distinguishing various types of occurrence at Elandsfontein, Cape Province, South Africa. *Palaeoecology Africa* 19:213-219.

BEHRENSMEYER, A. K. 1978. Taphonomic and ecologic information from bone weathering. *Paleobiology* 4:150-162.

BUTZER, K. W. 1973. Re-evaluation of the geology of the Elandsfontein (Hopefield) site, South-western Cape, South Africa. *South African Journal of Science* 69:234-238.

COMPTON, J. S. in prep. Holocene evolution of the Sixteen Mile Beach barrier dunes and the Yzerfontein-Geelbek dune plume, South Africa.

CONARD, N. J., T. J. PRINDIVILLE AND A. W. KANDEL. 1999. The 1998 fieldwork on the Stone Age archaeology and palaeoecology of the Geelbek Dunes, West Coast National Park, South Africa. *Southern African Field Archaeology* 8:35-45.

DU TOIT, L., A. REHDER AND H.J. DEACON. 1998. Report on the Archaeological Survey of the West Coast National Park. Department of Archaeology, University of Stellenbosch.

FELIX-HENNINGSEN, P., T.J. PRINDIVILLE & N.J. CONARD. 2001. Palaeoecology and archaeology of the coastal dunes of the Western Cape, South Africa: I. Sequences of paleosols on ancient dunes as stratigraphical markers and palaeoenvironmental indicators. In: *Proceedings of the 1st International Conference on Soils and Archaeology, Százhalombattta, Hungary. May 30th – June 3rd, 2001*, György Füleky (ed.). Szent István University Gödöllő, Matrica Museum Százhalombattta, pp. 157-159.

HENDEY, Q. B. 1968. The Melkbos site: An Upper Pleistocene fossil occurrence in the South-Western Cape Province. *Annals of the South African Museum* 52:89-119.

INSKEEP, R. R. & Q. B. HENDEY. 1966. 'An interesting association of bones from the Elandsfontein fossil site.' *Actas del V Congreso Panafricano de Prehistoria y de estudio del Cuaternario, Santa Cruz de Tenerifo*, 1966, pp. 109-124.

KLEIN, R. G. 1974. On the taxonomic status, distribution and ecology of the blue antilope, Hippotragus leucophaeus (Pallas, 1766). *Annals of the South African Museum* 65:99-143.

KLEIN, R. G. 1975. Palaeoanthropological implications of the nonarchaeological bone assemblage from Swartklip I, South-Western Cape Province, South Africa. *Quaternary Research* 5:275-288.

KLEIN, R. G. 1980. Environmental and ecological implications of large mammals from Upper Pleistocene sites in Southern Africa. *Annals of the South African Museum* 81:223-283.

KLEIN, R. G., G. AVERY, K. CRUZ-URIBE, D. HALKETT, T. HART, R.G. MILO AND T.P. VOLMAN. 1999a. Duinefontein 2: an Acheulean site in the Western Cape Province of South Africa. *Journal of Human Evolution* 37:153-190.

KLEIN, R. G., K. CRUZ-URIBE AND R.G. MILO. 1999b. Skeletal part representation in archaeofaunas: Commetns on 'Explaining the 'Klasies Pattern': Kua ethnoarchaeology, the Die Kelders Middle Stone Age archaeofauna, long bone fragmentation and carnivore ravaging' by

Bartram & Marean. *Journal of Archaeological Science* 26:1225-1234.

KLEIN, R. G. A. K. CRUZ.-URIBE. 1991. The bovids from Elandsfontein, South Africa, and their implications for the age, palaeoenvironment, and origins of the site. *African Archaeological Review* 9:21-79.

LYMAN, R. L. 1984. Bone density and differential survivorship of fossil classes. *Journal of Anthropological Archaeology* 3:259-299.

LYMAN, R. L. 1994. *Vertebrate Taphonomy. Cambridge Manuals in Archaeology.* Cambridge University Press, Cambridge.

NETTERBERG, F. 1978. Dating and correlation of calcretes and other pedocretes. *Transactions of the Geological Society of South Africa.* 81:379-391.

PRINDIVILLE, T. J., N. J. CONARD & P. FELIX-HENNINGSEN. 2001 Palaeoecology and Archaeology of the Coastal Dunes of the Western Cape, South Africa: II. Spatial Archaeology and Taphonomic Processes. In: *Proceedings of the 1st International Conference on Soils and Archaeology, Százhalombattta, Hungary. May 30th – June 3rd, 2001,* György Füleky (ed.). Szent István University Gödölló, Matrica Museum Százhalombattta, pp. 153-156.

ROGERS, J. 1980. First Report on theCenozoic Sediments between Cape Town and Elands Bay. *Geological Survey* 1980-136.

SMIT, B. 1964. *Insects of Southern Africa: How to Control Them.* Cape Town: Oxford University Press.

SMITHERS, R. H. N. 1983. *The Mammals of the Southern African Subregion.* Pretoria: University of Pretoria.

TINLEY, K. L. 1985. *Coastal Dunes of South Africa.* Vol. Report No. 109. National Scientific Programme.

VOLMAN, T. P. 1984. 'Early Prehistory of Southern Africa,' in *Southern African Prehistory and Paleoenvironments.* R. G. Klein, ed. Rotterdam: A. A. Balkema. pp. 169-220.

www.ingramcontent.com/pod-product-compliance
Lightning Source LLC
Chambersburg PA
CBHW051306270326
41926CB00030B/4737